THE GAMBLER'S GUIDE TO THE WORLD

Also by Jesse May

Shut Up and Deal

**The Inside Scoop from a
Professional Player on Finding
the Action, Beating the
Odds, and Living It Up
Around the Globe**

JESSE MAY

Broadway Books • New York

THE GAMBLER'S GUIDE TO THE WORLD

Broadway Books titles may be purchased for business or promotional use or for special sales. For information, please write to: Special Markets Department, Random House, Inc., 1540 Broadway, New York, NY 10036.

BROADWAY BOOKS and its logo, a letter B bisected on the diagonal, are trademarks of Broadway Books, a division of Random House, Inc.

Visit our Web site at www.broadwaybooks.com

Library of Congress Cataloging-in-Publication Data
May, Jesse.
    The gambler's guide to the world: the inside scoop from a professional player on finding the action, beating the odds, and living it up around the globe / Jesse May.
        p.   cm.
    Includes index.
    1. Casinos—Guidebooks.   2. Gambling—Anecdotes.   I. Title.
GV1301.M275 2000
795—dc21   00-031188

FIRST EDITION

Designed by Bonni Leon-Berman

Maps by Folio Graphics.

ISBN 0-7679-0552-0

00   01   02   03   04   10   9   8   7   6   5   4   3   2   1

ACKNOWLEDGMENTS

The author wishes to gratefully acknowledge assistance from the following people, without whom he would still be standing at one hot and dusty bus stop. Tina Pohlman, Heather Schroder, the Mays, the Kjaersides, the May-Weinsteins, Jon Tare, Mike Luber, John Hennigan, Gerry Jordan, and Lothar Landauer.

CONTENTS

Introduction   1

Part 1—SOUTH OF THE BORDER   17

Chapter One—San José, Costa Rica   19

Chapter Two—Mar del Plata, Argentina   61

Chapter Three—San Juan, Puerto Rico   79

Chapter Four—Panama City, Panama   99

Part 2—ABC ISLANDS, NETHERLANDS ANTILLES 119

Chapter Five—Aruba   121

Chapter Six—Bonaire   137

Chapter Seven—Curaçao   145

Part 3—THE EUROPEAN TOUR   171

Chapter Eight—Baden and
   Vienna, Austria   181

Chapter Nine—Amsterdam   189

Chapter Ten—Paris, Helsinki, Slovenia,
   and Dublin   195

Part 4—THE EASTERN BLOC   203

Chapter Eleven—Moscow, Russia   205

Part 5—THE U.S. OF A.   223

Chapter Twelve—Atlantic City, New Jersey 225

Chapter Fourteen—Las Vegas, Nevada   257

Index   291

TIDBITS AND TALES

Jesse's Besties	9
Glossary of Basic Terms Used in This Book	12
The System	22
What's the Line?	28
Costa Rican Poker Schedule	34
Ticos and Gringos	36
Why Not?	40
Granola Gamblers	44
The Lollapalooza	45
Lock Your Doors	58
Banca Gana	70
Cuidado	101
Poker in Aruba	125
Adventures in Card Counting	149
Ringside Seats	167
Gambling in Europe	173
The European Poker Tour	175
Marijuana	193
Money in Moscow	206
A Little Green Can Grease the Wheels	260
The Gambler's Book Club	268
Party On	280
Morty the Hammer's Top 5 Spots in the Land of the Damned	288

GAMES IN DEPTH

Rommy	26
Baccarat	69
Canal 21	104
Blackjack	149
Craps	231

INTRODUCTION

ABOUT THE BOOK

The question. Are you a gambler. That taboo word associated with bread lines and threadbare clothes. And I say, what is the definition of gambling? What makes a gamble?

I have my definition. Gambling is when you have a vested stake in the outcome of an occurrence, an outcome that has not yet been resolved. You may know the likelihood of that outcome, and you may know the stake you have vested and the reward and loss for the possible outcomes, but that outcome has not happened yet. In my mind, this is a gamble.

Taken like this, almost everything in life is a gamble, and I prefer to think in terms of whether or not something is a good bet. It's a bad bet to go for a suntan in Chernobyl. It's a bad bet to play poker in Panama. In Atlantic City, while craps may not be a good bet, it is a fair bet, or almost an even gamble.

I may go through life as a gambler. And though I may have made plenty of bad bets in my time, I do not go through life looking for bad bets. What I am on the lookout for is good bets.

This book is written first for people who want to gamble for fun, and second, for people who want to gamble for profit. But the thing is, in order to gamble for profit, you must have two things. You must have skill, and you must have knowledge. And there is no way to acquire these two things without study and practice. No way at all.

Who the hell cares if you're a gambler.

This book took a lot out of me. For this book I was hugging a toilet, racking with heaves. For this book I was twenty hours in a blackjack seat, stuck to the gills. For this book I have been insulted by floormen, laughed at by dealers, and hustled by pimps. My pledge was that I would not recommend or criticize something without firsthand experience, and I held that ideal alight, if at times letting other components of the book's construction skip to the wayside. Sometimes notes are my memory. Details are my brain. If the accuracy of any of my claims suffered, know it is not a lapse in honesty. Put it down to logistics, to checking your bag in Moscow and finding it returned drenched in vodka and broken glass. To arriving in Buenos Aires in the pouring rain with no map and no hotel reservation on a Sunday. To walking into a Panama City pool hall too late at night. And to deciding to play just one more hundred at the craps table. At least I been there.

WHAT'S IT LIKE?

People want to know what it's like to be in action every day. What it's like? It's a different way of looking at life. Because you see, then life becomes the poker game, one series of hands coming right after another, even when you're outside the casino.

When I first proposed the idea to a publishing company about a no-nonsense guide for gamblers the world over, I said I would never consider writing about or reviewing a casino without actually gambling in it, real gambling being necessary to properly evaluate each locale. Toward that end, I proposed that in addition to an advance, the publisher would provide me with full traveling and hotel expenses, and a modest gambling stipend for every casino. They came back and said, in essence, are you drunk?

While the book sounds interesting, we're not paying for the research. We'll give you half of the advance you asked for, you have to pay for all your travel expenses, and you have to fund all of your own gambling experiences. Now, no sane person would accept that deal, but I was unemployed, broke, and I figured I could count on a little ace up my sleeve that I hadn't told the publisher about, a little piece of information that every gambler knows. Simply put, it's this: If you gamble all night long, then you don't have to spend money on a hotel room.

But with a very limited budget and so many casinos to experience, I realized that good money management was going to be essential. What I did was, I divided all my money up into different envelopes, a big white envelope for each country. Then in each of those white envelopes I divided the money up into smaller colored envelopes. A different sealed envelope for each gambling game or traveling expense. Red envelopes for blackjack, green envelopes for craps, orange envelopes for food and hotel money. By adhering strictly to my expense system and using the envelopes only for what they were intended in the country they were intended for, I thought that I could modestly gamble on every game, have a place to stay and food to eat, and return safe again with the travel information for the guide.

My first destination was Las Vegas. I arrived in Las Vegas at approximately 11:35 P.M. on the Wednesday evening before Super Bowl Sunday and hit the town running. By Saturday morning I had been up fifty-nine hours in a row, played golf, been to fifteen or sixteen casinos, and gone through the envelopes. And I spent the next eight weeks traveling through Central and South America with one small light blue envelope that was to have been for laundry money.

And the point of this story is that a gambler needs to be flexible.

Flexibility is a key ingredient in the makeup of a gambler. One card, one word, or one bet can change an entire night, and small decisions can affect an entire vacation. I really never know what to do next. When traveling, my general rule of thumb is adapt on the fly and don't ignore your first instincts. Consider how I came to leave Mar del Plata, for example. I am a blackjack player, new to the game but full of gusto. I put in the time before my trip with the books and the simulators, memorizing the charts and practicing the strategies, and even though I had managed to lose $20,000 to my computer in the month before I left, I felt ready. After all, my only realistic goal was to break even. I mean, given that I had to visit twelve countries I'd never seen before and gamble every night in every one with no expectation of finding more than a few poker games, breaking even was quite a mountain to climb in the first place.

I had found myself in the beachside resort of Mar del Plata, a town on the coast of Argentina, where I'd come to take some sun and check out the biggest casino in South America. While I'm charmed by the happy-go-lucky vacationing families, the late nights, and the all-you-can-eat parrilla joints where the entire cow, pig, and chicken are sliced up and put on the grill, the $20 minimum in the casino is just a little steep for my meager bankroll. And while I enjoy the blackjack conditions, my luck is something less than fortunate. So after only four days in the town I check out of my hotel and head over to the bus station to catch a ride back up to Buenos Aires. Alas, everyone else has the same idea as me, and no seats are available before late afternoon. This won't bring me into Buenos Aires until after midnight, a little late to find a hotel and get good value for a night's sleep. I decide to take this turn of events as a sign, so I purchase a ticket for a midnight bus that will get me into Buenos Aires in the early morning, put my luggage in a locker, and figure that fate wants me to return to the casino for one more day of gambling.

I'm the first one in when Casino Central opens its doors at three o'clock, and wouldn't you know that it happens to be the first day that the casino has decided to lower its minimum bet to $10 instead of $20. Armed with these extra bets and the winds of change, I manage to win $500 over the course of the next five hours, when I figure it's a good time to escape for a leisurely dinner before my bus. But even though not much has changed, now everything has changed. Who wants to leave town in the midst of a winning streak? I'm a gambler, and I figure fate has dealt me a new hand, and I must act accordingly. So I eat my $25 bus ticket, recheck into my hotel, and figure now I'm gonna win all the money in town.

Over the next two days, I manage to lose back my $500 plus $1,100 more. I go to the bus station and just like the time before, there's no seat until late afternoon, too late to get into Buenos Aires and get good value for a hotel room. But I still believe a gambler has to rely on fate, because what the hell else do you have to go on?

If my grandma had wheels she'd be a trolley car. If I had only bet black. If I hadn't sat in that seat. If I had put it all on Denver. If my grandma had wheels she'd be a trolley car.

Every gambler knows all the permutations of if. Intimately. We're faced with it every day and every bet, and while some people hold a belief that small actions can spin their lives in a million directions, the gambler lives with it all the time. It's just that in gambling you're faced with so many decisions, and while they are muddy at the time, often it is only seconds or minutes before the effects of those decisions become crystal clear, and while a gambler is free to take it all with an impassive equanimity, there's no way to keep from thinking about it, from lying awake at night caught in a half reflex and trying to will your hand to move those chips over to the number seventeen black and away from all things red.

Everything in gambling is like that, should I or shouldn't I? Will it or won't it? What the hell to do next? And with little or almost no practical input from the world around us, on some level we all have to resort to our own personal brand of voodoo, religion, or decision-making.

Let me tell you my friend Steve's story about the history of religion. Back in the day, back in the old days, man decided it was time to stop being a hunter-gatherer and develop some roots, so he settled down in the Tigris–Euphrates River Valley and started to grow crops. And as every farmer knows, once you start to grow crops, you begin to rely on the whims of the rain like the randomness of the little steel ball. And every few years, the rains would stop for a while, a drought would develop, and the crops would be in jeopardy. And don't you know those farmers would try anything they could think of to make it rain. They'd jump up and down. They'd pray. They'd dance in a circle. And whatever worked, whatever made it rain, that became their religion. And like the random distribution of points on a short bell curve, some things, say the sacrificing of young lambs, always brought the rain for a period of hundreds of years, while other things, like the building of mud towers, never worked and so they never seemed to attract any followers and died out. Random but effective. Nothing works, but yet some things do work.

And so it is with the gambler. Nothing works, but superstition is our middle name and we'll go down dying with it as long as it works. Some folks have lucky underwear. Some people know it helps to close their eyes when they make a big bet. Others never change their socks on a winning streak, or only play with a certain dealer. We're always on the lookout for signs, I personally am willing to consider any and every minute piece of random information as the basis for changing my mind or determining even the largest decisions in my life.

But we've got free will. We do. Oh, there are consequences, you better believe it, and we may not know what they are or what they will be. But value your decision-making process, because, baby, you've got free will.

I realized this when I checked out of my Argentine hotel and went to the bus station, but the next bus wasn't for four hours, so I put my bags in a locker instead and went back to the casino, and because I won I decided to go get my bags and check into another hotel, because who could leave town on a major heater? But over the next two days I lost everything I had won plus twice as much in addition and then I broke even for a day and on the fourth day I checked out of my hotel and went back to the bus station and again there was no ticket until the evening, so I put my bags in a locker and went back to the casino and went on a ten-hour winning streak and got back about three quarters of what I had lost and then sat in a restaurant and tried to figure out if I should check back into a hotel again, because who can leave town on a major heater?

Anyway, I went and got on that bus and rode out of town and into the sunset, and now I'm here to tell you that you've got free will, and don't believe what some other Joe schmo will tell you about how life is out to get him and he can't do nothing right and how everything he touches turns to rotten pineapples in his path. Because even though that may be true and fate may just have it in for him, you tell him, son, value your decision-making process, not the decision but the process, because you've got free will. You really do.

Sometimes, the most profitable thing you could ever do is to lose a little bit. You'll never realize it at the time. At the time, all you want to do is to get even. You just want to get even and you don't care how long or how much money it takes you and you're just glued to your seat as the hours fly by, but later on, and trust me, later on, you'll realize that the most profitable thing you could ever do is to lose a little bit. Life ain't about always going forward, it's hills and valleys, and sometimes chasms.

Addiction. I call it passion, loosely. Without passion, you're a dead fish. With passion, you have to deal with addiction. It's a paradox, because what you love kills you. We, the lovers of life, are the passionate addicts of all things, whether they be romance or sports, gambling or drugs, eating or drinking. What you love to do can kill you. Those are the demons of passion. Gambling is a more dangerous passion than most. It can wipe you out, tear your heart away, and make you grovel. It can get you high, lift you up, and bring you cash, the god of material pleasures.

How does a person deal with this, with the danger, with the demons? You have to be strong. First, you must study your opponent. Know what battlefields you can attack him on, where his weaknesses are. Know your own weaknesses. Be aware of where your opponent will attack you, when he will come calling with his lights and bells and shiny promises. Playing the game is to be on the edge, but the better you know that edge, the more secure it becomes. And then sometimes there is no foothold at all. Sometimes there is no foothold at all, you can't rest no matter which way you turn and the rock is crumbling away at your feet and every step is a landslide, a landslide. Then you must get out. You must just get out. Because down there is a pit of no return. Addiction? It's tough out there.

A common mistake of most gamblers is that they figure that just because the odds are slightly in their favor, there's no way they can lose. Brother, I've lost more money with the odds slightly in my favor than any reasonable person has the sense to admit. Don't worry, I've also lost plenty of money with the odds against me, but that's not the issue here. What I'm trying to say is that when the odds are in your favor or when the odds against you are greatly reduced, that's all it is. Nothing more than that, and as to what the outcome of any individual wager will be, only fate can say. Those odds only mean something when they get pounded over the course of a thousand or a million or ten million bets, and what I'm trying to say is that there is no substitute for bankroll, no substitute at all for having the cash to withstand the losses. And that's why most players get ground into the Nevada dust.

And I just keep trying to tell myself the same thing, over and over. Cards have no memory, the cards have no memory. Yeah, my ass they got no memory. On my right is a deaf mute. Hell, I didn't know he was a deaf mute, I just thought he was crazy, he's over there waving his arms and speaking tongues at me every goddamn hand giving me the hand signals when he doesn't like my decisions, which is just about every hand.

And he's jumping up and down out of his seat and waving his arms at me like a windmill, and I move all the way over to the other side of the table 'cause I figure he's off his goddamn rocker, and believe me, even for a deaf mute he's a little goddamn weird and he's drinking beers to boot and for a guy who can't talk he's making so much noise and doing so much waving and pointing that I got a goddamn earsplitting headache and meanwhile I'm trying to keep track of the count, the cards spitting out of the shoe by some hotshot dealer who's trying to show off by how fast he can deal, and I tell you I'm losing it.

Meanwhile, over on my left is a voodoo Chinese fellow betting either $50 or $100 each hand who looks like he's ready to punch me because every time I take a hit with my $3 hand, I take the dealer's bust card. And even though it's a hit by the book and if you know the count, it ain't no hit according to the voodoo way they play Canal 21, and I've probably cost the guy about $800, which is most of his stake, and he's slamming the table and cursing me in Chinese and I'm just thinking, brother, I know exactly how you feel.

Because I was on the other end of that just the night before when I'm playing the dealer head up and just when the count hits Jesus Christ mode and I plop down a $70 bet, some fifteen-year-old Panamanian kid comes over and buys in for eight singles and plops four of them down in the spot next to me and then he has to go ahead and hit twelve into the dealer showing a six and take my double down ten and instead, when I double down my ace-eight into the dealer's six I end up with seventeen, and the dealer goes ahead and makes nineteen and I lose 140 smackers all in one hand which is the last hand of the shoe with the running count at about plus thirty and all my money on the line and it's just because good Leroy has gotta hit twelve into a six and I'm just shaking my head and saying, the cards have no memory. Brother, if you don't think about even a little voodoo, then there isn't nothing but ice water in your veins, because the shit is just turning me white, and I thought when it came to gambling that I'd seen it all.

There was twice in the Casino Central in Argentina when I'm playing third base (the last seat) with a thirteen or fourteen and the entire table sticks on between twelve and sixteen with the dealer showing a face card, and I hit. I get twenty once and twenty-one the other time, and the dealer gets twenty and nineteen, so I push once and win once, but both times the whole table lost and glared at me. And a Chinese lady with eighteen who would have beaten the dealer's seventeen if I hadn't taken a card, she let out a yelp like a wounded puppy when I said, *"Carta."*

It doesn't matter where you sit. They'll curse you from the first seat, they'll curse you from third base, they'll pound the table when you're sandwiched in the middle and mutter in Spanish or jabber in Cantonese. It's tough to take a lot of cards and be popular.

Hell, you're a moron if you don't think about it. The problem lies somewhere along the lines of if a tree falls does it make any sound. The simple idea is this. In Central and South American blackjack, the dealer waits to take his second card until the whole table has acted on their hand. In Las Vegas, the dealer takes two cards at the same time as everyone else, but in Argentina the dealer waits until the players have busted or stuck until he takes his second card from the shoe. And what this means is, this means that whatever the last card is taken by someone at the table as a hit, whatever that card is would be the dealer's second card if the player sticks. And the question is, does it matter?

The answer, the simple answer, is no. The cards have no memory, and even though if you stick, then the dealer can take your bust card, even though it doesn't matter. And me, I just call it voodoo.

If you really want to think about it, it can keep you up nights. I'm not sure the human mind is programmed to conceptually get a hold on it. The only people that don't play the voodoo game, the ones who hit all those cards because they understand it, they're all book players, got to believe in the book because they ain't got nothing else to grasp onto. Like Bible thumpers, they sound unreasonable, it makes no sense, but they'll die clinging to what that book says if it's the last thing they do. When I put it in that light, it makes me want to be a voodoo player. At least it seems to make sense because I can see it. I can see that if I had stuck then I wouldn't have taken the dealer's bust card and the whole table would have won. I can see that.

Now I ask you, what makes more sense, what you can absolutely see would have happened, or the notion that it doesn't matter because the odds are completely random and it could have just as easily have been another card in there? But it wasn't. I'd like to be a voodoo player, but I can't. My self won't let me. Not after all those months of studying the books and practicing blackjack on the computer. I need Stanford Wong to be right, just like a guy who's gone through four years of private college needs to believe his education was just worth $100,000. Because if he's wrong, then he's a big fool. Better to drown with a sinking ship than get washed up on shore, naked and homeless. Anyway, I find plenty of places for voodoo. I save it for roulette and baccarat. Craps is something else all together. That's what I save my octane for.

I still don't know if they thought I cut a dashing figure in my charcoal suit, or if they liked the fact that I played different than everybody else at the table and had the perversity to ask for a card with sixteen when the dealer showed an eight. But I do know one thing, if they weren't voodoo players before they saw me, then they sure went home voodoo, because I busted all of them, every last lady who backed me, and a good part of the rest of the table while I was at it. And lying here now in my $18 a night hotel room, with my back propped up against the wall giving me serious pain on account of my sunburn and the fan on high clicking its way through the night into the sultry morning, I'm just glad to have gotten out of there even. And I haven't sweated so much or felt so much gamble in me since I was playing $200 and $400 and was throwing the chips around like a machine on water. It takes balls to gamble in Argentina.

The Luma Kid told me one thing. The Luma Kid told me a lot of things. But he said, he said one time, a good sleep after a big win? Ain't nobody who can sleep well after a big win. But when hammered, man, when you're broke, you sleep like a baby. Nothing can make you appreciate a big meal and a good sleep better than being flat busted on your ass. He's right, of course.

JESSE'S BESTIES

I just drank six cups of double espresso, I could tell you about anything. I could tell you about watching the Lennox Lewis–Evander Holyfield fight in a sports bar in Curaçao with three hundred Caribbean natives screaming in Papiamento and drinking sea-water-distilled nine-ounce Amstel Lights and the riot that ensued when they declared it a draw, I could tell you about being holed up in a private poker club in the middle of Costa Rica playing no-limit Hold'em with a local whorehouse owner who always wears a Yankees cap and smiles crookedly at you every time he raises a pot. I could tell you about going toe to toe with a bunch of Argentine maniacs who can eat an entire grilled cow at 1 A.M. washed down with their own bottle of wine and then gamble all night and still look rosy-eyed come 8 A.M. and time to hit the beach. Or I could tell you about going to Vegas with Morty the Hammer, who wears a pinkie ring, smokes Cuban cigars, bets $5,000 a hand, and drinks three bottles of Dom Pérignon a day before spending all his nights at the Olympic Gardens strip club, or I could tell you about Chuck, grizzled and gnarled Vegas denizen since the forties, who watched a town grow from one-horse to a one-eyed monster, and through it all Chuck was always in action and watching everybody who's anybody come and go.

When I let on about my mission, to visit every casino in the world and come out alive, the question I'm asked again and again is the same. Which is the best casino in the world? If it were that easy, my friend, the book could just be two pages long, I'd be out of a job, and there'd be no need to travel. Variety is the spice of life and I would no more want to spend the rest of my life in one casino than I would never to gamble again or be forced to survive on only bread and jam. Different casinos are good for different things, and the true gambler, the connoisseur, will take my advice. Certain places are better for certain things. I would never play craps in Argentina and I would never go to Costa Rica looking for a slot machine, but to satiate the truly impatient quick fix gambler who needs everything broken down into X's and O's and needs the short list, here is my attempt at the ultimate ratings, Jesse's Besties:

Best cocktail: the Bloody Mary at the El San Juan, Puerto Rico

Best casino for blackjack: Casino Curaçao Resort, Curaçao

Best casino for craps odds: Wild West Casino, Atlantic City

Best casinos for craps ambiance: Trump Taj Mahal, Atlantic City; the Bellagio, Las Vegas

Best casinos for service and luxury: El San Juan; Caesars Palace, Las Vegas

Best casinos for gambling high: the Bellagio; Casino Cosmos, Moscow; Trump Taj Mahal

Best casino for sweating a basketball game: Colonial Casino, San José

Best casino for a sauna and wet steam when fighting a hangover: Caesars Palace

Prettiest waitresses and dealers: San José Palacio, San José; Casino Cosmos

Best place to get robbed: Panama City, Panama

Flat-out best food: Mar del Plata, Argentina

Best room service: Caesars Palace

Best place to get free alcohol and cigarettes while spending no money: Colonial Casino

Best place to pick up free women: El Pueblo, San José

Best place to pick up professional women: Night Flight, Moscow

Best strip club: Olympic Gardens, Las Vegas

Best booze and cigars: El San Juan

Best site for a honeymoon: the ocean suites at the El San Juan

The best gamblers: the European Tour

MY PERSPECTIVE

What makes this book different? Well, first of all, it's written by a gambler. I am not a pawn of the casinos, a stooge propped up by casino dollars to promote their industry, nor am I some quack promising a get rich winning system that's made me $1 million and now I'm selling it to you. I'm a gambler, pure and simple, and I've won and lost with the best of them. And I'm telling it to you straight.

I am pro gambling, but I am not promoting gambling. If you are going to gamble:

1. You should be aware of the rules.
2. You should be aware of the odds.

3. You deserve to be treated like a gentleman.
4. You should be in a place where you will get the most value for your gambling dollar.
5. You should be able to rely on the absolute integrity of the game.

I've spent a lot of time in casinos. If you put a quarter in my mouth and pull my arm, my eyes will spin.

"NO, THANK YOU"

You may wonder at the proliferation of prostitutes, drugs, and other deeds of mortal sin throughout this book. You may question my morality, integrity, and general lecherousness. But I am not interested in preaching my personal views about these issues. Those are for me. Make up your own mind.

It's just a fact that when you're around gambling, there's a lot of other things you're gonna be around. It just happens. Prostitution, alcohol, drugs, money lenders and borrowers, I neither advocate nor condemn the existence of all of these things.

Gamblers move in a circle where there are always large amounts of cash money on hand. And cash money attracts everything. Like flies. It's all there when you're gambling, and, brother, it's all dangerous.

It's just like this. These are the things that you encounter in the gambling world. Be prepared. Be prepared to make your own choices, because if you're gonna travel, if you're going to move in the circles that gamblers do, every step is a trap, pitfalls are common. You must know yourself, and be prepared to say no, thank you.

People can be very insistent. My advice? Just repeat these words over and over in a firm but polite voice: "No, thank you." Don't be belligerent or overaggressive. Just say, "No, thank you."

GLOSSARY OF BASIC TERMS USED IN THIS BOOK

BACCARAT A card game played between the player and the bank, where the object is to make a hand totaling as close to nine as possible.

BANKROLL The total funds that you have to gamble with.

BIG WHEEL A casino game featuring an upright spinning wheel. A simplified version of roulette, but with odds that are more to the casino's advantage.

BLACKJACK A card game played against a dealer where the object is to get a hand with a point value as close to twenty-one as possible, without going over. Aces can be used as a value of one or eleven, picture cards have a value of ten, and numbered cards have their own face value.

BLIND (1.) A bet that is made without seeing your cards. **(2.)** A forced bet to begin the action in a poker game.

BUST A blackjack hand that totals more than twenty-one.

BUSTED Out of money.

CAGE The place in a casino where you exchange chips into cash money.

CARIBBEAN STUD A simplified version of poker in which you play against the house rather than other players.

CHOP GAME A game impossible to win at in the long run because of the large amount charged by the house to play. A chop game is not illegal, nor is it cheating.

COME, DON'T COME, THE FIELD Craps betting options that are available after a point has been established by the shooter.

(THE) COUNT A number, usually expressed as an integer, that reflects the ratio of high cards to low cards remaining in a blackjack shoe.

CRAPS A game played with two six-sided dice. Players wager on whether or not the person rolling the dice will roll an established number (the point) before he rolls a seven.

DIME $1,000.

DOUBLE DOWN Doubling your blackjack bet after you've seen your first two cards, in exchange for receiving one and exactly one more card.

DRAW (1.) An incomplete hand in cards, a series of cards needing one more to make a complete hand. **(2.)** To take an additional card.

HEADS UP One on one. Competitive between two people, excluding everyone else.

HIT To draw a card to a blackjack hand in order to increase your point total.

HOLD'EM A variation of poker. Every player gets two cards facedown, and then five community cards are turned faceup. The object is to make the highest-ranking five-card poker hand out of seven available.

HOLE CARDS Cards that can't be seen by any player except yourself. Your facedown cards.

HOUSE The casino.

LINE BET The craps bet you make on whether the dice will pass (roll the point), or don't pass (roll a seven before the point).

MONEY IN THE DITCH A game in which it is impossible to ever win.

NATURAL A two-card blackjack total of twenty-one consisting of an ace with a face card or ten.

PASS AND DON'T PASS The two opposing betting options that constitute the basis for a craps roll.

PIT The place in a casino where the table games are located, usually blackjack and craps and roulette.

(THE) POINT The number established at the beginning of a craps roll that must be rerolled before a seven in order to make the dice pass. The point is either four, five, six, eight, nine, or ten, depending on what has been established on the come out roll.

POKER A card game where the object is to make the highest-ranking five-card poker hand. Poker has many variations, including Hold'em, Omaha, and stud.

PUSH A tie. A dead heat.

RAKE The amount of money that the house takes out of a pot as a charge for running a card game, usually poker.

ROMMY A variation of blackjack played in Costa Rica.

ROULETTE A casino game in which a steel ball spins around a wheel divided into thirty-seven sections numbered zero through thirty-six. American roulette features an extra section numbered double zero.

SHOE The rectangular holder for multiple decks of cards, used primarily in baccarat and blackjack.

SHOOTER The one who is rolling the dice in a craps game.

SLOTS Slot machines.

SOFT (AS IN "SOFT SEVENTEEN") A two-card blackjack hand containing an ace. A soft total cannot be busted (go over twenty-one) with one card, because an ace can be used as a value of one or eleven. A soft seventeen is an ace with a six, it can be counted as seven or seventeen.

SPLIT A PAIR A blackjack option offered when your first two cards are the same in value. You double your bet and play two hands, each card of the pair becoming the first card of a new hand.

STAND To decline your option of taking more cards.

STRIPPED DECK A deck of cards that has had the cards numbered two through six removed from the deck, leaving thirty-two cards.

STUCK Losing. Behind money.

SURRENDER A blackjack option of resigning your hand after you've seen your first two cards for a return of half your bet.

TOKE A casino employee's tip, usually given in appreciation for a winning bet.

VIGORISH (VIG) The house edge, the odds that are in the casino's favor.

WHALE A gambler who has the capacity to win and lose very large sums at one time. A gambler who gets the highest level of service from casinos.

SOUTH OF THE BORDER

CHAPTER ONE

SAN JOSÉ, COSTA RICA

LAY OF THE LAND

"Ten thousand to you sir . . ." The dealer's voice brings me out of my reverie, I was staring at the cocktail waitress and thinking about her short dress and my mighty fine Chilean wine. I look at the raiser, a heavyset bearded man with an impatient twitch, and then down at my cards, where a jack and a six lay side by side like clothes that don't match. *"Mala suerte,"* I mutter as I return them to their rightful place in the muck.

◆

Sweat two basketball games on twin big-screen TVs over beer and a chicken sandwich. Enjoy fresh fish and then step next door to a nightclub with three rooms for three different types of dancing. Play live-action no-limit Texas Hold'em for only $18. Have a swim before meeting your date. San José has a lot of action. Costa Rica has a lot of beauty, but San José has got the action.

◆

A graying New York wise guy sits behind a counter talking on a portable phone, spitting out lines to someone on the other end. Behind him, a white magnetic chalkboard lists all the sporting events taking place and the line for each one. On the seven TVs spread across the room, Latrell Sprewell and the New York Knicks are fighting a losing battle against the Miami Heat. The Knicks are -4.

A scattered crowd of varied Americans wearing tropical button-down shirts lounge in the deep armchairs and sweat their day's bets in the cool comfort of the air-conditioned room. It might as well be Vegas, but we're in San José.

San José, Costa Rica
GENERAL INFORMATION

YOU'RE NOT IN KANSAS ANYMORE It's amazing there aren't more people going to Costa Rica. It's amazing that salesmen all over aren't ringing up their bosses and talking about the sales potentials down in that part of the world, because you could do a lot worse than to take a sales trip down to San José.

Costa Rica has now developed as a tourist and American expatriate destination in such a way that you not only begin loosening your tie on the airplane ride down there, you take it off altogether and stuff it in a side pocket in your suitcase.

WHERE Costa Rica is located in Central America, wedged between Nicaragua and Panama. The capital, San José, is in a hilly area where it may be warm in the daytime, but evenings are cool and you don't need air-conditioning because there's always a breeze blowing through.

WHEN It's always nice to visit San José. Costa Rica's high and dry season is from December 20 to February 28, so expect rooms to be more expensive during that period. Dry season is best if you're visiting rain forests or beaches.

CLIMATE The weather in San José is extraordinarily pleasant. The temperature averages between seventy and seventy-five year-round. Humidity is not terrible, but it always helps to wear shirts that breathe. The only tickle is that between May and October, there's about eight inches of rain per month.

TELEPHONES International phone code for Costa Rica is 506. To dial from the U.S., 011-506 + number. Calling cards are available on the streets of San José, usually from the same guys selling the lottery tickets. These can be put into a public phone and used for international calls. Calls to the U.S. are expensive. Don't expect to be able to talk for longer than ten minutes internationally on any one card. Calls within the country don't cost much at all.

CURRENCY The colón is the Costa Rican unit of currency. At the time of this writing, $1 = 275 colones. The colón is fully convertible in the country, as in you can just walk into a casino and get dollars for it. Don't expect to reconvert colones from outside Costa Rica, however.

There are 10,000-colón notes ($36) all the way down to little raggedy old torn, ripped, and dirty 100-colón notes ($0.36). Beware of ripped money. People are constantly trying to pass off old or torn money to you, casino cashiers notwithstanding. Once you get old or torn money, good luck getting rid of it yourself. I don't even think a bank has to take it. Don't be too meek to not accept torn or old money when cashing out of the casino cage. That's one place I don't mind being insistent.

ATMS There are ATMs in Costa Rica, but they are not conveniently located in casinos or hotels. All casinos, however, allow you to charge chips directly to your credit card, a service which usually allows you to receive more chips without having to leave the table.

¿HABLA ESPANOL? There is a lot of English spoken in San José, enough so that you won't really have a problem. But you will find some basic Spanish very helpful. Spanish is the official language of the country.

SAFETY It's basically safe to walk around in the downtown area at all times, if you're not a fool. I carried money around in a money belt with little fear. Cabs are safe, the most they'll try to hustle you for is about $3 extra. I spent a lot of time out at night and had no problems. I talked to one fellow who had been approached and hassled by a group of women who had surrounded him and begun to reach for his pockets. He ran.

There are always policemen in the large park next to the Gran Hotel Costa Rica, making it a fairly safe proposition to stroll down Avenida Central at 4 A.M. Of course, I'd still prefer to be in a taxi.

WHAT THEY WEAR People don't wear shorts in San José proper, they just don't. You'll be far more comfortable in khakis than jeans. Lightweight sport shirts with collars are the way to go. You can pick up some nice shirts along the pedestrian mall at Avenida Central that are a good value at 5,000 colones ($18), come in short or long sleeves, and seem to provide the perfect combination of style and comfort in a tropical setting. I picked out six shirts when I was down there and just wore them. Who needs a suitcase?

None of the casinos are very elegant with the exception of the

Camino Real, but you could dress up to go there and there would be no one there! I usually find the best thing is to wear nice but comfortable clothes to the casinos, and if you feel like dressing up, go to El Pueblo.

TIPPING Cab drivers don't need a tip because the fare's negotiated, but a small one for good service doesn't hurt. Some restaurants have the service included in the bill and some don't. Check your bill and tip accordingly. In some luncheonettes, tips are not expected.

INTERNET AOL has local access number. Most hotel phones support modem hookup. Internet Café located in shopping plaza right next door to Gran Hotel Costa Rica.

The System

I found out about the system by accident—honest. I mean, it was my last day in Costa Rica, Lord knows how I went so long without finding out. And I only found out about it because when I went to check out of my hotel, I noticed that there were three extra $18 charges on it. "What are these charges for?" I asked the cashier.

"For the ladies," she said, and she laughed. I laughed too. It was a funny joke.

"What ladies?" The señoritas . . . It turns out that prostitution is legal for women over the age of eighteen. Prostitution is so legal, in fact, that every hotel has its own staff of hookers, and guests are encouraged to charge them to the room (how's that for a business expense!). And not only had someone ordered three women and charged them to my room on the same night, they were of the $18 variety.

My taxi driver Coco called it "el sistema." He said he was forever having to drive prostitutes back and forth from hotels and they always wanted to know if he wanted to be paid in cash or sex. "Cash, it's safer," he said with a laugh.

Finding an escort in San José is like finding a needle in a sewing shop. If you're willing to pay, stay at one of the nicer hotels and talk to the concierge. Talk to the concierge at any hotel, for that matter. And don't forget your condoms.

I'll Walk There Barefoot
TRANSPORTATION ISSUES

LEGAL Americans need only a valid passport to enter for ninety days, and judging by the number of Americans who are down there, extensions are not difficult. Arrival is free, but they'll charge you a $17 departure tax, which is basically bail money.

FLIGHTS Juan Santamaria International airport is twelve miles outside of San José and is your number-one gateway to the country. American cities with direct connections are Los Angeles, Miami, New York, and Houston. I had no complaints with Lacsa, the Central American airline. Request the fruit plate. For very cheap fares try *www.expedia.com* or Sunday paper bucket shops. Continental and United also run regular flights. Reconfirm or risk being bumped.

It doesn't seem possible for a gringo to get anywhere from the airport for under $15, but isn't that like all airports anyway? The airport taxis are altogether different animals than local taxis. Different cars, different colors. Airport taxis are bright orange and usually Nissans, and as far as I can figure, there's no way to avoid getting ripped off by them. Flying into San José, just accept that it'll cost you $15 to get anywhere from the airport.

STREETS Downtown San José isn't that hard a place to find your way around in. The streets are in a grid. Avenidas run essentially east-west and Calles run north-south. The twist is that going north from Avenida Central, you have Avenidas 1, 3, 5, 7, and so on. Going south, the Avenidas are 2, 4, 6, 8 and so on. It's the same with the Calles. Heading east from Calle Central, the Calles number up 1, 3, 5, 7, and heading west from that spot are the even-numbered Calles. House numbers aren't bothered with here, locations are determined by the cross streets.

WHERE THINGS ARE The only things that aren't in the downtown area are most of the luxury hotels. The downtown area of San José is nice to walk around in, if only to get a feel for the city. The park abutting the Gran Hotel and the national theater is called the Plaza de Cultura (Avenida Central, Calle 3 & 5). It's a prime people-watching place and a fine place to catch the sun. The same goes for Parque Central, located around Avenida 2, Calle 2.

TRANSPORTATION AROUND TOWN In San José, everywhere is just a cab ride away, and you would be wise to keep it that way. In a city where traffic lights are a guide rather than a rule and cars hurtle around corners with their klaxons bleating, where there are shortcuts to take and streets to avoid if it's raining, if you want to gamble in the driving department, then it shouldn't get beyond sitting in the passenger seat.

Notes about Costa Rican taxi drivers. First of all, only get in the red taxis with the signs on top. The drivers are registered and won't roll you. I found all of these cab drivers to be friendly and reasonably honest. There are taxi meters, but they're usually not used for the tourists. Agree on a price before you leave. Of course, if your driver is so kind as to turn on the meter, better for you. From town to somewhere on the outskirts of town is about 1,000 or 1,500 colones.

A great alternative to renting a car is to find a driver with a cellular phone who is available twenty-four hours a day. Coco (Jose Cascante) owns his own taxi, speaks English, and knows San José like a postage stamp. He's cheaper than a rental car too. Taxi man Jose Cascante (Coco), cellular 506-390-1520.

The Money Plays
GAMBLING SETUP—THE QUICK FACTS

CASINOS With more than ten fully operational casinos, one private poker club, and more sports books in the woodwork than even the government dares to estimate, San José does provide variety for the gambler. All except for the Casino Colonial are attached to hotels and are privately owned affairs that lease out the casino space from the hotels.

HOURS Vary. The Casino Colonial and the casino in the Gran Hotel Costa Rica are open twenty-four hours. Other casinos close at 4 A.M.

ADMITTANCE No entrance fee. No dress code. Minimum gaming age is eighteen.

AMBIANCE AND AMENITIES The casinos are smaller than your Vegas casinos and tend more toward stately than fantasy themed. The Central Americans aren't going for the gimmicks. That said, each of the casinos in San José has a distinct flavor.

All casinos provide free drinks and cigarettes to players. The Colonial and the Irazú provide snacks, the Holiday Inn has a buffet on Friday and Saturday nights, and the Palacio and the Colonial have the best liquor.

GAMES ON OFFER Canasta (roulette), Rommy (like blackjack), craps, slots, Tute (Caribbean stud), sports betting, poker (Texas Hold'em), Pai-Gow poker.

LIMITS From 500 colones ($1.80) to about $500. Higher limits are available at the San José Palacio.

MONEY Casinos allow you to play in either colones or dollars and cash out in same. Some casinos require you to cash in your chips at the table, for which you receive a check that you take over to the cashier cage. It works fine.

LEGALITY The casinos and sports books operate in the gray area of a 1920s gambling statute that forbids certain types of gambling. The law forbids blackjack, for example, so the casinos have Rommy, and the law prohibits roulette, so the casinos have introduced canasta.

TIPPING POLICIES IN THE CASINO Tipping in the San José casinos is sort of like if you want to then go ahead. It's not expected. Most of the locals don't tip at all, and in the poker games a small tip is included as part of the rake. The dealers do not keep their own tokes, there is some sharing system. I found that a 100-colón ($0.40) tip every once in a while did wonders for dealer morale.

AND . . . ON THE SQUARE Casinos that possess absolutely no reason to be visited include the Hotel and Casino El Presidente on Avenida Central across from the Balmoral and the Royal Dutch Casino. They're small, never have any people in them, and don't strike me as well heeled enough to sustain the kind of loss I'm looking to put on them. Some casinos will only welcome you if you lose. You know a good casino because they don't mind if you win.

I mean it, I wouldn't go to the El Presidente casino. In my mind it's for the riffraff, and I find it hard to watch the cards and the dealer and keep all hands on my money at the same time.

I'll Take the Odds
BREAKING APART THE GAME

CANASTA (ROULETTE) The only difference between canasta and roulette is that instead of spinning a small steel ball around a roulette wheel, they spin a steel cage with thirty-eight numbered Ping-Pong balls and draw one at random. The layout and the payoffs are the same. I want to believe there's a bias. I mean, what if one of the balls gets dented?

CRAPS If you know that you want to play craps, try the Casino Colonial or the Aurola Holiday Inn.

PAI-GOW POKER Go to the San José Palacio for Pai-Gow poker played with cards.

TUTE POKER (CARIBBEAN STUD) Tute is one of those games that I sometimes watch in vain just to find a person who is winning at the game. It moves slow, and I guess it's fun, and the best advice I can give is to find a table with a huge-ass jackpot, because if you do hit that thing, it had better be worth your while.

ROMMY It looks like blackjack, and it plays a lot like blackjack. But Rommy has enough different rules that a casual player sitting down at a table could fast become confused. No worries.

It's at least as fun as blackjack, so it's a shame that the average odds against the player are at least 1 percent more than they are in your typical Vegas blackjack game. But then Las Vegas has among the best blackjack rules in the world.

Like blackjack, Rommy is a card game where players compete against a house dealer, the object being to get twenty-one, or to get as close as possible without going over. Aces can be used as one or eleven, face cards are ten, and other cards have the value of their number. After the player sees his own two cards and one of the dealer's, he has the option to hit (take another card) or stand (let the dealer act on his hand).

The main difference between Rommy and blackjack is that in Rommy, all twenty-ones are the same. Ace and ten does not pay 3–2, but rather, even money. A three-card twenty-one by the player will push a dealer blackjack.

Then there are the Rommy bonuses, which provide no small amount of excitement to the game. Should your first three cards all be the same (e.g., three threes or three sixes), your bet gets paid 5–1. The same goes if your first three cards make a straight flush in any order (e.g., four five six of hearts).

You can double down, or double your bet and receive one card, when you have a Rommy draw, for example if you have two fives or a six and five suited. Then, if you hit your draw, you will be paid 5–1 on double your bet. It's kind of fun.

As in blackjack, you are allowed to split pairs and double down on any two cards. They also allow you the option of early surrender, surrendering for half your bet before the dealer has seen his second card. This is especially useful when the dealer shows an ace or ten. Early surrender is always recommended when the dealer shows an ace, unless you have nine, ten, eleven, or greater than seventeen.

There are some times when it may make sense to double down on what would normally be considered blackjack, ace and a ten, because there is no 3–2 payout. You would most likely do this when the dealer shows a six, maybe a five.

Decisions regarding the Rommy draw come into play most often when you are dealt pairs. I would continue to split eights except into a ten, where I would either surrender or draw. I would not be as liberal with splitting twos and threes, however, except into a six.

The good news is that there is basically no heat for the card counter. With the exception of the San José Palacio, Costa Rican floor people wouldn't know counting techniques if you conked them over the head with a book by Stanford Wong. At the Colonial and the Holiday Inn Aurola, you can spread your bets from 500 colones ($1.60) to $200 with no heat save a puzzled stare. Shuffle tracking is very possible in all the casinos. Deck penetration varies from 60 to 80 percent.

The bad news is that the game is tough to beat. Blackjack only paying even money adds a whopping 2 percent to the house edge, but early surrender gets you back about ½ percent, and the Rommy bonuses and unlimited draw on the aces get you a little extra more. Using either the $25 match play coupon at the Holiday Inn or playing the joker game at the Gran Hotel should put you close to thinking you can beat it. I had middling success by playing the minimum 500 colones bet and then raising it to one or two hands of $50 each when the true count reached +4.

If you're serious about beating the game, my advice is to cut the match play coupon out of the *Tico Times*, an English-language weekly available all over town, and go over to the Holiday Inn Aurola at noon for some head up play. (See Holiday Inn Aurola, Rules and Notes.)

SPORTS BETTING There's a lot of sports books in San José, but you won't necessarily see them all when you're down there. The big ones don't mess with local action, they have their headquarters in some office building where they field telephone and Internet bets from other countries, primarily America. If you're interested in betting big (sky's the limit), give Servicios Internacionales de Informacion a call. Located in an area called Sabana Sur, phone numbers 506 + 220-3922, 220-3928, 220-3932, 220-3936, 220-3937, 220-3283, 220-4428.

If $10 up to a few hundred a game more suits your fancy, check out the books at the San José Palacio, the Casino Colonial, and the Gran

Hotel Costa Rica, in that order. You can pretty much bet on any game taking place in America that day, college or pro, laying 11 to win 10 on standard line bets.

CRIS, Costa Rica International Sports, is a reputable outfit with a lot of money behind them and friendly service. Their motto is "We can't pay you fast enough." Offices at the San José Palacio and Barcelo Amon, and a website at *http//www.crissports.com*. Hours: 9 A.M. EST until the last game starts, seven days a week. Telephone Numbers (506) 256-4568. Jimmie at the Barcelo Palacio 011-506-291 0740. 1-800-5-YOU-WIN, 1-800-596-8946. 011-506-296 6205.

What's the Line?

The sign on the door reads SERVICIOS INTERNACIONALES DE INFORMACIÓN. Inside, rows of operators sit plastered to their computers and their telephones, spitting out names and prices to callers. From the plate-glass windows to the twenty-five-inch computer screens, no expenses have been spared in making this the most modern of all business offices.

The office building is located in a prestigious complex on the outskirts of town. On the first floor are the offices of Citibank, upstairs those of the Japanese Ambassador. And here, inside Servicios Internacionales de Informacion, is the headquarters of one of the largest sports betting operations in the world. Here, inside San José, Costa Rica.

Forget Las Vegas. "We own Las Vegas," a clerk named Marty brags to me, "Their lines follow us." In Las Vegas you can't make a bet bigger than $10,000 without having to report it to the government. Here, a 10 dime wager (gambler's slang, a dime is $1,000) barely evokes a stifled yawn.

Sports betting is one of the largest American pastimes. Betting on the Super Bowl alone, is estimated to be in excess of $1 billion worldwide. Yet Nevada sports books, the place a bettor would traditionally go to place a legal bet, reported this year a betting handle on the Super Bowl of $70 million, a large sum but less than 10 percent of the estimated worldwide activity. Does this mean that Americans wagered $900 million this year illegally in only one week? Not exactly. And that's where Costa Rica comes in.

Costa Rica, land of opportunity. The country is stable, the government is democratic, and as one American operator down here put it to me, "The only things they arrest you for are rape and murder."

Dave has been in the booking business his whole life. He ran a local operation in Sarasota, Florida, until about two years ago when the heat came down and police grabbed hold of a bookie and confiscated his Rolodex. They started arresting clients, plastering the names of local attorneys, doctors, and politicians on the front page of the paper and basically embarrassing members of the community and scaring everyone else out of business. So

Dave moved shop down to Costa Rica, got his own website, and now he's legitimate. Or at least gray enough not to worry about prosecution.

Just how does a booking operation like Servicios Internacionales de Información operate? With a telephone account, players need only pick up the phone from anywhere in America and they are instantly connected via a toll-free number to the most up-to-date lines on the planet. And if you want your money and you're in Milwaukee, don't worry. A certified check will be sent by overnight mail or the money can be waiting at a Western Union depot in a matter of hours. Or you could leave something in your account just in case. After all, the Yankees play almost every day.

Now we've all heard of the neighborhood bookie. And we've doubtless also heard about those fly-by-night booking shops in the Caribbean, with a phone line, a web page, and a shack on the beach. And the reason some people don't bet is because they're scared they might not get paid if they win a bundle. Now it's amazing that places can exist that have a credit rating similar to the Las Vegas Hilton, but Servicios handles and pays some huge bets.

One of their clients is a movie star, long known in gambling circles as a whale, someone whose action is courted by casinos worldwide because of his capacity to lose more than $100,000 in a single gambling session. During 1998 to 1999, the star reportedly lost $11 million sports betting with Servicios Internacionales, including a $4 million wager on the Super Bowl. (Unfortunately for him, he picked the Falcons.) Now that's big.

It seems the only reason Servicios Internacionales de Información doesn't have more clients is because the average bettor fears prosecution. But just what is the current legality of these operations?

It seems like no one is sure what's legal anymore, including the U.S. government. In the past, the government prosecuted bookies for taking bets and in some cases, bettors from making them, using phone records and betting slips as evidence that the 1961 Federal Wire Act had been violated. But what if the wagers are not taking place in America? What if the bets are being made in a foreign country where they are not illegal?

Are the books breaking the law by accepting bets from Americans? Is an American breaking the law by making the bet in a foreign country? Does it matter if it takes place over the Internet?

The answer is no one knows for sure. The Attorney General's office has been attempting to see the bounds of the law by pursuing some cases, but their headlong rush for settlements on some and foot dragging on others as they make their way to the courts or are dismissed seem to point toward an acknowledgment that it will take legislation to stop the new wave of gambling. And into the void stepped the Kyl Bill.

Introduced by Senator Jon Kyl of Wisconsin and dead on the floor in 1998, the original version of the bill sought to make all forms of gambling illegal that take place either over the telephone line or via computer modem. It would have clarified the gray area by making it not only illegal to take the bets, but also to place them from the United States via phone or Internet. Except for the special exemptions made for the state owned on-line lotteries, which already feature ways for Americans to purchase lottery tickets on line. The states are loath to give up that boon.

The Kyl Bill is a study in irony. On one hand, Senator Kyl trumpets the bill as taking the moral high ground, protecting average citizens from the evils of having legalized betting creep into their homes where the dangerous addiction of gambling can't be controlled. On the other hand, funding for this bill comes not from anti-gambling puritan activists, but rather from Nevada casinos who are worried about offshore and Internet gambling cutting into their share of the gambling market, or taking it away completely. The bill has also gained the support of the thoroughbred racing industry.

The moral argument about the ills of gambling just aren't holding water anymore. Like the Volstead Act, which sought to impose a puritan opposition to alcohol on an unwilling majority, the explosion of casinos has obliterated the idea that Americans want to be protected by a law prohibiting gambling. Ten years ago, a person had to either fly to Las Vegas or go to the racetrack to participate in legal gambling. The thirty-two states that now boast some kind of legal casinos and the others that have signed on to lotteries of some kind have made a situation where it's more than likely that if you want to place a wager, you're only driving down the road.

Why, then, is everyone so scared of Internet and telephone wagering? Taxation and fear of their products losing big when it comes to open market competition. If the government is truly concerned about the ills of gambling, why the giant billboards, why the TV commercials, why the saturation and publicity associated with the state lotteries, which fill state coffers with an easy source of funding, or state income from racetracks. But of all the gambling options available to people worldwide, nothing could be worse for the informed bettor than betting at the racetrack or on the lottery.

Let's examine horse racing first, long popular with Damon Runyon–esque citizens and having a reputation as only beatable with inside information or uncanny good fortune. Maybe this is because the racetrack and the state hold on to an average of 20 percent of the betting handle, making a horse wager one of the worst bets in the country, comparable only to a few unregulated slot machines that are tighter than your steel drum. What fool in his right mind would bet on a horse race where he's giving up 20 percent of his money when he can place a craps bet and only be fading 1 percent to the house? Any wonder why the tracks these days resemble ghost towns more than they do hotbeds of gambling activity? Any wonder why the image of the horse player is threadbare clothes and two dimes to rub together?

The other state supported gambling activity is the lottery. This addictive get-rich-quick scheme is almost exclusively the domain of the lowest income section of the population, making the lottery a great disguise for a poor tax.

Forget that and look at what the state keeps. Should you be one of the one in 8 million people who does win the lottery, then you have two options about how to get paid the jackpot. One option is to get it paid out over twenty years, the government taking the interest on the money for twenty years and in effect paying out little more than that interest. Or you can take a lump sum payment, which usually amounts to less than half of the total. And then you've got to pay taxes on the money to boot, so not only does the state keep most of the money, it then taxes you in addition. Compare that to your average 11–10 sports bet where the bookie takes a modest 5 percent, or your average casino game where the bulk of paybacks range from 95 to 99 percent, and you'd have to be crazy to play a state-run game with an option. Is it any wonder why the government fears open market competition in the gambling business? They would lose their stranglehold.

A new version of the Kyl Bill, introduced in early 1999, shows a good deal more leniency all the way around. First of all, gone from the bill is the casual bettor provision, which means the bettor of the gambling site would no longer be subject to prosecution or fine or jail term. There are also numerous exceptions in the bill, including one for overseas sites as long as the games are legal in the countries where the bettor is participating. Hello, Costa Rica, the Caribbean, and Servicios Internacionales. It would still remain illegal, however, to accept interstate bets over phone or wire lines, and Indian reservations would similarly be banned from having wagering sites.

As of this writing, the Kyl Bill (called the Goodlatte Bill in the House) is so mired in murky backroom deals, weird amendments, and flat out ambiguity, that no one is sure what it will mean if the law should even be passed. One thing is sure, however. The most honest and up-to-date site for accurate information regarding the legality of Internet gambling, as well as the best place for a frank description of which online sites are reputable, is "The Prescription." Go to www.theprescription.com, and believe what they say.

Where sports booking used to be the registered domain of the Mafia, the bastion of shadiness and organized crime, the business is now a billion-dollar semilegal operation, where bettors have nothing to worry about, lines are coordinated worldwide via the Internet, and betting is approximately as safe as walking your dog. Maybe.

Here in Costa Rica, the passage of the Kyl Bill in its current form would be looked upon as the green light. From telephone betting shops like Servicios Internacionales to online poker sites like Planet Poker to web-based pari-mutuel betting sites like All Sports Bets, the exceptions in the current bill would turn the gray area of legality into business sunshine. It could be that the gambling gloves are off.

Who are the Yankees playing today?

SLOTS The story is that all the slots in Costa Rica are owned by three guys. Technically slots are illegal, but they made a deal with the government some years ago and I guess a small percentage of the profits go to the Red Cross or something like that, but the casinos don't own those slots or run them. And if you hit a jackpot, a special representative from the slot guys has to come out to pay you. I'll take the under on the slot pay back rate. If you really have to, why don't you just hire someone to shine a flashlight in your eyes and take your wallet. Easily the worst bet in Costa Rica.

But I will say this for the Costa Rican slots—with the exception of the Hotel Irazú, they're the quiet kind. The Irazú is the only place where the slot noise can get a little annoying, but the place is a fuckin' zoo.

I have thirdhand information that the slots in San José pay back 85 percent, but that is an absolute maximum. I would not be at all surprised by much lower numbers. There's no one to regulate and there's no competition!

POKER Right now San José is a haven for a poker player. All the games are good, and all are on the square. Poker winnings are taxed. Though the rake is very reasonable (less than $1 per hand in most cases, including tip), 3 to 5 percent is taken off the money you cash out for by the state. Winners must play at least two hours (three at the Corobici). No hit-and-run. There is no missing of blinds, either in a tournament or live game. It just gets taken off your stack if you're not there. You still get cards. Throwing cards or cursing can get you into trouble. A buy-in is called a *camisa* (shirt). The dealer gets a small tip as part of the rake, anything extra is optional.

The live-action no-limit Hold'em game, which rotates between the Palacio and the Irazú, is exciting and very beatable. Expect an average win to be in the $100 to $500 range.

Poker is being played at three San José locales. The Casino and Hotel Irazú (pronounced *ear-ah SUE*), the San José Palacio, and the Brennes' poker club at the Hotel Corobici. During the week, the Hotel Irazú and the Palacio alternate hosting tournaments followed by open poker games. The tournaments usually last about three to four hours and the live games continue on until 4 A.M., when most of San José's casinos close. The games are well run and attract a steady mix of tourists, locals, and in-betweens.

On Mondays and Wednesdays, the action gets under way at the Irazú at 8 P.M. A low buy-in tournament is immediately followed by live-action play, no-limit table stakes Hold'em with a minimum buy-in of only $18. On Fridays, the tournament is eschewed in favor of just the live-action games, and they usually start up one regular table and then one larger stakes table, where the minimum buy-in is around $72.

Tuesdays and Thursdays, the setup is pretty much the same over at the Barcelo San José Palacio. The tournament starts at 8 P.M. The only nettling thing is that paying for your initial buy-in is at the discretion of the card room manager, which means some people get into the tournament for free. No worry, the action in the live game after makes up for anything, and the Palacio is a comfortably friendly place to play.

More serious poker in town can be found at the Hotel Corobici. On the second floor of the Corobici, in a conference room next door to the Japanese restaurant, is the home and headquarters of a private poker club run by the Brennes brothers, a Costa Rican poker family who have made a name for themselves on the international poker scene. Humberto is a familiar figure on the world tournament circuit, him being the rightful owner of a World Series of Poker bracelet. And he's not bashful about it either. If you're locked up in a big pot with him and you push in your stack, he's prone to asking in his thick Spanish accent, "Do you know who I am? . . . I'm Humberto!" He's brought full-scale poker to Costa Rica, and the natives have been quick to learn. The games here are a tad more serious, the stakes larger, the buy-ins bigger. Visitors are welcome, however, as long as they bring cash and know-how, and conduct themselves like gentlemen. Throw the cards here, or curse someone out, and you're likely to be shown the door. The poker club at the Corobici lists among its clientele many prominent and wealthy Costa Ricans, including one regular player who is the wife of a former president of the country.

Games get under way seven days a week, usually around 3 P.M., with the exception of Sunday, when players don't arrive until the eight o'clock tournament time. A typical day sees one table of $15 to $30 limit half Hold'em/half Omaha Hi-Lo, and a table of pot-limit Omaha with blinds of $5–$5–$10, which can quickly become expensive. The games have a buy-in of only $300, but you're liable to see several thousand on the table. The pot-limit game plays especially big and a person could win or lose $5,000–$10,000 without stretching the imagination. The club has a three-hour minimum for winners, so don't try to hit-and-run.

The best deal in town is the club's Sunday night tournament, limited to fifty players, where a mere 5,000 colones ($18) will give you a shot at a prize pool that is regularly $7,000 or more. Why so much money? Not only are there ninety minutes of unlimited rebuys, but players are permitted to make more than one rebuy at a time according to how many they've already purchased. It is not uncommon for a player to make twenty or more buy-ins in the space of that hour and a half, and while you might object to the structure, no one objects to the overlay they're getting on their money. Arrive there before eight o'clock and get 50 percent extra on your first buy-in. This tournament doesn't usually end until about 3 A.M., but the live games start up as soon as enough people are knocked out to fill a table.

You can order directly from the next door Japanese restaurant or the downstairs coffee shop and eat at the table. Poker and prime sushi.

COSTA RICAN POKER SCHEDULE

DAY	PLACE	TIME	GAME (BUY-IN)
Mon.	Corobici	3 P.M.	Cash Games ($300)
	Irazú	8 P.M.	Tournament ($10), Cash Games ($18)
Tues.	Corobici	3 P.M.	Cash Games ($300)
	Palacio	8 P.M.	Tournament ($10), Cash Games ($36)
Wed.	Corobici	3 P.M.	Cash Games ($300)
	Irazú	8 P.M.	Tournament ($10), Cash Games ($18)
Thurs.	Corobici	3 P.M.	Cash Games ($300)
	Palacio	8 P.M.	Tournament ($10), Cash Games ($36)
Fri.	Corobici	3 P.M.	Cash Games ($300)
	Irazú	7:30 P.M.	Cash Games ($36 or $72)
Sat.	Corobici	3 P.M.	Cash Games ($300)
Sun.	Corobici	8 P.M.	Tournament ($18), Cash Games (varied)

Casinos and Lodging
THE POINT

(BARCELO) SAN JOSÉ PALACIO

The Palacio is where the big gamblers hang out. It's where you come if you got $1 million and you want a private table and want to get treated with the professionalism and respect that you deserve. Or you could fly to Vegas. But who needs Vegas when you've got the Palacio? Bob, the casino manager, understands gambling; hell, he's been in it his whole life. But don't worry. They take the $5 bets too. And you get treated the same way and get to look at the same pretty dealers.

Bob broke in at the old Union Plaza in the 1970s, worked for Benny Binion at the Horseshoe and at the Fremont and at Caesars Palace Las Vegas before he hooked up with his present employer. Bob's learned from the best, and his casino reflects it. The dealers are excellent (not to mention the prettiest in San José), the casino is quiet and classy, and it's the only place in town where you can set your own upper limit (à la the OLD Horseshoe).

Bob burns a card every hand if you're playing Rommy heads up, and that is a fairly effective foil for the counters. He says one fellow came in once and won $14,000 the first night and $10,000 the second night and then Bob thick cut and started burning cards on his ass and the guy didn't want to play anymore. So he seems to feel like that's pretty good evidence that Rommy can be beat if a counter really knows what he's doing.

The Palacio is the only place in town that has a good Pai-Gow poker game dealt regularly. I saw a local heavy come in and want to play Pai-Gow for $500 a spot across six hands a deal. And Bob didn't say anything, just got the dealer and opened the rack and stood there at the side of the table with a cup of coffee and his cell phone on his hip and made sure the game was dealt right. Three thousand dollars a hand.

He leases out casino space to Jimmy, a young straight arrow American who runs the sports book there. Jimmy has another office in town and he's hooked up with CRIS (Costa Rica International Sports), who have a big operation down there and even have brochures and sports schedules put out on display for perusal. But Jimmy just manages the book at the Palacio, and he's got a bunch of telephone accounts and a lot of local action from guys who work at other books, and he was telling Bob that he just got hammered on the Super Bowl. Darn near everybody did. Now he feels like he worked the whole year for free. But he always had a smile for me, and I wasn't even betting very big, just parlaying some action from the Oscar De La Hoya fight over onto a Utah Jazz game.

Casino

HOURS 2 P.M.–4 A.M. daily, sports book daily until start of last game.

LANGUAGE English and Spanish.

LAYOUT The casino is on the second floor, occupying a wing. The casino is not big, but its atmosphere is the pièce de résistance for the hotel. Vegas style, and so professionally run it's a pleasure to spend an evening there. Sports book seats six.

GAMES Pai-Gow, Rommy, craps, Caribbean stud, slots, sports book, poker.

LIMITS $5–$500 posted; however, the Palacio regularly has people who play higher and the casino manager, Bob, will probably give you anything you want.

RULES AND NOTES In the poker tournament on Tuesdays and Thursdays, your first buy-in is either free or 2,000 colones ($7.20), depending on management discretion. It's not the greatest of tourneys, but the live no-limit Texas Hold'em game following more than makes up for it. When playing blackjack heads up, the dealer will burn a card almost every hand and cut it thick.

FOOD AND DRINK The buffet at the restaurant is unimpressive. Good liquor in the casino. Try the crème de menthe or the house red wine.

THE PEOPLE THERE Bob, the casino manager, arguably knows more about running a casino than anyone in Costa Rica. Wise guy know-how is uniquely American, if you ask me. The dealers and waitresses are the prettiest in San José. The clientele is mostly tourists and wealthy Ticos. No riffraff.

Hotel

The Palacio is a luxury standard edifice just off the highway into town. It is owned and managed by the Barcelo group, who also own the Amon Hotel in town. The lobby is spacious and broad, the bar has comfortable couches and a big-screen TV. Room rates are in the $120 per night range, plus tax.

PRACTICALITIES
Hotel Phone Number: 506-220-2034
Casino Phone Number: 506-220-1310
Internet Address: *www.barcelo.com*
Location: Near the area called La Sabana Norte. Just outside of city central, a five- to ten-minute cab ride to town and fifteen minutes to the airport. In close proximity to both the Corobici and the Hotel Irazú.

Ticos and Gringos

I find the Ticos, as the Costa Rican people like to refer to themselves, friendly to strangers. One night we're in the heat of a four-table tournament over at the San José Palacio, and a big beefy American sits down with a bad attitude and a very vague idea of what poker's all about. He clearly has never played in a tournament before, can't seem to grasp that the chips aren't real money and that they can't be cashed out at any time. Several locals at the table who speak English patiently try to explain the situation to him, but he refuses to listen and keeps waving them off with a "You shut up. I don't want to hear nothing from any of you. I want the dealer to tell me what's going on." Unfortunately, this particular dealer did not speak English so well, and she only knew that this threatening fellow seemed poised to upturn the table for no reason and start slugging Costa Ricans. He finally left in a huff with a puffed-out chest and a scowl on his face, and all of us at the table were bewildered, to say the least. One player, a pleasant middle-aged lady in a jumpsuit and bright red lipstick, asked me, "What was wrong? We were only trying to help." What could I say? Some people come in with a bad attitude and the assumption that everyone is out to get them, and if you feel that way, traveling won't be much fun for you, regardless.

I was heartily welcomed in every poker game I played in and received numerous invitations to dinner from some of the players I became friendly with. The only time I felt severe animosity directed toward me was one night over at the Casino Colonial when some severely unpopular Rommy decisions that I made caused some fellows to lose a great deal of colones. Or so they thought. The truth was that these guys played Rommy so badly that they were in big trouble regardless, but they certainly didn't like when I found ways to hit fifteen and sixteen and by some voodoo analysis of what coulda shoulda been I take the dealer's bust card. From three seats away, mind you!

Guy next to me yesterday says, most of the expatriates down here are rummies. Like me. I looked and sure enough he had the requisite red and misshapen nose. "I don't care about the money," he said, "I just like to fuck around in here and drink for free." And the way he was downing those gin and tonics, you'd have to think he got the best of it. Just bet the minimum and make your money last, and fill 'er up. "Neat!" he said every time the dealer got a bust card.

Some guy was telling me about the woodwork. "You ain't never seen nothing like it!" he exclaims while we're sitting in the Casino Colonial. "When they had the Super Bowl here, the line to bet went around the room. They had guys coming out of the woodwork you never seen before!" Americans will come out for the Super Bowl. And there's a lot of Americans in the wood-work in San José.

Take Big Jim, who tried living in Reno for a while, then he came down here. And he said after a few weeks he came to the realization that Costa Rica was just better in every way. I mean, every way. He racked his brain and couldn't figure out a single reason not to be here.

Big Jim stares down and to the left in that off in space expression of I've got it made and you have no idea. He trades stocks by computer and bets sports and spent some time in Kiev, where he says the prostitutes look like models and are chemical engineers and will sleep with you just because the radiator is on in your hotel room. But here in San José he's got a cheap apart-ment and everything else he could ask for. As for sports betting, his com-ment is "Well, I don't bet a lot of games." Yes, you mean not like Pete Rose.

Big Jim's not more than thirty-five, and he's one of those guys who's just kind of big everywhere without being fat, and he wears a baseball cap pulled down that is a bit too small for his crewcut head, and it's like he might have been a lineman or something.

I guess you might as well retire as soon as you can.

Then there was Joe. Joe had a pretty nice setup. I met him while bullshitting with the guys about basketball in the Colonial sports book. He was in his early sixties and sported a beard and he was trying to be trimmer in his running suit. Joe hailed from upstate New York, I think, and he had some business that he left his sons in, and he's been down here a year now and he's having the time of his life. He's got a girlfriend maid who comes three days a week and cleans his apartment and he gives her lunch and $36 a week and she's twenty-five years old, beautiful, and happy as shit. She makes twice as much as the cardiologist lady who comes twice a week to give him Spanish lessons and would like to be his girlfriend herself, as there aren't many jobs for a cardiologist in and around San José. But Joe rents a condo in a gated community and he bought all his own furniture and he walks from his apartment into town and hangs at the Casino Colonial, where he likes to make big sports bets on the basketball totals, or else he pops on over to the Holiday Inn for a little Rommy with that match play coupon they've got. He eats well, he gambles, he feels great, he loves the life. Costa Rican women are different, he says to me. Age is not so important to them. They want a man who can support them and who will treat them with respect.

And he tells me about the time his girlfriend maid came over when his cardiologist Spanish teacher was there, who is quite a looker herself, and his girlfriend turned purple and started throwing things and he said there was gonna be some violence if his cardiologist Spanish teacher didn't start explaining pretty quick. "They're jealous, these Tican women," he said.

CASINO COLONIAL

Housed in an old restored mansion, and permanently tended by a twenty-four-hour gorilla at the door, the Casino Colonial has got the most flavor of any joint in town. There's always something going on inside, whether it's señoritas bringing around trays of bacon-wrapped plantains or fried cheese, or someone stopping at your side every five minutes to find out what it is you'd like to drink, and then looking genuinely sorry if you ask for a glass of water. Personally, I got into the fruit milk shakes myself. They have papaya or mango or chocolate, but the bar is well stocked with booze that is liberally free to customers. I just have a problem counting down a four-deck shoe when I'm soused.

The Casino Colonial is quiet. Not the kind of quiet that's real empty, but the kind of quiet where they're serious about gambling and there's no noisy bells and the ceilings are yea high and absorb all the noise and it's downright pleasant, from the big European-style dining room in front, with plush chairs, to the large horseshoe-shaped well-stocked bar. Nobody gives you a hassle if you gamble or not, as long as you look presentable. I have to tell you, the place reminds me a lot of the old Concord Casino in Vienna, Old World charm, tuxedoed staff, and professionalism all around. And the sports book upstairs is a class act. These wise guys aren't stiffing you. They're in business because of their reputation, and you're not gonna be their first louse up.

Casino

HOURS Twenty-four hours a day, sports book open daily until about 6 P.M.

LANGUAGE Spanish. Some English spoken.

LAYOUT Large casino, tall ceilings, sports book up the circular stairs in back located on its own floor. Day in and out, the busiest casino in town.

GAMES Craps (1 table), canasta (6), Rommy (6), Tute (6), slots, sports book.

LIMITS 500 colones or $1.80 to $100, depending on which currency you're using.

RULES AND NOTES In the Rommy they let you take insurance when the dealer has a ten as well as when she has an ace. If you take insurance when the dealer is showing a ten and she turns up an ace, it pays 10–1.

In craps, placing the six for 600 colones, or just over $2, is a cheap option for fun. You can lay every point across for a mere 3,200 colones ($12)! When it gets off the ground, the craps game at the Colonial is as good as any in town. It is not uncommon to see the table full around eight in the evening.

The sports book is the most pleasant place in Costa Rica to watch a game. Seats fifty people with no problem, complete with seven TVs. It's the place of choice for gringos to sweat their action. Run by Richard, phone accounts are welcome.

FOOD AND DRINK Bocas (snacks) come on the average of twice an hour, and they don't skimp. Pass on the fried pork pieces. The restaurant is full service twenty-four hours. Plate of the day or Tom Evans meat loaf, 1,300 colones ($5). The bar is well stocked, and they can make you a martini or a milkshake. When you order a beer, it comes in a beer glass, a tall and tapered stein with a perfectly foamed head in a glass that isn't even allowed to get below halfway before being replaced with a fresh one. Now that's service.

THE PEOPLE THERE Casino is owned and run by Americans with longtime interests down here. Richard, graying wise guy type from New York, runs the sports book during normal business hours. The clientele is local. Very local. It can get a bit boisterous late at night.

Hotel

No hotel attached.

PRACTICALITIES
Casino Phone Number: 506-258-2807
Location: Avenida 1, Calles 9 & 11. Located in the downtown area, right next door to the Hotel Del Rey.

Why Not?

Gamblers come in all shapes and sizes, but one shake and they separate, instantly distinguish themselves inside of five minutes as to what types of bettors they are. Take the scene that I stumbled in on in the Casino Colonial. Five guys surrounding a Rommy table, their leader interrogating a casino floor person about the rules. She spoke not a lot of English, and he was using the tried-and-true communication method where when they don't understand your language, speak louder. So he's yelling at her at the top of his lungs, "Blackjack? Is this BLACKJACK?" What do you pay for blackjack? And the poor señora is looking a little flustered and his gang of five is gathered around him and I just took a wild guess that they were new in town.

We commandeered a Rommy table in the corner. One of them bet the minimum every time, win or lose. One of them never took a hit. One made a big bet and then got scared to double down with it. And one of them, John, bet all of his chips in such an alarming fashion that within no time he had put all of his cash in, and then you should have heard him whoop like a little kid when he found out you could draw chips directly from a credit card. This man had done a little gambling, he had a recklessness which piqued even my interest and considering I'd seen some pretty mad fellows, that was saying something. John was from Michigan and I guess he was vaguely in business back there and he wore a baseball cap and was full on, all the time, from his throwing back the tall beers to playing his blackjack hand to the hilt, he had more gamble than you would normally see in a twenty-something vacation breaker.

You know what I liked about him? He was funny. He was gambling and he was losing, and he was funny. He knew what it meant.

He hated to surrender. They allow you to surrender in Costa Rica, concede your hand for half your bet after seeing your two cards and the dealer's one, which I do a lot, especially if the dealer has an ace show-ing. "Wipe your ass," John called it. To signal a surrender, you do have to wipe your finger across your cards, horizontally, and so every time we'd surrender we'd say, "Wipe my ass," and we were having a hell of a time playing Rommy, drinking and talking and me trying to keep a running count on the decks at the same time.

And here's the kicker. Somehow we ended up playing roulette over at the Del Rey, it had something to do with wanting to see all the strumpets at the Blue Marlin bar.

So my man John is betting it up pretty heavy there, he keeps asking to go over the limit betting on black, and they keep no betting his ass every time he tries to put down 40,000 colones. Maximum bet on the outside is 20,000 colones, they say. Now who ever heard of that shit? Seventy-two-dollar max bet on the outside of a roulette table?

My man has 70,000 colones in chips on the table, all of it his money by the way, and the management refuses to bring him a beer. *"No hay cerveza,"* they say. "Scotch?" They only serve booze because it's cheaper and because they got that rotgut house well liquor out back that I wouldn't serve to a dog as paint thinner. Classy joint. And the Del Rey is small and noisy and Cuban cigars average $15 each and the bar is stuffed with old men and young whores. Severely past its prime. Meanwhile, next door at the Colonial, they won't even let my beer get empty before they replace it. If I leave it sitting there untouched for six minutes, they figure it's gone flat and serve up a fresh one.

And while we were over there, my man John got hungry. He wanted carne, he said. *"Mas bocas,"* said I to the floorman. He snapped his fingers and said something strong to a waitress and fifteen minutes later we had not a little snack, but a parade of bountiful hors d'oeuvres coming our way. First a tray of salchichon wrapped in tortillas, followed by finger sand-wiches, fried chicken tenders, and some kind of pork meatball. Plus ciga-rettes coming fast and furious. Casino Colonial is a real joint, and they'll take care of you if you're gambling. And why not?

HOLIDAY INN AUROLA

The fellas liked the Holiday Inn. There were four of them and they were from Alabama and they were staying two to a room and their only prob-lem was that two of them had to wait upstairs in the casino and play Rommy with me while their friends were in the rooms with their dates. And they weren't very good Rommy players. They had just come from two days up on the Caribbean coast and they were sunburned from play-ing golf, but they said that besides playing golf there wasn't much else to do up there in the resort. Not like San José, where they'd already gambled and eaten lobster and picked up escorts, and they just got into town!

Isn't it worth the trade-off for a beach, if you've got a place with a nice pool and an exercise room and just a host of activities at your fingertips? I was in Costa Rica three weeks and I never left San José, and I was just budgeting my time at the end because there was so damn much to do. And all the restaurants. You will not lack for sustenance, or ever eat the same meal twice. Unless you want to eat it six times.

Casino

HOURS Open 2 P.M.–4 A.M. daily.

LANGUAGE Spanish. Lots of English spoken.

LAYOUT The Holiday Inn Hotel Aurora has got a pretty sweet deal up on the seventeenth floor. It's a beautiful view of the city at night from the penthouse casino, as the Holiday Inn is the tallest building in the area. The casino is a halfway pleasant place to relax even when you're not gambling. Deep plush red velvet armchairs and sofas let you sink into the room. Comfortable gambling.

Nice house music soundtrack. In succession, the Doors—"Don't You Love Her Madly," Romantics—"Talking in Your Sleep," and Survivor's "Eye of the Tiger."

GAMES Rommy, canasta, craps, Tute, slots.

LIMITS 500 colones ($5) to 50,000 colones ($200).

RULES AND NOTES Best place in town to play Rommy heads up with the dealers, in the afternoons. Don't forget the $25 match play coupon in the *Tico Times*, there's one in every issue. The great thing about the match play deal is that for $25 you get five $5 match play chips. Contrary to every other place I've been, if you win your bet, you get to keep playing with the match play chip. You can keep getting paid $10 for the same $5 bet as long as you keep winning. Now that's pretty sweet. No word on how often you can use this coupon either. I did it three days in a row with nary a raised eyebrow, and I won each day.

Good selection of slots, for Costa Rica. Two kinds of video poker, deuces wild, bars and cherries.

Don't get sucked in by the raffle. I carried a hoard of raffle tickets around for a week—just forget it.

FOOD AND DRINK There is a nice but pricey restaurant adjoining the casino on the seventeenth floor. The casino has a well-stocked bar and they will bring you a tasty-looking ham and cheese grillwich free of charge at all hours. The mixed drinks I sampled were exceptional. There is a free dinner buffet with live music on Friday and Saturday nights.

THE PEOPLE THERE The casino is owned by the same fellow who owns the Colonial Casino, an American named Shelby Addleman. The stickman at the craps game has either been to Vegas or seen some Frank Sinatra movies, because he knows the slang on the numbers, calls nine the center fielder, and runs a rocking craps game. The Aurola also allows you to buy numbers. The craps games I witnessed there cooked, with no sweat during $100 pass line bets or $180 each on the six and eight. The craps game, however, does not go every day. For a sure game, try the Colonial Casino.

Unfortunately, a few of the female dealers are bored and surly. The clientele consists mainly of guests from the hotel, which frequently hosts business conventions. There is also a smattering of locals and backpackers.

Hotel

The Holiday Inn is a sleek businessperson's hotel with all the services. Pool is indoors, but this is made up for by the addition of a sauna and exercise room. Rooms with numbers ending in 01 or 17 are corner rooms with two sets of windows. These should be pursued at all costs, because the Aurola is the tallest building in the area and views are pretty sweet. Feels like Windows on the World from room 1117. The staff is top-notch. Facilities are clean and well provided for. Room rates are reasonable for the area at $110 plus tax.

Presidential suite has Jacuzzi and sauna and full kitchen and reception room and banquet table. 188 rooms, 8 suites, including 1 presidential and 4 junior. El Mirador restaurant with French cuisine, coffee shop, underground parking, executive services, and business hookups.

PRACTICALITIES
Hotel Phone Number: 506-233-7233, or 1-800-Holiday from the U.S.
Casino Phone Number: 506-233-9490
Internet Address: *www.ticonet.co.cr/hotel/aurola/ aurola.html*
E-mail: *aurola@ticonet.co.cr, aurola@sol.racsa.co.cr*
Location: Avenida 5 and Calle 5. On the north side of downtown, easy walking to any downtown location.

Granola Gamblers

The girl reminded me of that character from *Let It Ride* who's just a little bit cheesed off at losing her $20 and bound and determined to get it back. She and her boyfriend were backpackers, skinny world travelers with him sporting a goatee and her thin as a rail and both of them wearing the one thing they had that wasn't ripped and wrinkled, and it was flowery and flowing. They're at the Rommy table when I come in, two people behind one $2 bet and he's got his fingers rubbing his goatee as he deigns to make out what cards are coming next, and he's usually wrong.

Later they're sitting in the comfortable couches off to the side, talking about what to do next. The girl absolutely can't believe she's lost gambling. All is not right in the world. She is concocting some sort of roulette scheme that can't lose like betting half the money on black and then betting again on red and the guy is rubbing his goatee and looking like he just wants to gamble but is out of dough. He can't be more than twenty-one. Later on they are at the roulette table and then I see them the next night too, so I guess they were finished with the hiking and eco living.

HOTEL HERRADURA

You won't make the mistake of thinking you're in downtown San José. The Hotel Herradura is a large luxury complex located a hop, skip, and a jump away from the airport and a hearty cab ride away from downtown. That aside, it's quite a nice place with lots of tennis courts and an eighteen-hole golf course. The pool is a sight to behold and you have all the other services and restaurants associated with a luxury hotel.

My complaint is that it's far enough from town to make it a little bit of a hassle getting back and forth. It's also not a real busy place. When I was there, it was quite empty. Golf is theoretically available to people not staying in the hotel, but I would suggest calling well in advance for tee times.

Casino

HOURS Noon–4 A.M. daily.

LANGUAGE Spanish. English spoken.

LAYOUT Medium size, with a thoughtful separate area for slots.

GAMES Rommy, canasta, Tute, big money wheel, slots.

LIMITS 500 to 70,000 colones or $5 to $300, depending on which currency you're using.

RULES AND NOTES In the Rommy, it's the only place in town where the dealer takes his second card before players act on their hand, so if you're pining for a more American style of blackjack . . . Also the only place where they deal from a six-deck shoe rather than four decks.

Canasta (roulette) is played on a traditional wheel rather than a steel cage with Ping-Pong balls, technically illegal. When I questioned the floorman about it, he smiled and said, "Shhh!"

FOOD AND DRINK 3 hotel restaurants.

THE PEOPLE THERE Management is friendly and helpful. Clientele is solely tourists.

Hotel

The hotel has everything. The pools are outdoors and curve around. Golf, tennis, spa, and massage. Room rates in the $150 plus tax range.

PRACTICALITIES
Hotel Phone Number: 506-239-0033
Internet Address: *www.westnet.com/costarica/herra.html*
E-mail: *hherradu@sol.racsa.co.cr*
Location: Three miles from the airport, about fifteen minutes by cab to downtown.

The Lollapalooza

One rule twist in the Rommy game at the Hotel Herradura is quite bizarre. If you get dealt two red nines, you get to go and spin the big money wheel for a bonus. Of course you could play all night and never see that hand. Actually, when I got dealt it, being that I was the only one in the casino at the time, I kind of thought they might be taking the piss out of me with that rule. Making me run over to the big money wheel and give it a spin to figure out how much I would get paid in bonus. I got $1. I was thinking about the story of the Lollapalooza.

You must know about the story of the Lollapalooza. Seems a card shark by the name of Action Joe came into the town of Nevada Flats in the hopes of finding a poker game, and he was rewarded when he found one currently in progress at the local saloon. No one objected, so Action Joe sat in and it wasn't long before it was his turn to deal and he wasted no time in setting up the deck to give himself three aces. A monstrous hand ensued, with the pot coming down to Action Joe and an old geezer with white sprouts out of his chin for a beard. The geezer turned his cards over at the end—he had a two of spades, a six of hearts, a nine of diamonds, a ten of hearts, and a queen of clubs. In short, nothing. Action Joe flipped over his three aces and reached to take the pot, but the old geezer stopped him short with a "Wait a minute, young feller. I got a Lollapalooza!" "What's a Lollapalooza," asked Action Joe? "Why, you're looking at it right there! In this town, a Lollapalooza beats every other hand!"

Well, Action Joe was a bit skeptical, but there wasn't much he could do, and he figured it would be his deal soon enough again. He was right. The deal came around and Action Joe resolved not to mess up. This time the pot came down again with the old geezer and it was twice as big as before as Action Joe gleefully put all his money in and when the old man turned up the four aces that Joe had dealt him, Joe triumphantly showed his hand— the Lollapalooza. He reached to take the pot and was again stopped up. "What do you think you're doing?" "I got a Lollapalooza," cried Joe. "I win!" "Sorry, son," said the old geezer, "but in this town we only allow the Lollapalooza once a night."

CAMINO REAL SAN JOSÉ HOTEL AND CASINO

This beautiful piece of paradise is located in Escazu, a suburb of San José that is a minimum ten-minute ride to downtown and more likely twice that. Escazu is where all the rich Ticos and gringos live, and the Camino Real is primarily for business folks and guests of people in Escazu. The casino is small but very fancy, not open until 8 P.M. each night. The pool is stunning, the rooms are deluxe, the restaurants are French. Cheapest rooms are around $150 plus tax, but if that's where you gotta be for business . . .

Casino

HOURS 8 P.M.–4 A.M. daily.

LANGUAGE Spanish. English spoken.

LAYOUT Very small but formal casino located next door to the gourmet French restaurant. Appropriate dress required.

GAMES Rommy, craps, canasta, Tute.

FOOD AND DRINK Food is pricey but recommended. French restaurant.

THE PEOPLE THERE A guy I met gave a cocktail waitress a very big tip, and he still had to ask three times for another drink. And the casino was not busy at the time. Not the level of attention or service that I would expect. Camino Real is where Mark stays. Mark is from Chicago and he comes down on business once a month and he stayed at the Camino Real and then tried the Palacio because it's got just a little bit more action, but next time he's going back to the Camino Real, he says, because you can't beat the pool and the French Restaurant. But you do have to make your own action there, and the casino doesn't open until eight at night and you're in Escazu, which is a good fifteen- to twenty-minute drive to get anywhere, anytime. So while it may be nice, you'll probably end up missing most of the excitement of San José.

Hotel

The Camino Real receives high marks in everything except action and atmosphere. The outdoor pool is beautiful, the grounds lush, the rooms magnificent. Very open and airy, the hotel is only five stories high. Rooms start at $130 plus tax in the low season.

 PRACTICALITIES
Hotel Phone Number: 506-289-7000, fax: 506-289-8930
Location: In Escazu. Fifteen-minute ride to downtown or the airport.

COROBICI HOTEL AND CASINO

At first glance, the Corobici is an exercise in magnificence. A beautiful marble atrium stretches up four stories. A flautist plays mellow jazz for bar patrons who are sunk into deep red plush armchairs and love seats. A classy Japanese restaurant promises authentic food and quality. Rooms are $150 plus tax, but look to be worth it. The swimming pool is a stunning treat surrounded by palm trees that rustle in the cool night air. Like old man Tony says, Costa Rica is just better in every way.

The Corobici is one of two places I've found where they have Pai-Gow poker in Costa Rica. Probably because the hotel was built and owned by a consortium of Japanese businessmen and the hotel still has a lot of Asian clients. But I couldn't find any reason to gamble in that casino. It's shoddily run and the staff is surly. You're much better off on the second floor, where the poker club is (right next to the Japanese restaurant).

Casino

HOURS Noon–4 A.M.

LANGUAGE Spanish.

LAYOUT The dour-faced floor lady sitting behind a big desk in the center of the tables sets the mood for the whole casino. Glumly, sternly, she surveys the operation, making all gamblers feel like either leaving or losing. I pull out a notebook with which to jot down a few notes and she comes behind me, stands over my shoulder with her arms folded on her chest trying to read what I'm writing. I'm writing that a person shouldn't come here and expect to feel welcome. Thank God the poker room is an entirely separate operation.

GAMES Pai-Gow poker, Rommy, canasta, Tute, slots.

FOOD AND DRINK Japanese restaurant is recommended. The sushi is good, but the real winners seem to be some of the salads and grilled dishes that the kitchen turns out.

Hotel

Luxury hotel with facilities just a notch above the others in the same proximity to town. Nice outdoor pool and spa, the lobby stretches all the way up four floors. The only knock is it's a bit stiff and cold. Room rates start at $150 plus tax.

 PRACTICALITIES
Hotel Phone Number: 506-232-8122, fax: 506-231-5834
Internet Address: *www.centralamerica.com/cr/hotel/corobici.htm*
E-mail: *corobici@centralamerica.com*
Location: In an area called La Sabana Norte. A very close cab ride to town, fifteen minutes to the airport.

HOTEL AND CASINO IRAZÚ

Run by Best Western, the inside of the Hotel Irazú is akin to a large Motel 6 in Nashville. The casino isn't much more pleasant with the exception of pretty cocktail waitresses and exceptional free bocas (small plates of snacks).

Monday finds me there for their 8 P.M. tournament. The buy-in is cheap ($16), but fast play, unlimited re-buys for ninety minutes, and the propensity of many players to go all in with queen-nine suited prop up the prize pool to a worthy level. As is my usual, I play hard and end up three places out of the money. Oh well. I hustle over to the live game, already in progress, to try and get even.

Casino

HOURS Noon–4 A.M.

LANGUAGE Spanish. Little English spoken.

LAYOUT The casino is in the basement of the hotel. Not much in the way of atmosphere and charm. And it's not worth a special trip unless you're gonna play poker. The place is a zoo on Friday nights, when live music blasts the small casino. You're a big bettor here when betting over 5,000 colones ($18).

GAMES Rommy, canasta, poker, Tute.

LIMITS 500 colones to 10,000 colones or $1.80 to $36, depending on which currency you're using.

FOOD AND DRINK Don't forget about the bocas at the Irazú. I tell you, by the third time I'm going there, I'm going for the bocas, licking my lips as I wonder what little treats the casino chef's gonna come out with tonight. Pork chop and mashed potatoes on a small plate, or meatballs with rice, or ceviche or a small salad. Plates consist of about six bites and are free to casino players. Just signal the waitress and say, *"Tráigame bocas, por favor,"* or ask at the casino bar. Authentic Costa Rican snacks are quite tasty and not filling, pleasant for the palate.

While the downstairs kitchen has a creatively accomplished chef, the one upstairs looks rather subpar. The $12.50 buffet there contained warm slop and a mayonnaise salad.

THE PEOPLE THERE The hotel does big business with North American charter tourists. The casino staff is on the whole competent, the poker dealers are especially friendly.

Hotel

The hotel has little to recommend it in the way of feeling like you're in Costa Rica. That said, room rates include a breakfast buffet and a free happy hour at the hotel bar and there is a swimming pool and all the other facilities. Official room rates start at $100 per night plus tax, but I met some businessmen who had secured a $65 corporate rate, and that seems like very good value.

 PRACTICALITIES
Hotel Phone Number: 506-232-4811, fax: 506-232-3159
Casino Phone Number: 506-232-7910
Location: A few miles outside of town, just past the Corobici Hotel and the San José Palacio.

GRAN HOTEL COSTA RICA

What's the Gran Hotel Costa Rica good for? Get there about 10:30 A.M. when the lines are going up. Have a startlingly good cup of coffee and watch the sexy gals post the lines on the big white magnetic board in black Magic Marker. The lines change fast, and sports books should make note of how much it means to prospective bettors when the lines are adjusted by women with shapely bottoms. It bodes well for a day of sports betting. It gets so you're just praying for the line to move.

The Gran Hotel is where the action's at. That's where the backpacker action, the tourist hubbub, and the closest thing you'll get to an American tuna sandwich is—all crowded on the patio of the Gran Hotel, the fading elegance of the thirties with the prime real estate location in San José.

Remember that this hotel is not officially called the Gran Hotel. Tell a cab driver you want to go to the Gran Hotel (big hotel) and you may have a problem. The place is properly known as the Gran Hotel Costa Rica. Go figure. Anyway, it's the central tourist landmark in town. Like all tourist hot spots, the service is shabby, the food is completely average, and the rooms are dingy and overpriced. And it's still a legitimate contender for a great place to stay because you're where it's happening twenty-four hours a day, and you're plugged into the entire tourist traveling young people network for the whole country. Housed in a beautiful old 1930s mansion, the Gran Hotel had its last thorough cleaning around that time.

Casino

HOURS Twenty-four hours a day.

LANGUAGE Spanish. English is spoken and understood.

LAYOUT My feeling is it's not a casino, it's tables in the lobby. The place is always heavy with the traffic of people walking in and out of the hotel. But, hey, if young tourists is what you want to see. Don't expect to be playing heads up with the dealer, as the tables are consistently full. The sports book is comfortable but a little noisy with seating for about fifteen. The lobby is always bright.

GAMES Rommy, canasta (roulette), Tute (Caribbean stud), sports book.

LIMITS 1000 to 20,000 colones, or $5 to $100. There is usually one table with a minimum limit of only 600 colones, but don't expect to get a seat.

RULES AND NOTES In the Rommy there is a unique rule. They put a joker in every four-deck shoe, and whoever gets dealt the joker gets a 1,000 colones (approximately $3.60) bonus. Definitely worth a percentage, especially if you're the only one playing and watch the joker and always cut it near the top of the shoe. Then you've got a 50 percent chance of getting it, and when I achieved that situation one time at 7 A.M. on a rare deserted morning, I tortured them.

The floor people are authorized to give out $5 match play coupons at their discretion, and they're usually liberal with them. Don't be afraid to ask.

FOOD AND DRINK The Café Parisian coffee shop, open twenty-four hours, is also in the lobby of the hotel. Half of it abuts the casino and sports book, the other half is just outside the front door, where lovely tables on the patio look out onto the National Theater, the park, and the bustle of San José. They pour one of the best cups of coffee in town, a damn fine place to greet the day.

The food is mostly tourist fare, at least don't get the chicken sandwich. The free beverages plied by the casino are severely substandard.

THE PEOPLE THERE The place to be for the bustling backpacker industry, the Gran Hotel Costa Rica crawls with Americans of every ilk. Don't bother shaving. The dealers and waitresses are generally unengaging.

The sports book manager, David, is one of the friendliest guys in San José. They take a lot of local and tourist action in addition to the bets they get from phone customers. David is a dapper man, mild-mannered and genteelly graying. His cell phone is always attached to his hip or his ear, and while he's always talking on it, he never shouts, he doesn't curse, and he doesn't have anyone in his employ with biceps and a name like Thugley. David is a well-dressed bookie.

Hotel

The good news is that you're in the center of everything. The bad news is that the rooms are shabby, the hotel is dirty, and the whole place looks like a tinderbox. Rack rates are $54, $71, $78 (single, double, triple). Suites start at $100, and the presidential suite is $157. Plus 18.5 percent taxes. There is no pool.

 PRACTICALITIES
Hotel Phone Number: 506-221-4000, from the U.S., 1-800-949-0592
Internet Address: *www.centralamerica.com/cr/hotel/gran.htm*
E-mail: *gran@centralamerica.com*
Location: Avenida 2 & Avenida Central, Calle 3. In front of the National Theater. The center of downtown and the tourist area.

HOTEL AND CASINO DEL REY

The Hotel Del Rey is a famous San José landmark that's fading fast. It still lives on its reputation as a semiwhorehouse, the street-level bar called the Blue Marlin is permanently staffed and stuffed with prostitutes of every ilk. They're legal, they're happy to negotiate, and there's tons of 'em twenty-four hours. Joe was joking how most of the prostitutes in there work shifts so regular that you know what time it is just by walking in and seeing who's on the stools.

The casino is in the lobby, kind of crammed into the space between the front desk and the Blue Marlin Bar. There's one roulette table, and about eight tables combined of Rommy and Tute poker. They have a sports book, but it was temporarily "closed for remodeling" while I was there. Yeah. Like they're gonna paint the magnetic chalkboard. I get a bad feeling about this place from top to bottom.

The hotel is a big pink five-story building one block from the center of town. It's popular with men interested in the sex trade and organizing deep-sea fishing trips.

Casino

HOURS Noon–4 A.M.

LANGUAGE Spanish. English spoken.

LAYOUT Casino is in lobby, put into whatever available space there is.

GAMES Canasta, Rommy, Tute, slots.

LIMITS 600 colones to 20,000 colones, or $2 to $72, depending on which currency you're using.

FOOD AND DRINK The Blue Marlin Bar is open twenty-four hours. Alcohol and more.

THE PEOPLE THERE Prostitutes. A lot of prostitutes.

Hotel

Rooms are in the $50-per-night range, are clean and have safety boxes.

PRACTICALITIES
Hotel Phone Number: 506-221-7272, fax: 506-221-0096
Location: Avenida 1, Calle 9. Next door to the Casino Colonial.

HOTEL BALMORAL

I ended up staying at the Hotel Balmoral for quite a long time. It's a family-run place, small enough that after a few days you know both the women who clean your room and the doorman who smilingly and uncomplainingly lets you in when you return at four-thirty in the morning.

Personally, I think it's the best hotel in the city if you're looking for a combination of value, location, and friendly surroundings. It's just that you have so many options. I mean, it's true there's no casino at the Balmoral, but the Gran Hotel, the Casino Colonial, and the Hotel Aurola are all within easy walking distance. And the Irazú, the Palacio, and the Corobici are all a mere 1,000 colone (approximately $3.60) cab ride away. Foodwise, your options are limitless.

Casino

No casino.

FOOD AND DRINK Hotel restaurant is completely average, but just outside your door, you have a myriad of delicious and inexpensive options. Nice lunch spots on Calle 7 or 9, and the bakery shop across the street is open at dawn with fresh-baked goodies.

THE PEOPLE THERE You can trust your stuff in the room. The maids have all been there from ten to twenty-eight years. Everyone has a smile for you.

Hotel

Rooms are very clean, and come with air-conditioning and television. Be sure to request a room with a window to the outside. They're about five dollars more, but worth it. Sometimes the hot water is a little slow in arriving. Rooms are a good value at $50 per night, but if you reserve well in advance or are planning to stay for a while, reductions can be negotiated from even this price. Laundry, while not cheap, came back to my room the next day still warm and smelling like a fresh day.

116 rooms, 4 suites. Minifridge on request, safety deposit boxes in a room adjoining the front desk are very safe.

 PRACTICALITIES
Hotel Phone Number: 506-222-5022, fax: 506-221-7826, from the U.S., 1-800-691-4865.
Internet Address: *www.balmoral.co.cr*
E-mail: *reservas@balmoral.co.cr*
Location: Avenida Central, Calles 7 & 9. Nice downtown spot that fronts onto the pedestrian street of Avenue Central. Close to everything.

COSTA RICA MARRIOTT

The Marriott is the newest hotel on the block. Though lacking a casino, it has received raves about its luxurious facilities, which are everything. Might become the new businessman's place of choice.

Casino

No casino.

THE PEOPLE THERE Businessmen.

Hotel

252 rooms, pools, tennis courts, golf range, gym with sauna and Jacuzzi, a restaurant at the side of the pool plus lots of fancy food options make the room rates starting at about $150 worth considering.

 PRACTICALITIES
Hotel Phone Number: 506-298-0000, fax: 506-298-0011
Location: In an area called San Antonio de Belen. Close to the airport, at least a fifteen-minute ride to town.

Entertainment and Nightlife

EL PUEBLO

El Pueblo Commercial Center is an attractive setup that houses at least seven different restaurants, a horde of souvenir and cigar shops, and a discotheque named Infinito that is as fun and happening a place as you could hope for. El Pueblo is essentially open twenty-four hours, and it is the entertainment and nightlife capital of the city.

My first time at El Pueblo happened kind of all of a sudden. I had hooked up with a crew from Michigan over at the Casino Colonial who were dead set on having a good time their first night in San José. One of the fellows had heard that El Pueblo was the spot to meet local girls, so after we were pretty well liquored up from a few shoes of Rommy and a particularly forgettable experience trying to get drinks while playing roulette at the Del Rey, four of us hopped into a cab and said, "Take us to El Pueblo." It was wild enough so that I only bumped into the guys I was with every so often. There was one room for house music, one room for salsa, and one room that I guess was Latin romantic tango or something, but all three rooms were cooking, plus there was a big bar in the middle. But we had a few tequila shots when we came in, so I had no need to be spending too much time there. The women love to dance, they just love to dance, and I didn't see a guy there who wanted to dance who wasn't finding somebody to dance with. One of the guys from Michigan got a date for the next night and another tall and shy fellow named Todd was flailing in a sea of women for hours on the dance floor. The place hops seven nights a week after 10 P.M.

Remember "Take me to El Pueblo." These are the most important words in San José, because when spoken to a cab driver at any time of the day or night, he will deliver. Food and dancing and drinking, and dancing and drinking and food. Every time.

I ran into Tom at the Palacio. Tom was from Long Island and here on business and Tom could put you to sleep inside a four-minute conversation. But he told me he had been to El Pueblo and he had a hell of a time on the dance floor and he hooked up with a girl and danced and everything. And if Tom can have a blast dancing the night away with a strange and beautiful woman in El Pueblo, then we've all got a shot. Go get 'em.

Infinito Discoteca en Centro Comercial El Pueblo: Cover is about $3, the music and dancing really go all night.

STRIP/NIGHTCLUBS

The Bikini Bar is located in the downtown area, it doesn't get going until very late at night. While it's not the most elegant joint in the world, and all the action takes place in the upstairs bar, where they have a winding bar with a countertop wide enough for a girl to walk back and forth on, it is the real thing. This Hawaiian fellow I was out drinking and gambling with who was only eighteen, spending his last night in San José after a month surfing down in Quepos, was definitely in the mood for some action, and he parlayed a rather liberal 3:30 A.M. lap dance into a $40 trick in the back room they have expressly for the purpose—and outfitted with a bed, I'm told. She was a screamer, he said.

There's also some five-star joints where drinks are $15 and you sit at your own table with your own little couch and the guys from Alabama were raving about some joint they went to that they found in the center of their hotel tourist magazine, but they did spend a bundle. They also could've called the concierge.

FOOD IN GENERAL

San José is a delight for the eater. I like to go for a walk just before lunchtime, when the sights and smells of the busy streets and shops provide tantalizing temptations for my eyes, nose, and stomach. I start in the pedestrian street behind the Gran Hotel Costa Rica and walk up the even-numbered streets, stopping in a small park along the way to hear some mariachi players, three old men amazingly spry on xylophones and drums. Sometimes I make it to the Central

Market (Avenida Central & Avenida 1, Calle 6–8), sometimes I don't. There's so many little joints to eat in. I just look for the word *casado* and then get that. Among other things, the Central Market is a nice place to look for belts and not too expensive leather, as you weave your way through butchers, fishmongers, and comestible retailers of every ilk. The adventurous may be rewarded.

CASADOS Meaning "married" in Spanish, *casados* are both a national dish and the most common of meals in Costa Rica, and no two are the exact same. I never tired of the endless variations on this meal, which is a large plate of white rice, black beans, some type of vinegary cole slaw, possibly a potato salad, plump fried plantains, and then some type of meat or fish, either *bistec* (steak), *chuleta* (pork chop), *pescado* (fish), *pollo* (chicken), or another *carne* (meat) on top of the lot, and then usually finished off by the accompaniment of tortillas and some raw onion. Choices are usually listed on the menu or on a board in the restaurant (e.g., *casado con chuleta, casado con bistec*, etc.) . . .

While the *casado* is not an inherently spicy dish, the different tastes, textures, and flavors in it make it a rather exciting eating experience. And there's always a bottle of take-the-paint-off-the-walls hot sauce on the table if you really want to kill all the bacteria.

Always an inexpensive option for quite a bit of food, *casados* are usually in the 500 to 1,500 colón range (approximately $2 to $6).

CEVICHE Ceviche is another delicious dish with many variations, commonly ordered as an appetizer or snack. Fresh seafood is marinated in lime juice and coriander and chopped onions and some delightful other things and eaten with crackers or toast. It is out of this world.

BEVERAGES Costa Rican beer is called Bavaria. It comes in Bavaria or Bavaria Light, and I think it's a damn fine, nice, rich taste. *Batidas* and *fresas* are fruit shakes, one made with water and one with milk. To be honest with you, I can't keep them straight myself, but they're delicious. They have some luscious fruits in Costa Rica that you've never heard of before, along with all the standards.

RESTAURANTS

PAPAPEZ Lunchtime is best for Papapez, the seafood place, where the lunchtime light spills through the windows, and the clatter of the lunchtime crowd of business people makes for a lively atmosphere. The old-time service makes you feel right at home, and the seafood is the freshest you'll see this side of the Atlantic.

You can't beat the fresh Ceviche Papapez washed down with a beer and crisp garlic toasts. Young secretaries dine with their jacketless bosses, folks smile and eat with gusto at the clean wooden tables.

The bar is well stocked. Two open-collared gentlemen share a medium-sized bottle of Johnnie Walker Black. The waiter hovers with tongs and a bucket of ice, replenishing one man's soda and the other's water.

You can eat fast or slow at Papapez, no pressure. I told the guy I wanted to relax over my meal and an hour later I had to trip him in the aisle to get the check. It's a fun place. Don't miss the *postres* (desserts).

Papapez, located in El Pueblo Commercial Center. Open for lunch and dinner daily. About $20 per person.

LUKAS' Lukas', another restaurant at El Pueblo, has the distinction of being open twenty-four hours a day, perfect for the appetite one can build up after a full night of drinking and dancing next door at Infinito. The menu runs the gamut, prices are reasonable.

RIAS BAJAS Rias Bajas comes highly recommended for the shrimp and lobster, but expect to pay. It is also located in El Pueblo. While lobster will most likely be the most expensive thing you order in San José ($50 to $60), treat yourself at least one time for a lobster that is quite unlike its Maine brethren—and delicious.

An evening beginning with a late dinner at Rias Bajas followed by touring the bars and discos in El Pueblo will be fun. Don't forget to go to Infinito. Rias Bajas, located in El Pueblo Commercial Center, phone 506-221-7123. Mon.–Sat. 12 P.M.–3 P.M. and 6 P.M.–11:30 P.M.

SODA PERLA Three A.M. and I got three mariachis serenading me with "Guantanamera." If it's late at night, really late, and you're mostly done drinking and you're done gambling and you just want to be someplace where you can sit and stare and have a snack and maybe finish that goodnight beer or coffee, then head on over to the Soda Perla on Avenida Central and about Calle 8. It's twenty-four hours, well lit, and there's usually some musicians either winding down a night of work or just waiting for some tourists to serenade. If you're lucky, you'll get a beefsteak and "Guantanamera" in three-part harmony.

LA HACIENDA STEAK HOUSE Well above average, both in service and quality. Don't make the mistake of trying to go cheap by ordering the lunch specials or the lowest-priced items. Just go nuts and have a tasty steak, everything's delicious and you'll be out for $10 to $15 and filled like a plump hog. Don't forget the garlic bread.

La Hacienda Steak House: Calle 7, Avenida Central & 2, phone 506-223-5493, open for lunch and dinner.

BILLY BOYS Avenida Central, Calle 5, serves up a loaded hamburger and a milk shake that can be thick or thin (corriente). The coffee milk shake has me licking my lips at the memory. They have a pickup window out on the street, for that ever important shake on the go. Management is beaming smile friendly. $5.

JAPANESE FOOD There's a popular Japanese restaurant in the Hotel Corobici with an extensive menu that goes from sushi to bowls of noodles to teriyakis and stir-fries. Perk is that you can get full service while playing poker just next door at the poker club, which permanently resides in one of the hotel's conference rooms. $40 per person, lunch and dinner.

OTHER STUFF

CIGARS I didn't think the prices were that great, but Cuban cigars are readily available. Shop around a little bit in the downtown area or El Pueblo and negotiate. Cigars that you buy on the street could easily be fake Cubans.

OUTSIDE OF TOWN Possibilities include deep-sea fishing, visiting the rain forest, seeing an active volcano, and whitewater rafting. No problem in booking a last-minute tour once you're down there, there are tour operators in every hotel and you'll probably save money. Day trips to see the volcano come highly recommended.

SPORT FISHING If you want to go sport fishing, the easiest place to go from San José is to Quepos, three hours by car, twenty minutes by plane. It is usually no problem to organize something when you get down there, but December to April is the busy season. One outfit recommended not for being cheap but for outstanding service and professionalism is Costa Rican Dreams: phone 506-777-0593, fax 506-777-0592. Ballpark of $400 for a full day of fishing. Boats usually take two to four anglers.

Lock Your Doors

There're certain games that are no fun to play alone. Like craps and roulette. Being alone at a lonely roulette table is like pitching quarters against a wall. Nobody's around to even see when you hit a great shot. Now, that said, nothing turns me on more than a roulette table piled with clattering chips, stacks of multicolored wonders that zing back and forth across the table like revolving doors and every number that's hit has a bevy of opportunities, and some granite-faced Chinese fellow is betting the absolute maximum on number thirty-two time and time again with the stubbornness of a mule.

When the croupiers look at the floor person with a blank face in trying to figure out how to pay out a number that has been hit with twenty-six chips at 17–1, at 8–1 with eleven chips and thirty-seven chips, on the side for 6–1 with a stack of pinks, and three or four times by the skinny-faced and worried-looking fellow who's covered every number on the board and is just hoping to get enough chips back to play one more roll. Yes, roulette can be a game of delirium.

I'm playing roulette at the Casino Colonial, and the only reason I even sat down into the game was because I liked the style of the Chinese guy who played while standing and was accompanied by another man and their dates, but the other guy had since busted out and he was just kind of slumped in the corner as the first fellow stayed alive. At first he had no pattern. He would fling huge stacks of chips out every spin. Sometimes to a number. A row. A corner. A column. He was all over and he would make his decisions very quick, *whoosh*. And he was winning. Well, not winning, but he was staying alive, and he hit some numbers and collected some big chips and so he was able to remain about even or ahead a little bit while his compatriots got wiped out and I came over and sat down and right from the start, I started betting with him. I mean, I wasn't gonna let him get hot and me be betting the wrong color, so while I only bet one or two chips in place of his thirty or more, I began to cover his space as well.

But he had one hell of a way to bet. I mean, sure, a lot of guys bet all their chips every spin, but they usually spread them around the whole table. My Chinese roulette partner would send out stacks of chips, twenty-five and thirty chips high, and surround one number so he had four stacks around the edges and one stack in the middle. And then, if he had another stack or two, he'd pick a row of three or six numbers, so he only had to hit a little corner of something to get money back, and if he ever hit a number dead on, watch out, because he might break them.

At some point he went on a little run and got some of the larger value chips together and then he fell in love with the number thirty-two. Or maybe we fell in love with number thirty-two. Because I wasn't gonna sit there and see it come in and have just got off the thing so we both started betting number thirty-two every spin, he would put a huge stack of chips on the number and around all the edges and on the corner every roll. And it didn't hit. No, it didn't hit, and we kept betting on thirty-two and got stubborn, and that's a mistake to make on the roulette table. You don't want to ever get stubborn, because no one is as stubborn as the odds.

After about fifteen rolls and most of my chips, I left my Chinese friend there and went over to play some Rommy, the fun had gone now that we were just riding thirty-two to the poorhouse. He gave no sign of my leaving, he just reached in his pocket for his wallet and the goods to buy more chips. About twenty minutes later I hear a *whoop* from the roulette table and I sprint over to look. My man has switched from number thirty-two to number eight, some numbers just don't ever hit, and he's hit it square on, with the max on the nose and every side and a row as well, and they were still trying to figure out how much to give him when I went back to the blackjack game.

After a few days on the gambling circuit, San José is just like anywhere else. You keep seeing the same people in different places. "And don't ask any of these Ticos what they do for a living," the guy from Georgia says to me when we start to warm up to each other after playing together four days in a row. "Most of 'em are in the numbers business."

We're sitting at a Rommy table at the San José Palacio in the time between getting knocked out of their small Tuesday night tournament and when the real game is gonna start, no-limit Hold'em with a 10,000-colón initial buy-in and then anything you care to place on the table after that. And believe me, people are putting some money down, you can win 200,000 colones if you pick up some reasonable cards.

Anyway, we're kinda having fun playing Rommy, even though we're both getting creamed. The dealer is a hot young Costa Rican lady, just like all the dealers there, and she can count fast, but she's trying to bring the cards out of the shoe too fast and they keep flying up in the air and either falling on the floor or dropping into this hole she's got in her rack. And every time a card goes in the hole or on the floor, she comes up and she's got twenty-one. Now I promise you it's a coincidence and this game is on the square if any game is in Costa Rica because the casino is managed by an American named Bob who's seen the shit and knows about gambling and I'm telling you you don't have to worry about nothing there, but it does seem like every time a card goes off the table, the dealer's getting twenty-one.

So me and my man from Georgia start putting up the stink, just for fun really and as much to flirt with the dealer as anything else, and we tell her that we ain't playing with the cards in the well and we're taking back our bets every time a card goes off the table, win or lose, because you can't expect us to play in that kind of game where they're switching cards. And we're laughing our heads off and having fun, even though we are getting slaughtered at the game, and I'm having trouble keeping my mind on the count because Fred is one hell of a storyteller and he's telling me about the craps game that he used to run up above his furniture store in Atlanta.

Fred's from Georgia, and I have no idea what the hell he's doing here in Costa Rica except it's some kind of weird business and he's been in a lot of them. He keeps regaling me with stories about traveling through Argentina and Chile in the old days, looking for classic cars to ship back to the States, and he said the women were so loose and beautiful down there that you had to lock your car door to keep them from climbing in!

CHAPTER TWO

MAR DEL PLATA, ARGENTINA

LAY OF THE LAND

It's 11 P.M. here, which must mean it's getting close to dinner-time. I'm serious. A restaurant wouldn't even think of opening down here until after nine, and they're all open until at least 2 A.M. So much for going to bed on a full stomach giving you indigestion. In Argentina, you better just get used to it.

♦

Don't hurry. Life is a business taken seriously in Argentina.

♦

A typical Argentine breakfast consists of hot black coffee, a piece of toast, and a lot of cigarettes. Why? They've been up gorging themselves until 2 A.M. It's a wonder anyone can even sleep with the kind of heartburn that must be going on in this country. Hell, it takes them until about nine at night to even work up an appetite again.

You should do it this way. Wake up at eight, or no later than nine and have pastries and coffee from a confiteria, mmm, freshly baked lovelies. Make your way to the beach with your deck chair and *paraguas* (umbrella), or rent one. Lounge in the sun or shade, or swim until two or three o'clock. Be careful, the sun is hot. Return to your hotel, stopping along the way to grab a small snack of a *Milanese* or little ham and cheese sandwiches.

Go siesta away the hottest part of the afternoon and arise around 7 P.M. Freshen up, take a shower and get spiffy, put on your evening clothes. Have a nice walk to whet your appetite and then find a churrasceria or a pastaleria about 9 P.M. for the serious business of dinner. When dinner's over, it's time to hit the casinos for some serious gambling. And don't forget to grab an ice cream cone on your way home at 3 A.M.

Don't hurry. Life is a business taken seriously in Argentina.

I never encountered a people who know how to gamble like the Argentineans. I'm not talking about the casinos, the way they run them or anything. I'm talking about people who know how to gamble the real way, where every bet is everything you've got, all or nothing. *Punto* or *banco, pide* or *planta, negro* or *roja.* They don't get tied up in the lily-livered discrepancies, placing the four and Chuck-a-Luck red dog or Caribbean Pai-Gow. That ain't gambling. Gambling is sitting at a table with seven other men, a crowd in back craning their necks and betting from their feet, the dealer in a high chair with a long wooden paddle, reminiscent of the Mississippi boys' academy disciplinary crew.

Mar del Plata, Argentina
GENERAL INFORMATION

YOU'RE NOT IN KANSAS ANYMORE Argentina—heaven for the beef-eater. For a long time, the only things I had heard about Argentina were that they lost the war of the Falkland Islands, they played a pretty good game of soccer, and they raised beef on the Pampas. Little did I know that this South American gem boasts travel and vacation spots that can make even the most demanding of sourpusses smile. And once you get out of Buenos Aires, your pocketbook won't even feel a thing.

The beach resort of Mar del Plata is known as the Happy City. It is a nice place, and people don't eat dinner until after ten o'clock, at the earliest. And at three in the morning, everyone's still walking around, including kids eight to fifteen who have their 3 A.M. ice cream cone before bed. The only time the streets are deserted is about 6 P.M.

WHERE Argentina is located at the bottom of South America. The climate is somewhat similar to America, but on an opposite schedule. Remember, we're below the equator. Time in Mar del Plata is two hours ahead of EST, which puts you all alone way out in the middle of the Atlantic Ocean.

WHEN Summertime is best, from December to March.

TELEPHONES The international telephone code for Argentina is 54. From the U.S., 011-54 + number. In Argentina, some phones are better than others. The local phone system is not as good as it could be.

CURRENCY The peso is the Argentinean unit of currency. Inside the country, the peso and dollar are basically equivalent. Dollars are not accepted everywhere, but they can be changed in banks or casinos at a ratio of 1:1, or nearly so. And pesos can easily be exchanged back into dollars, inside the country. I wouldn't advise taking pesos out of the country, where the exchange rate, if you can find one, is at least 15 percent lower.

ATMS There are ATMs all over Argentina. There is an ATM in the Casino Central that you can use for cash withdrawals.

BANKS Banks in Argentina are all very crowded. Better to find a currency exchange and do your business there. There's a good one in the pedestrian mall on San Martín.

¿HABLA ESPANOL? Argentina is tough on no Spanish at all. But you will do remarkably fine on only a very little bit of Spanish. I know only a few words from high school and did fine with a bit of patience.

C is for *caliente*, which is hot, not cold, and *f* is for *frío*, which is cold, not hot.

Did you know that Alf made a full-length movie? I just watched it dubbed into Spanish. The commercial break had Erik Estrada pitching a weight-loss pill. I love Argentine television.

SAFETY I feel about as threatened as if I'm in Omaha, Nebraska, on the Fourth of July. It's a safe place. Really safe.

INTERNET Internet access on Moreno between Corrientes and Entre Rios, $9 per hour.

CLIMATE I'm gonna say this one time, even though I'm fairly certain it will have absolutely no effect on you and you'll heed me just like you do your grandmother when she tells you to put on a sweater. The sun is very strong, and if you're not careful it'll fry you like a turkey, crackle your skin like fresh drippings. I only laid out for an hour on my first day and my back looked like a fire engine. And felt like it needed one.

Bring a sweater, or better yet, don't bring one because it's much nicer to buy one down here, very good quality sweaters are made locally and only cost about $20 and are perfect for the cool breeze that blows at night. Thin but beautiful sweaters, some sort of fine wool.

I'll Walk There Barefoot
TRANSPORTATION ISSUES

LEGAL Americans need a valid passport.

FLIGHTS Buenos Aires is a long flight. I got a $500 round-trip ticket on Aerolinas Argentinas from Miami, which I thought was an incredible value. I got that ticket through *expedia.com*. New York is another city offering nonstop flights. Check on the Internet and in Sunday travel sections.

AIRPORT Manuel Tienda León Airport, utilize the Tourist Info just outside of customs! Fourteen dollars gets you to the bus station in a nice air-conditioned bus where they check your bags and give you a ticket. There's signs everywhere that say you shouldn't negotiate privately for a cab, and who are we to disagree? They'll juice you when you leave with a departure tax.

BUSES It's only $14 to get a nice air-conditioned bus directly to the central bus station, which is in the southern part of Buenos Aires and far from the airport. That's a good deal. Ask about the bus, which leaves like every half hour from right as you walk out the door of the airport. Be sure to use that tourist information center at the airport. That may be your last outpost where you can 100 percent use your English.

There's no reason to even stay a night in Buenos Aires if you don't want to because you can get a bus to the central bus station from the airport and then a bus down to Mar del Plata from the bus station and buses leave pretty much twenty-four hours. But maybe you can't hack it. Maybe you can't hack a twelve-hour plane ride down there followed by an hour ride to the bus station followed by a four-hour bus ride down to Mar del Plata. That's certainly understandable. But I did a plane trip from Panama to Costa Rica, followed by one from Costa Rica to Miami, followed straightaway by a flight from Miami to Argentina plus both buses, and when I found myself looking out the window at 8 P.M. as the bus drove through the sleepy streets of the Happy City, I was so glad I'd come all the way. It was just so pleasant.

The bus station is no problem. It's large, it's a twenty-four-hour affair, and it bears no resemblance to Port Authority in New York, thank God. Every bus company has a different ticket window. Information can give you all the lines that run to your destination. You buy your ticket, go to the bus, and *voilà*. The buses are, on the whole, much nicer than Greyhound. Much nicer. The slightly more expensive buses are also newer and nicer. You'll appreciate this over a four-hour bus ride, or if you're taking the twenty-hour ride to Viña del Mar in Chile, which I certainly considered, you'll like a nice bus seat. Reclining seats, footrests, snacks, AC, movies, bathroom. Get on a nice bus. El Condor, Tony Tur, and Micromar all run lines down to the Plata.

The bus ride down to Mar del Plata is quite pleasant, especially if you haven't slept for four days. I can't say enough about positive first impressions for this sleepy seaside town. First of all, the bus station is tout free. And hassle free, and the only person that stopped me on the street wanted to tell me that my knapsack was open.

Mar del Plata is first and foremost a beach town and a tourist resort. During the summer (December to February, remember we are below the equator), the town swells to capacity with sunburned Argentinean families of every shape and size who pack the beach, the casino, and the many barbecue joints late at night. I had a brilliant time arriving at the end of February, when the weather was still plenty warm for sunbathing but the crowds were not as large, and I was able to procure a $100-a-night room in a four-star hotel for only $28. My corner windows looked directly onto the grand old casino, which is really the heart of the town. Its imposing size (it takes up an entire city block) dwarfs every other building in town, even though it's only four stories high. Of course, those are some rather large stories.

Buy your return bus ticket early—the mornings are crowded—to return to Buenos Aires.

There aren't a whole lot of gringos here, however. In fact, the only non-Latinos I did encounter in a week here was an Australian couple at the casino, but I hesitated to introduce myself because they were getting crushed at blackjack and didn't appear to be in the mood to meet anyone.

WHERE THINGS ARE Western Union is on Córdoba, the 1700 block, Mon.–Fri. 9–1:30 P.M. and 4 P.M.–8:30 P.M., Sat. 9 A.M.–1 P.M., if you need it.

TRANSPORTATION AROUND TOWN To Argentinean drivers, stoplights are an intrusion. They drive like they gamble, double every bet. Careful crossing the street. Why they drive with their headlights off is beyond me, but there it is. Running around at night trying to save battery power? Hurtling across the no-traffic-light streets with reckless abandon. Having a car can be a bit of a problem, as parking is pricey.

The Money Plays
GAMBLING SETUP—THE QUICK FACTS

CASINOS Virtually all casinos in Argentina are state owned and operated. And they do a pretty fair job of it, at that.

HOURS Afternoon until late evening, usually 2 or 4 A.M.

ADMITTANCE Varies. In Mar del Plata, entrance is $5. Gaming age is twenty-one. They reserve the right to refuse admission to anyone, basically if you haven't freshened up.

AMBIANCE AND AMENITIES Drinks and snacks must be purchased. Ambiance is quite formal and stately. Cigarettes are only $2, all brands.

GAMES ON OFFER Blackjack, roulette, craps, baccarat, slots.

LIMITS If you play baccarat, $10 up to sky's the limit. Other games have a $500 maximum bet.

MONEY Dollars or Argentine pesos are accepted, with an exchange value of 1:1.

LEGALITY Casinos are legal and licensed by the government. Winnings are not taxed.

TIPPING POLICIES IN THE CASINO Tips expected. The dealers work for their tips. They give you change regularly, and you're expected to deliver.

AND . . . In Argentina, they play blackjack like baccarat, the team game where everybody wins or everybody loses. But blackjack's not a team game. And they play craps like individuals, and there's a team game if you've ever seen one. Rolling dice all by yourself is a lonely proposition in my book.

I'll Take the Odds
BREAKING APART THE GAME

Every game in the Argentine casinos is based around baccarat, also called *punto y banco* in Spanish. I say every game is based around this, because no matter what you are playing, thinking is reduced to a minimum. A gambler should not have to make many more decisions other than yes or no, it will or it won't.

CRAPS Limits are $20 to $400. The shooter must put up a bet, which goes on a special square in the center. It plays just like a line bet, but like everywhere else in the casino, the croupiers will automatically let a winning bet ride unless you tell them to take part or all of it down. The shooter loses the dice not only if he craps out, but if he rolls two, three, or twelve craps on the come out roll. So much for hitting ten straight passes. Come, don't come, and the field are all standard here, as are place bets with a $20 minimum. You may not, however, get true odds at any time by backing up line or come bets, and the whole net effect is for there to be not very much money on the table, not much action, and no excitement. Look, if you really needed to play craps, you should have stayed in America, for that's the place to play craps, and Argentina is far better for baccarat, roulette, or their interesting brand of blackjack.

The Argentineans have no clue how to play craps, and even when full the game has about as much energy as a dead fish.

BINGO Bingo del Mar is a bingo house one block from Central Casino, on the corner of Moreno and Buenos Aires. They've got a big bingo room in the back, and in the foyer are some slots and a giant roulette slot-type game that seats eight players and you play with quarters and it does look like fun. There's usually a line to sit at it. At night there's usually a line to get a seat in the bingo game also, but it's a big room. Popular place to go on a rainy day. Play is in Spanish, but you can follow along on TV screens where they post the numbers visually. You'll do fine. They get several hundred people playing at a time.

ROULETTE I'm not a huge fan of the roulette down here, I have to admit. While there are well over 100 different tables at the Central Casino, none of the layouts are especially big. In addition, they only have four different colors of the smallest denomination color chips, the $2 chips, so you rarely have more than four or five people playing at any one table. They have two different types of $3 chips and two types of $5 chips, but when I'm playing roulette my philosophy is more is always better, and if I want to bet $10 I'd rather do it with five chips than with two. Also, because of the strange $10 maximum on the inside (if you go into the special room, you can bet a lot more, but 95 percent of the gambling goes on in the big room), it's hard to get a big payout. To me, this takes one large element of excitement out of the game. That and sitting around a giant table with fifteen or twenty people and the felt covered in every which way imaginable with colors, patterns, and chaotic number mania. The game is sedate, regular, and in my mind a little boring here.

On the positive side, however, the wheels only have one zero, which cuts the odds against you in half as compared to American roulette, 2.8 percent. As opposed to 5.5 percent, and that is very significant. So if you bring your own interest to the game, Mar del Plata is a fine place to play.

If you like to bet black or red, odd or even, the simple chances, bets can range from $20 to $400 on the even money bets and $20 to $200 on the 2–1 bets. There again, the spread is a tad small. For all you systems players out there, there are no electronic screens that keep track of the numbers as they are spun, but the house is happy to provide you with a paper if you deign to keep track yourself.

It's fine, I just like the tables more crowded and huge towering stacks of chips moving across the layout. The fact that there are over 100 roulette tables in the Central Casino is sort of appealing in itself.

BLACKJACK The dealer sits at the table with you, a horseshoe-shaped table with low chairs for everyone. They use eight decks here, which is about as big a shoe as you'll see anywhere, and the effect it had on me is that while it's still very possible to count, the shoe lasts so long that I lost my concentration about once in every three shoes and had to play half a shoe blind.

All the cards are dealt facedown to the eight players, and under no circumstances are you to look at your cards before it's your turn to act. If you can't stand the suspense, just sit in the first chair, first base, and then you always go first. The man playing third base, the eighth seat clockwise from the dealer, must have a stronger constitution than most. You will at once become the most popular and reviled person at the table, but often no one else wants your job. This is because the last card that you choose to take or not to take is also the dealer's second card. Basically everyone either blames you if the dealer doesn't bust and you're a hero if the dealer does bust.

Lots of the rules are different. First of all, you can only double down on ten or eleven. The dealer only takes one faceup card and waits to take his second card until the table has completed acting on their hands. Unless the dealer shows an ace, that is. If the dealer's first card is an ace, an insurance option is given immediately. Then the dealer's second card is dealt and turned faceup! If it's blackjack, the hand is over and tie blackjack hands get paid one half of their bet. So if you had a $30 bet out and you and the dealer both had blackjack, you would get your $30 back plus $15 more. If the dealer's second card is not a face card, then the hand just continues on as normal, players get to act on their hand with the knowledge of the dealer's first two cards! I think this is a big advantage for the player.

Another interesting rule here is that not only do split aces get one card, but split ace blackjacks get paid 3–2, the first time I've seen that, and if you split your two face cards and get blackjack, you also get paid 3–2. While you might gasp upon hearing someone splitting two face cards, in Argentina it's done all the time, and card counters know that this can be a very profitable play in a certain situation if you can do it without raising any eyebrows.

It's also quite a common practice in Argentina for someone to play behind your bet. They do this by putting their own bet next to yours. Even if their bet is larger than yours, you still make the decisions in the hand. Don't be intimidated. On a busy night, most of the blackjack tables will have several people standing and watching and putting bets down next to other players, sometimes on every hand on the table at once. If you have a $20 bet down in your seat and someone comes and puts $300 behind it, you are still in charge. And it happens quite frequently.

BACCARAT Baccarat is clearly the game of choice down here. It ideally suits the temperament of the Argentinean gamblers, who are most concerned with the age-old question: Will he or won't he? Contrast this, if you will, with the common temperament of the American gamblers, who prefer to ponder I'm damned if I do and I'm damned if I don't.

Here are the basic rules to baccarat, James Bond's preferred game of chance. Cards are dealt from an eight-deck shoe. The shoe is passed around the table in a circular fashion. The person who has the shoe is called the bank. The person with the highest wager placed in opposition to the bank becomes the player. If nobody wants to bet in opposition to the bank, then the casino plays the player's hand. The shoe does not move as long as the bank continues to win.

The object is to get to nine in three or less cards. The closer hand wins. Each hand gets two cards to start, which are flipped over with much fanfare. Aces count one, face cards count zero, and everything else is face value. Six plus six equals two in baccarat, not twelve. If either hand totals eight or nine, it's a natural, and the hand is over. If the hands have from zero to five, a third card may be dealt. There are really no decisions for you to make along the way, except once in a blue moon when you're playing bank and you have a five.

It's very easy, and very dramatic. As far as the percentages go, the bank has a slight edge over the player, and to compensate for this you must pay the house 5 percent commission on every winning bank bet. That is their edge. But they do strange things with rounding up and down here, so be alert.

The shoe moves around the table, passing every time the player hand wins. When someone goes on a streak, wins five or six hands in a row while holding the bank, that's the game of baccarat.

Even though your odds are slightly better when betting on the player, who wants to bet on the player all the time? Basically it means you're betting against everyone, you're hoping for the shoe to move around the table in a series of fits and starts, and you never get to experience the thrill of a crumply eyed rheumatoid old man with a Zen-like expression rediscover the spring in his wrist and flick the cards out of the shoe like a fireball pitcher in the World Series, never breaking stride and never changing expression as his $20 original stake gets parlayed up into the hundreds, as oblivious to the money as he is oblivious to the cheers of the table, his team who rides him all the way to the bank. No, all he knows is the cards come out of that wooden shoe and then after the bank wins again, he's on to the next hand. That's why you play baccarat, my friend, and if you've gotta give up the whopping extra percent to sit there in your tuxedo and feel like a true gambling gentleman, then they can take my money in Argentina anytime.

Furthermore, in Argentinean baccarat, you are not able to bet on a tie. A tie is a push, and the hand is replayed. What does all this mean? Well, in my mind, it makes baccarat a much more attractive game to play here as opposed to in some other locales. And of course you can't beat the atmosphere. Now if I could only get myself some of those green-tinted glasses that James Bond had with which to see through the cards . . .

Banca Gana

It's my first time holding the shoe, that wooden rectangle of polished fate containing the plain-backed lovelies. Seven seated players, a crowd of standing onlookers and side bettors, the floorman in his high chair and tapping his long wooden paddle, and all stare expectantly at me across the green felt. I have to admit my hands fumble as I try and remember just how Jordan slid the cards out of the shoe in my favorite gambling book, *Fools Die*. A card for the player, a card for the bank, a card for the player, a card for the bank. The floorman expertly scoops up the player's cards with his paddle and delivers them to a man across the table, someone so foolish as to bet against me on

my first try with the shoe. Doesn't he know about the luck of fools, the terri-
tory of the ignoramus? The man rubs the cards one time and then flings them
up on the table for all to see. Eight-four, or two, in baccarat terms. Not much.
I turn my two cards over in one smooth motion. Ace-seven, a natural eight.
"*Banca gana,*" intones the floorman, the bank wins. The dour-faced woman
with glasses on my left flashes me a smile. "*Muy bien!*" she says, and I feel
like I've really done something. Baccarat, after all, is a team game, the man
or woman with the shoe is the captain, and you have to ask yourself, "Will I
be led on to victory?" Meanwhile, I've won myself $20.

HORSE RACING I visited the Buenos Aires racetrack. They have ten
horses running a kilometer around no turns. Now I know why Balmoral
only has the longest stretch run in North America. Somehow the grand-
son of Cryptoclearance managed to find his way down here and go off at
6–1 odds. I lost a bundle.

Casinos and Lodging
THE POINT

CENTRAL CASINO

The Central Casino in Mar del Plata deserves the title of the biggest
casino in South America. It's grand. Housed in a giant beachfront edifice
from the 1930s, when the casino is full—and it's usually full—you still
feel small inside. I mean, the ceilings are forty feet high if they're an inch
and basically you've just got one grand room, suitable for an opera but
not ill suited in its present capacity as a casino. Everything else is understated. No flashy carpets or decor, just a few impressive wooden bars
with old clocks hanging on the walls. Central Casino has no need to hide
what time it is. If it's after ten o'clock, it's time to gamble and that's that.
At least half of the tourist population must show up on any given night. It
is quite simply, the place to be. And don't expect to show up with a hundred bucks and nurse it all night for the free drinks. First of all, you have
to pay for the drinks. You come to the casino to gamble, minimum bet
$20, and it goes fast. You can get away with making $2 bets on the inside
at roulette, but that doesn't last long either.

A long-haired studly fellow sits at the blackjack table, smoking a cigarette and sporting a tan. His white shirt is unbuttoned almost to his
navel, exposing his gold chains, hairy chest, and rippled ribcage.

Casino

HOURS Casino is every day from 3 P.M.–2:30 A.M. (later during the height of summer). At 9 P.M. on a Friday, there's still plenty of seats, but forget about it by midnight.

ADMISSION No wearing of hats in Central Casino, why I don't know, but they do have a coat and property check. $5 entrance, free entrance to basement slot house. You get a free entrance card if you stay in a nice hotel, like the Hotel Riviera, for example, and get to ride up to the casino in a private elevator.

LANGUAGE Spanish.

LAYOUT The Central Casino is not a slot house. An entire room of slot machines is tucked away downstairs, and in a fitting manner, entrance to the slot room is free, if you're silly enough to want to be in there. Actually, the slots are pretty decent, and while there are no poker machines or video slots of any kind, the machines are all the modern reel sort with the cherries and the diamonds, so a slot player won't be disappointed. Although the slot room is crowded, the ceilings are low, the zoo is noisy, and a live band adds to the cacophony.

In contrast to this is the real casino upstairs, to which you have to pay a $5 entrance fee. Stately, somber, and regal. The size of the room dwarfs everything, including the more than 100 roulette tables, 30 or 40 baccarat tables, 20 to 30 blackjack tables, and 2 craps tables thrown in for show, which I wouldn't waste a wooden nickel on if my life depended on it.

GAMES Roulette, blackjack, baccarat, slots, craps.

LIMITS Even though the casino is laid out as one big room, it is divided into three *salas*, featuring different limits. *Sala común, sala intermedia,* and *sala especial.* Sala special features sky's the limit betting on both roulette and baccarat. The normal limits for roulette range from $2 to $400, baccarat $20 to $800, blackjack $20 to $400, and craps $20 to $400.

RULES AND NOTES In a strange twist to accepted gambling wisdom, you are not allowed to buy chips at the table. *Fichas,* or chips, must be purchased at the cashier. This means if you're stuck big and have just lost your last chips, you have to leave your seat, go to the cashier, buy more chips, and then walk back to the table before placing your next bet. As most gamblers would agree, the seventy or so seconds that it takes to perform that transaction is simply unacceptable when you're stuck to the gills and trying to get even. My advice, change all your money to chips when you walk in, just in case. I had to learn the hard way when stuck two hundred and playing blackjack and the count was up on +6, so I had my last hundred in chips on the line, my big bet, and I scored an eleven looking into the dealer's four, and wouldn't you know they wouldn't let me double down, even though I was waving the cash in their faces and putting up as big a stink as I could in my limited Spanish. So again, my advice to you is: Buy the chips when you come in. Just in case.

In general, if you win a bet, the house will automatically let it ride for the next bet. This has something to do with the Argentinean gambling mentality. In my experience, they refuse to get off of a winner, which could be why the house has such paltry maximum betting limits. They're scared of getting busted by every man who just rode in from the Pampas. In America, you see a guy win twelve straight bets and only $12. You give an Argentinean gambler twelve passes and he's likely to pay off the national debt, if they'll let him. Of course, the downside is: Most of the gamblers go home broke. I'm not seeing a lot of people who are walking out of there saying, "I broke even."

While dollars are readily accepted for purchasing chips, the cashier only pays out in pesos. Don't worry, though, the peso is fully convertible and dollars can be repurchased at most any bank. By the way, Travelers Cheques are not accepted at the casino, but they have an ATM machine with every major card provider covered. MasterCard and Visa are only good for ATM cash withdrawals, there are no cash advance facilities currently at the casino. Don't forget to reconvert inside the country.

You can reserve your seat by means of a small white hexagonal button if you tap out or have to go to the bathroom. Just ask for *reserva*.

FOOD AND DRINK Casino light menu, very light on food, but all the alcohol is there and bar the cheap stuff. When you order a drink, say Scotch, the waitress carries the bottle to your table on a silver tray so you can watch her pour it. Nice touch, no well alcohol here, but no free alcohol either.

The ice cream shops are always the last thing to close in town, never before three, so you can always grab a cone on your way home.

THE PEOPLE THERE Argentine gamblers are on the whole very likable and good losers. Smiling, laughing. Some are impassive and some are wrinkled into expressive caricatures. The ladies who sweep the floor and clean the ashtrays are young girls wearing tight bodices suitable for a floor show. But I don't mind. In Panama, the dealers are always talking to you—they talk too much. In Mar del Plata, they always tell you what you have and what your options are, and that's it. They're very well trained.

HOTEL

The Central Casino has no hotel.

ACCOMMODATION AND A SMATTERING OF HOTELS

There are so many hotels in Mar del Plata that I can't list them all in a helpful way. However, the tourist office in the Buenos Aires's airport is NOT TO BE MISSED as far as being helpful with hotels. There's also supposed to be a tourist office in downtown Buenos Aires, but I couldn't find it. And I really wanted to find it. I mean it was pouring rain and I'd made the bright decision to carry my computer around with me, jumping from overhang to overhang until I could buy an umbrella. I'd been up most of the night and came in on the night bus back from Mar del Plata, so I was needing to find a place to stay, but I didn't like the look of what I saw, so I really wanted to find that tourist office to get me a hotel room, and I was there and it wasn't. It wasn't. At least not that day.

From their computer, the tourist office employees at the airport will, at no charge, print you out a list of all the hotels in Mar del Plata in your price range. All hotels in Argentina are rated by a star system, and I guess it works okay. First I stayed in a one-star hotel, which was cheap and basic, but clean and friendly. Then I moved up to three stars, which was very comfortable and spacious with remote-control TV and big windows, though not quite as personable, owing to the fact that there were a lot of people staying there. Four- and five-star hotels are top-notch both in terms of service, quality, and price.

The list that the tourist office prints out for you has every hotel in your "star" range, the telephone number, address, and room rates for singles and doubles and triples, if they have them, which a lot of these beach hotels do. The hotels are nice enough, but it's expected that you'll spend a lot of time outside when you're not sleeping, which you inevitably do. Between the beach and the cafés and the restaurants and the ice cream shops and the park and the casino, things are always happening until well past 3 A.M. And I mean happening.

Rack rates for a two-star hotel are about $40 for a double. Prices waver, depending on if it's the beginning of the summer or the end of the summer and how full the town is. But there's a lot of hotel space in Mar del Plata.

Buenos Aires makes you smile and Mar del Plata makes you laugh out loud.

HOTEL RIVIERA is a three-star establishment less than a three-minute walk from the casino. Corner rooms are especially nice, with views of the ocean, the beach, and the casino. Casino ticket and breakfast come with the room. If you arrive at the end of the summer, like say the end of February, the best rooms in the hotel will be yours for a song. Belgrano 2118, phone 54-223-495-4021. E-mail *reservas@hotelriviera.com.ar*

HOTEL FLAMINGO has a good location, but no single rooms. Doubles start at $65. Three stars on Moreno, just off the park.

THE GALEON HOTEL is your family-run budget option. $15 a night in peak season, private bath, okay, but who spends time in their room? The people are oh so friendly, breakfast and smiles all around. Come in and out whenever you please, there's always someone there. Two blocks from the beach, casino, and everything important. Located on Buenos Aires 2431, phone 54-223-495-9200.

THE HERMITAGE is a four-star hotel directly facing the beach. If you want a room right next to the beach, rather than one a five-minute walk away. I don't think anything's wrong with a five-minute walk to the beach when you're in a beach town, but . . . Hermitage Hotel. $130 to $260 room facing the ocean, and $100 to $200 facing town. Phone 54-223-451-9081, 451-9633. Located at Boulevard P.P. Ramos 2657.

THE HOTEL DOS REYES is the class joint in town. Four stars on Avenida Colon and Buenos Aires. Exceptional facility for Mar del Plata, in the center of where it's happening. The Mustang Café across from the Dos Reyes has pretty young waitresses, a "clean well-lit place" that's open until after 4 A.M. at least, when you can't go home.

HOTEL BOULEVARD is next to the Central Casino and beach. In a very prime location, about 100 feet from the casino entrance and a block from the beach. A little noisy at night, however, and I would rather walk one extra block and be in a place that's a little quieter when I want to go to sleep. The rooms aren't looking that special. Also quite close to the bingo hall. Located on Moreno 2035, phone 54-223-495-9625, 54-224-495-9849.

HOTEL ROLAND, $24 single, $38 double, located on Corrientes 1965 and Moreno 2200, regular enough place in a good location. Phone 54-223-492-2069.

IF YOU HAVE TO BE IN BUENOS AIRES . . . Then try the three-star **Alpino Hotel,** nice because it's in a residential neighborhood in the city, which is what you want. Lots of lovely neighborhood restaurants and bakeries that make those lovely thin sandwiches for lunch that I can eat by the dozen. Or at least the half dozen. Cabello 3318 & Avenida Libertador 2500, Buenos Aires. Phone 54-1-802-5151. I didn't stay in Buenos Aires long, but the neighborhood where most of the business hotels are pales in comparison to this one. Rack rates are only about $75, good value for three stars in Buenos Aires, which features outrageous hotel prices. Rooms are large and comfortable with remote-control cable TV. The front desk clerk is a favorite to ask you if you wouldn't like a little company tonight, as he runs his hands up and down in the hourglass figure. If he doesn't ask, he won't be put off by you asking him.

Entertainment and Nightlife

A lot of Argentina reminds me of "A Clean Well Lighted Place" by Ernest Hemingway—read it if you haven't; if you have, it won't hurt you to read it again. It's only about three pages, in which a man can sit in a clean bright room at three in the morning and drink with dignity, signaling to the pretty young waitress with his finger for another bottle of wine and some soda water, or a saucer of whiskey. Argentina seems like a fine place to become a drunkard, because these men can hold their liquor. People are expected to get drunk with dignity in Argentina. The proprietor of the Mustang Café sits behind his cash register reading his paper—unruffled at 3:30 A.M. with a fan whirring roundly behind his head.

THE BEACH Lots of pretty Argentine girls with not much on? Yes. Lots of old people with saggy suits? Yes also. And lots of kids. Mar del Plata is popular with families.

Things that come by in rapid succession include *helados, ensalada de fruta,* Coca-Cola, sodas, *agua,* and pretzels. But no hard sells. A shout and then they move on. The sand's not the greatest in the world, but it's clean and fine for your feet. It's just poor for sand castles. The beach is packed during the day. Your best bet is just to come with your towel, umbrella (or rent one), and ten pesos for sodas, fries, and water. Who needs more?

OUTSIDE OF TOWN The Iguazú Grand Hotel Resort and Casino is located at the waterfalls of Iguazú. This is a several-hour plane ride from Buenos Aires, on the border between Argentina and Brazil and Paraguay. These are the widest waterfalls in the world, stretching four miles across. Not the longest or the biggest, but the widest. The casino and hotel sit just next to the waterfalls on the Argentina side. It's a deluxe hotel and casino. Puerto Iguazú. Phone 54-375-749-8000, 749-8050, fax 749-8060.

FOOD Fast food is an oxymoron in Argentina. At dinnertime, eat and prepare to sit for a while. Eaters! I tell you the food that these people can pack away is incomprehensible. They have to be the biggest per capita eaters in the world, barring the Eskimos at a whale feast. And while we Americans specialize in junk food north of the border, grease and fries, the Argentines won't settle for anything less than prime A, slow roasted. They spend time and then some on their meals, and they pack it in. I mean, it ain't like they're a skinny people, but wow. Don't leave your fingers on the buffet table, you might lose them.

A *lomito* is a damn good thinly sliced steak sandwich, *lomito completo* includes lettuce and tomato and melted cheese and shouldn't set you back more than $3, which is nice. A *Milanese* is a breaded steak sandwich, not bad either. *Milanese gigante* probably has lettuce and tomato and cheese.

Nobody ever said anything about Argentine chickens. So if you're not eating beef in all its forms, I can't help you. Yogurt crunchers stick to the eco tour. I did discover two vegetarian restaurants in Mar del Plata, but come on.

The area around Belgrano 2200 and Entre Rios has quite a lot of restaurants. **El Imperial Marisquería** and pizzeria directly across from Central Casino is a popular dinner spot. **Paella Liberto** on Alte Brown between Arenalle and Tommun, where two huge pots of sumptuous *paella* are always bubbling away in full view and only cost $4 for a nice size portion, or $7 for two. **Yo Tú Él Pizzas** on Belgrano 2175 makes pretty tasty pizzas and is open very late, phone 223-495-8763.

ICE CREAM A kilogram of *helado* (ice cream) is only $4! Argentina is an ice cream lover's paradise. *Dulce de Leche* should not be ignored. It is a flavor down here, a candy, an ice cream, a delicious everything. It is basically the flavor of caramel flan, and it's so good. When my wife and I first discovered the flavor in the Häagen-Dazs brand, we became so obsessed with it that we used to chant, *"Dulce de Leche! Dulce de Leche!"* over and over again on our way to the store to pick up a container. And don't miss those special boxes of chocolate and *Dulce de Leche* candies that they sell on the streets and in the shops.

WINES Argentina does pretty well in the vino business. Santa Ana is a good cheap wine. Try *vino con soda*, a fine drink, popular and quite refreshing—you get your own bottle of wine and your own spritzer and a glass, and you mix the wine and the sparkling water to your own specifications. This is the drink to have when you are whiling away the afternoons in a street café. Oh yeah.

GOLF Plenty of golf down in Mar del Plata, four courses. Mar del Plata Golf Club, 54-223-486-2221, $20 Mon.–Fri., $40 Sat.–Sun., affiliated with Sheraton Hotel, nine holes. Los Acantilados, 54-223-467-2500, eighteen holes. Golf Sierra de Los Padres, twenty kilometers from Mar del Plata, eighteen holes, 54-223-463-0062. Marayui Country Club, nine holes.

SHOPPING Mar del Plata is a shopper's paradise. Sweaters and clothes and all things nice, and everything is fairly priced. You might even find some bargains. There is a very nice pedestrian shopping mall at San Martín. And just in case, Brandinelli is a twenty-four-hour upscale flower shop at 2700 Colón.

SAN JUAN, PUERTO RIC'O

LAY OF THE LAND

Brother, if you can think of something more romantic than sitting on your terrace at sunset staring out between the palm trees at the sand and the waves and the setting sun, and sharing a chilled bottle of Chardonnay with the one you love, then here's my home number. Because it doesn't get any better than this.

◆

There are two parts to every day in San Juan. There is day, and there is night. And day does not go into night, and the difference is in how you dress.

If you ain't happening at ten o'clock on a Friday night at the El San Juan in the lobby bar, then, brother, you could be a clam in a tank top at a funeral. The place is cooking. Cocktail waitresses flashing as they walk, slit up to the hip in black. Latinas with the Lambada backside.

We canceled our dinner reservations for the cheese plate and a chance to watch the folks coming in the door, and if you're a people watcher, then it's not a bad idea. And the cheese plate is a work of art.

San Juan, Puerto Rico
GENERAL INFORMATION

YOU'RE NOT IN KANSAS ANYMORE Puerto Rico is an island. San Juan, the capital, has a beautiful beach near the airport called Isla Verde.

WHERE Southeast of Miami, the "51st State" lies in an area that sees the Atlantic Ocean to the north and the Caribbean Sea to the south. Eastern Standard Time during summer, and one hour ahead the rest of the year.

WHEN Puerto Rico is always nice, basking in the Caribbean climate. The busy season, however, is the end of November until April.

TELEPHONES It's just like being in the states. The area code for most of San Juan is 787.

CURRENCY Dollars.

SAFETY Most hotels have safes in the room. I wouldn't want to be carrying a lot of money around in San Juan. Not at all.

ATMS ATM machines are plentiful in Puerto Rico. You'll usually find one just outside the casino.

WHAT THEY WEAR In Vegas, people are differentiated by the size of their bet; in Puerto Rico, it's by what you're wearing.

¿HABLA ESPANOL? Most people you meet speak English perfectly, but there is a lot of Spanish spoken as well and a lot of things in Spanish.

INTERNET AOL has local access number.

CLIMATE Ahhh . . .

I'll Walk There Barefoot
TRANSPORTATION ISSUES

LEGAL Puerto Rico, officially the Commonwealth of Puerto Rico, is a state, sort of. I have no idea of its exact legal status, but Americans only need a driver's license to go there.

FLIGHTS It's easy and cheap to get there. Miami, Houston, and New York are gateway cities. Or you can fly there cheap from Aruba.

AIRPORT The taxi rates from the airport are fixed. Once you get outside, go to the taxi desk, tell them where you want to go, and they'll write you out a slip to give the driver that says how much it costs. That's nice. Total does not include tips, and you should tip as you would in any major American city. It costs $12 to go from the airport to Condado Beach, $8 to Isla Verde. More than two bags, fifty cents extra each.

WHERE THINGS ARE There are basically two tourist hotel areas in San Juan. The Condado area is a bit older, I believe, a bit more in a state of disrepair, and not nearly as happening as the Isla Verde area. Both areas have several hotels.

The Condado area has a twenty-four-hour Walgreens on Ashford Avenue and a twenty-four-hour supermarket called Pueblo Xtra at 114 De Diego Avenue.

TRANSPORTATION AROUND TOWN Taxi rates are fixed all over town, and they are a little bit high, considering how little driving there usually is to do. You get the taxis at the hotels, and at least most of the taxis are nice cars to ride in, big old bombers from the seventies that run good as new. A taxi ride to anywhere is usually either $8, $12, or $16.

The Money Plays
GAMBLING SETUP—THE QUICK FACTS

CASINOS are licensed and privately owned. There are about fifteen different casinos in and around San Juan. Williams Hospitality Group runs the casinos at the Condado Plaza, the El San Juan, the Wyndham, and the El Conquistador. You can expect a good level of service from them.

HOURS Condado Plaza Hotel and Casino is open twenty-four hours. Most of the other casinos close at 4 A.M.

ADMITTANCE Gaming age is twenty-one. ID sometimes required.

AMBIANCE AND AMENITIES The Casino at the El San Juan is a place you won't soon forget, unlike the casinos on the rest of the island. The Ritz Carlton's casino is stately, but somber and empty.

GAMES ON OFFER Caribbean stud poker, blackjack, roulette, craps, baccarat, slot machines.

LIMITS $5 to very high. One of the things about Puerto Rico is that the nice hotels have always catered to the high limit player. The high limit player. If you want to play high, just ask. Anyway, there's a good chance that no matter what limit you are playing, at some point you'll be shoulder to shoulder with someone who's really getting the money down. And that's always fun to watch.

MONEY All games are played in dollars.

LEGALITY Casinos are legal and safe.

TIPPING POLICIES IN THE CASINO Dealers share tips, and those tips make up a good part of their wage.

I'll Take the Odds
BREAKING APART THE GAME

CRAPS Double odds is standard for the island. Double full odds at the El San Juan means that you can back up a $20 bet $50 on a five or six point.

The El San Juan easily has the most rocking craps game on the island. Shoulder to shoulder, most nights, $5 minimum table. The craps table is packed in tight, the kind of table where you can expect a round of applause for the shooter after a good roll. It's only a $5 table, but with a $2,000 maximum, and at my table we had a $6 six sitting next to one for $900. Now that's fun. Five dollars on the pass line backed up ten and a guy two spots down is playing with $30,000 in front of him. C'mon, shooter.

BACCARAT The way they play baccarat in Puerto Rico is according to rigid rules. There are no options for the player save how much to bet and whether to bet on bank, player, or tie, which pays 8–1.

BLACKJACK Six decks. Double down only on nine, ten, or eleven. Doubling down on these numbers only takes a lot of play out of the game, in my mind. One card for split aces. Double after split, but only if you have nine, ten, or eleven. Dealer stands on soft seventeen. They are quite leery of card counters in Puerto Rico.

COCKFIGHTING At Club Gallistico, in Isla Verde. It is cockfighting, just like in *The Cincinnati Kid*, and the front row has an even-money chance of getting some blood. Tickets are from $5 to $25. There is some heavy gambling, but if you don't understand Spanish, you're gonna have trouble getting a bet down. All fights are not to the death, but some sure are.

A circular pit ringed by high-backed chairs—you enter at the top and look down on the action. There is a ringside announcer. A fellow circulates with a tray of empanadas, but I'm not exactly hungry. Now I know where the term "peckerhead" comes from.

Around the top of the ring, there are the cages so you can check the roosters out before the fights, and areas where the owners prep them, sharpen their claws. The fights are not a quiet affair—the crowd loves blood and *"Vamos!"* and pounding and clapping the roosters into a massive frenzy. A quote from a breeder: "Honor is everything here. This is a gentlemanly sport. Winning or losing comes second to friendship. We all shout our bets and our word suffices." Hmmm.

Fights are no longer than fifteen minutes, but there are about thirty-five fights a day, beginning at 3:30 P.M. First they weigh them, then they warm them up, then they get them good and mad. Tuesdays, Fridays, and Saturdays. You have to be down in the front three rows in order to gamble. Bring your camera.

Club Gallistico, next door to the Hampton Inn and the Metropol Restaurant. Isla Verde Avenue, corner of Los Gobernadores Avenue, telephone 787-791-1557, 791-6005.

Casinos and Lodging
THE POINT

WYNDHAM EL SAN JUAN HOTEL AND CASINO

I'm having trouble thinking of a better place for a honeymoon than the El San Juan. No splurge will be better appreciated than a few days in the ocean suites. TV, yes. VCR, of course. Full stereo system. It doesn't stop there. His and her bathrobes, separate toilet, shower, and Jacuzzi rooms, gorgeous wood furniture and a terrace or patio with lounge chairs overlooking the ocean. Full couch, armchairs, writing table, a bed with real blankets, sheets, and bedspreads. Why leave the room? Well, only to relax in the pool that's just for ocean suite guests or take four steps onto the beach and into the bright blue sea. Or to gamble, of course.

Don't have an ocean suite? Don't worry. The El San Juan is crystal, from top to bottom. No less than six pools curve and wind their way around the grounds, with bars, lounge chairs, massage areas, it's a paradise pure and simple.

Remember, you're not only paying for the room at the El San Juan. You're paying for the six pools, the poolside waiter drink service, the two-hundred-year-old banyan trees, the front of the line at Club Babylon, and the privilege of saying you're a guest of the hotel. You will feel the privilege.

If you're not coming to the El San Juan, you didn't actually get there. Drive in past a high wall, palm trees, and a sculpted garden. The bellhop is dressed in spotless whites and a Panama hat. We felt out of place arriving in a taxi.

You want service? I had left our bags with the valet early in the morning, as we had arrived more than four hours before the 3 P.M. check-in and our room wasn't cleaned yet. When we did get into our room, which was still well before three o'clock, I picked up the phone and dialed down to the bellhop to see about getting our luggage sent up. Before I could utter a word, the man on the other end said, "Mr. May? If you're calling to inquire about your five pieces of luggage, don't worry, they're already on their way up. Is there anything else I can help you with?" And with that came a knock on the door.

You want style? Try a lobby with a ceiling made entirely out of hand-carved mahogany. A crystal chandelier that would dwarf a large rowboat. Three open all-mahogany bars with baskets of fruit and lavish arrangements of fresh flowers in a stone vase. Steve Wynn, eat your heart out, for you will always be a boy from upstate New York with no claim on Old World charm. Whoever designed this hotel had a lot of money, but even more taste. Built in 1948, the eighth wonder of the world.

Casino

HOURS Noon–4 A.M. daily, until 6 A.M. on weekends.

LANGUAGE English and Spanish.

LAYOUT This is the casino featured in many James Bond films. That's really all you need to know. It lives up to the billing. You do feel like you're stepping into a movie when you walk in there. The casino is a nice space, elegant and giving the impression of lavish furnishings. There is a very separate and elegant Players Lounge, table games for high-limit players. Special high limits can be arranged. They play very high here.

GAMES 360 slot machines, 16 blackjack tables, 6 roulette, 4 craps, 3 mini-baccarat, 2 baccarat, 4 Caribbean stud. Slot machines have player tracking with Slot Players Club.

LIMITS Roulette $2 min. to $20 maximum, $1 chips. Only one $5 blackjack table at night, but good for them. One $10 table, one $15 table, plenty of $25, $50, and $100 tables to $2000 or more.

FOOD AND DRINK The Bloody Mary is lunch. As the guy sitting next to me said when the voluminous filled-to-the-brim goblet arrived, "Wow! Look at this. You got celery, you got green pepper, red onion, what is this, pepperoni?" Yes, it is, a beautiful garnish on a tasty drink. Finish one of these, and well, you'll probably need a wheelchair, don't worry they didn't forget the vodka or the tomato juice. Bloody Mary $7.50.

Tequila Bar and Grill is a Mexican place on the tenth floor that opens at five-thirty—which is a perfect time to get there in order to have a few drinks and watch the sunset. They do a decent rendition of tableside guacamole. Service is excellent, friendly staff, and good Latin music over the speakers. Go for the view and the margaritas and the guacamole. The menu is not broad, but the standards are covered and the view—well, the view is priceless. Barrel-size large margarita comes in six different flavors, if you finish it you may not be able to walk back to your room. Tequila Bar and Grill open from five-thirty to 11 P.M. Make a reservation if you want to be assured of a table with a great view of the sunset and the ocean.

Just an outstanding restaurant selection. You could stay there for a while and never eat anything remotely similar, and it's all delicious. Very authentic Chinese restaurant called **Back Street Hong Kong. Yamato,** authentic Japanese sushi restaurant. **La Piccola Fontana** for intimate Northern Italian in a romantic candlelit room. **Palm Restaurant,** your Peter Luger–style steak house where the emphasis is on simplicity and quality, which is what you want when you're eating steak. Plus Tequila Bar and Grill on the roof for Mexican, and the new **Ranch,** a barbecued ribs country bar and grill, also on the roof.

A bottle of very good wine at the wine bar (they have Simi?) $40.

NIGHT Looking for a place to wear your white suit? Have you always wanted to get a white suit but couldn't find an occasion? El San Juan on a Saturday night. Their motto here is "Please dress to impress." They enclose a card for guests in the room. Part of it reads: UNDER THE SUN. THE SUN, SEA, AND OF COURSE, OUR POOL ARE NATURE'S BACKGROUND FOR BEACH AND LEISURE WEAR. SO FEEL FREE! WHEN THE SUN SETS . . . AND AFTER. TANK TOPS, T-SHIRTS, SHORTS, OR ANY FORM OF BEACH WEAR OR BARE FEET ARE NOT ACCEPTABLE IN PUBLIC AREAS OF THE HOTEL AFTER 7:00 P.M. What this translates to is, wear whatever you want during the day, but at night, dress up. To the max. Especially on the weekends. Alternatively, you can rent a white James Bond dinner jacket from the hotel for $60 for three nights.

Pretty young Latin honeys in gowns and tight-fitting dresses? Yes. A prime spot for picking up a little action. A typical Saturday night. The casino is packed, the five lobby bars are packed. The El Chico Mambo Dance Lounge—packed. The Club Babylon—packed with a line to get in and rave.

The lobby is 13,000 square feet, and it looks like Havana in the heyday. Fifteen bars and lounges. Salsa every night in the Spanish saloon, live Cuban bands on Thursday nights, pops concerts by the Puerto Rico Symphony on Sunday nights, piano and jazz music all the time, a very happening disco in Club Babylon on Saturday nights.

El Chico Lounge—The red velvet, packed-to-the-gills home of the mambo kings, complete with a fantastic bongo player and two glittered dancing singers and a Latin beat so rocking that you involuntarily start dancing as you walk by and look for a free spot on the dance floor. Small circle tabletops and red chairs. A covered lounge bar in the back promises wonderful things.

Club Babylon!—By two o'clock the line stretches around a corner—hotel guests can pass. One lady checks prospective VIPs on the "list" in her hand. Lord knows how you get on that list. They check ID. But hotel guests are VIPs, they get in without paying the $10 cover. Minimum age twenty-three, apparently you have to be older to rave than you do to gamble. Bring your fashion. The club is empty on Fridays.

One of the bars is called the **Wine and Cheese Bar,** where for $17 you get a platter with generous wedges of six different cheeses, plump seedless grapes, blueberries, strawberries, sliced pears, two kinds of sliced apples, and a whole bunch of crackers. I'm not kidding, this hotel is the nuts.

Every Sunday night, the hotel offers **Philharmonic Pops** concerts in the lobby. A forty-one-piece orchestra made from members of the Puerto Rico Philharmonic, accompanied by an all-chocolate dessert buffet that is sure to make your eyes pop.

Cigars—One of the bars is a cigar bar, not in a separate enclosure, but part of the huge lobby. An excellent ventilation system keeps the rest of the lobby astoundingly smoke free. When you consider the amount of heavy smoking going on, this is no small feat. The hotel has its own cigar, patrons are allowed to rent private humidors, there is an on-site cigar roller on the weekends, and the smoke shop stocks everything fine. The cigar bar also offers a special martini menu.

THE PEOPLE THERE Want to feel as if you're among celebrities? This hotel is exclusive and expensive enough to have been host to some of the world's biggest names, including John F. Kennedy, Ronald Reagan, Sammy Davis, Jr., Ricky Martin, Rod Stewart, Bruce Willis. And the Harlem Globetrotters.

Hotel

The property is so well kept that everything looks brand-new and antique at the same time. 389 rooms, 21 ocean suites. Originally built in 1958, bankrupt in the 1970s, and reopened in 1985. Officially now called the Wyndham El San Juan, but everyone knows it as simply the El San Juan. If I could just interject one thought at this juncture, one concept here, the word would be "surrender." Stellar service, where they prepare your bed and re-clean your room for the evening. Local calls $1.50. Cigar bar open from 6 P.M.–1 A.M. weekdays and until 3 A.M. on weekends, hand-rolled cigars. Very nice shopping arcade in the El San Juan, bathing suits,

El San Juan logo wear which is really nice, and jewelry and art and shoes and stuff like that. Twenty-four-hour tennis on lighted courts. 700-foot white sand beach is the nicest I found in San Juan.

The grounds feature huge hundreds-of-years-old banyan trees.

The standard guest rooms are spacious, with seating areas as well as a work table. Iron, hair dryer, safe, entertainment center with VCR and stereo as well as TV, and all the other stuff.

The ocean suites are the premier rooms at the El San Juan, and if you can afford them, they're worth it. Right next to the beach, twenty-one suites in a two-level building. These suites are separate from the main hotel tower, they are next to the beach and the pools rather than the casino. Oh so private. They have everything. They are beautiful, luxurious, and incredibly romantic. You will smile and sigh all day and all night long. $760 per night.

The El San Juan also boasts one of the truly unique rooms in the world, the Royal Suite, at $3,500 per night, which has furnishings in it valued at more than a quarter of a million dollars. Originally furnished by a big player who was a regular guest there at his own expense, and now purchased by the hotel (read, exchanged for casino debts). Baby grand piano, Lalique chandeliers, Baccarat crystal, Limoges china in the kitchen, lavish black marble bath, Oriental ceramics, sculptures, lacquer cabinetwork. The ultra ultra jet set. The adjoining Celebrity Suite was for the player's female companion. In the main tower of the hotel, but overlooking the ocean.

Lately the hotel has been offering a very popular four day, three night "James Bond Package." And it's easy to understand why it's popular. Limousine at the airport, room service waiter named Q, champagne, strawberries, brandy, your own "007" embroidered bathrobes, a Bond martini, and all kinds of James Bond extras all for $1,137 for two people. Only $190 per person per night, which is a hell of a deal in that place. Special reservations number is 1-800-544-3912, ext. 1474, and tell them you are Bond.

It's true the room rates are at the upper end. But everything else at the El San Juan is very reasonably priced, all the food and the drinks, so you're not really spending that much for them at all. Rack rates May to November 22, $285 to $480 for standard to deluxe room. November 23 to April, $395 to $595 for standard to deluxe room. Ocean suites $600 to $800.

 PRACTICALITIES
Hotel Phone Number: 1-787-791-1000, 1-787-791-6985, 1-800-468-2818
Internet Address: *esjres@caribe.net*
Location: 6063 Isla Verde Avenue, Isla Verde. Only five minutes from the airport. Fixed taxi fare from airport is $8.

AND . . . Next door to the hotel is the El San Juan Towers, a high-rise of completely furnished apartments with fully equipped kitchenettes, plus use of fitness center, pool, in-room safe, and all the business services. Plus you're right next to the El San Juan for all the action you want and the nicest beach. Could be a nice business option. Phone 1-787-791-5151, or 1-800-468-2026.

CONDADO PLAZA HOTEL AND CASINO

The Condado Plaza is still nice. Service is five star and very helpful. Room service menu is everything it should be, standards along with some imagination and originality, prices reasonable, food available twenty-four hours. One imagines it's from the Max's Deli kitchen. Yuca and beef soup, jerk chicken sandwich, grilled tuna steak, *camarones al ajillo* (shrimp with garlic and rice). But the hotel, the building, is just a little past its prime, and if you swim at the beach you're right next to the highway. Condado Beach was apparently a nice area about fifteen years ago. It's not anymore, and that's a fact. Other than the location, it's a nice place. The hotel is professional and well run. But stay in Isla Verde, if you can help it.

Casino

HOURS This is the only casino on the island that's open twenty-four hours a day.

LANGUAGE Spanish and English.

LAYOUT On the second floor is the casino, in one large space. It's big enough, and clean, if not overly charming.

FOOD AND DRINK Some nice restaurant options. Tapas bar and grill, **Mandalay** has pretty authentic Chinese food plus a sushi bar, **Tony Roma's Ribs,** and **Max's Deli.**

Max's Deli is the kind of place where you absolutely can't go wrong. Nice menu, with large portions. Complete breakfast buffet. Twenty-four-hour restaurant. Late-night chicken and rice in a mammoth bowl. Bagels, rye bread, and all the accoutrements. Good value for what you get. Lovely view from the tables of the beach and the ocean, the waves slapping the shore down below.

THE PEOPLE THERE Popular with business travelers.

Hotel

Two towers of rooms. One tower with ocean views, one tower across the street with bay views. The bay views are okay. It's lovely to order breakfast in your room and eat it out on your balcony looking over the water. I'd still rather be in Isla Verde.

It's not the part of the beach that you choose to swim in and for the price you'd be much happier in Isla Verde. The pool doesn't impress me either. Rooms are worn and small, but clean with nice views and very nice wicker furniture. It's a very old property, you expect to see the ghosts of a 1950s Puerto Rican mambo band roaming the halls. 570 rooms. That's just too many.

Rooms are overpriced at $220 per night.

 PRACTICALITIES
Hotel Phone Number: 1-787-721-1000, 1-800-468-8588
Location: On the end of Condado Beach, next to the bridge that leads toward the old city. 999 Ashford Avenue.

HAMPTON INN

The surprise of the bunch is the Hampton Inn, which has all the perks that you don't think about, like a quality free continental breakfast with local papers and quick maid service and free HBO and free local calls (every other place in town is $1.50 every time you pick up the phone) and free parking for hotel guests, and the manager calls you and asks if you're enjoying your stay and your room. And very nice artwork in the brightly sunlit lobby all around.

Casino

No casino. Cockfighting arena located next door.

Hotel

Free local calls, the king suites have two rooms, are very spacious, and not very expensive for the island, checking in at a top rate of $184, but you can almost certainly do better if you don't walk in off the street when the hotel is 99 percent booked. Good hotel for a business person.

The pool is exceptionally pleasant, with a lunch counter and bar. The hotel has a one block walk to the beach. No worries. The El San Juan is right there and the Ritz Carlton is one door down. New property, all the TV channels, including two HBO channels for free. No pornos. Coin operated Laundromat.

Rack rate for a king room, which is quite nice with two TVs and a completely separate living room with a couch and microwave, is $184 plus 9 percent tax. Standard room twenty dollars cheaper.

FOOD AND DRINK Metropol Restaurant next door. Check it out. Lupis Restaurant is across the street.

PRACTICALITIES
Hotel Phone Number: 1-787-791-8757, or reservations at 1-800-Hampton.
Location: 6530 Isla Verde Avenue. Isla Verde area, directly across the street from the El San Juan. Great location.

MARRIOTT

The Marriott has at least got some atmosphere and action in the lobby bar, but it's in the wrong part of town—that is, the Condado area. Not new, but large and well-maintained property. If you're gonna stay in the Condado area, this would be my choice.

Casino

THE STELLARIS CASINO is in one room off the lobby, but it's a big room with high ceilings. Unfortunately, this has no effect on the noise, as the Marriott carves out its niche by being a slot house. The noise level when you're sitting at the table is very high, a bass back beat with the ringing of bells.

Blackjack tournament runs most weeks, could be interesting, but you only get ten hands to play in a round and they have to have enough people there to get it started. I waited around on two different days for them to get ten players together to put up the $200 for the tournament and finally just got my money back and left.

HOURS Noon until 4 A.M. daily.

LIMITS $5 to $200, $50 to $2000, Caribbean stud jackpot $26,000.

LANGUAGE English and Spanish.

RULES AND NOTES Table snacks are free when you're playing. Sesame chicken fingers, mini taquitos, or a Cuban sandwich. Drinks are also free.

FOOD AND DRINK Nice Italian restaurant, but the **Ocean Terrace** restaurant is more varied.

Hotel

Rack rates, $265 city view or $285 ocean view. It's a nice hotel, and the pool is nice enough, but for that price I'd much rather be in Isla Verde. 11 percent tax. 510 rooms, 15 suites, rooms have everything including in-room safe. Hotel features spa with saunas, two tennis courts, and twenty-four-hour room service.

PRACTICALITIES
Hotel Phone Number: 1-787-722-7000, 1-800-464-5005
Internet Address: *www.marriott.com*
Location: 1309 Ashford Avenue, on Condado Beach. Not
too far from Old San Juan, but you can't walk.

RADISSON AMBASSADOR PLAZA HOTEL AND CASINO SAN JUAN

This is not one of Radisson's star properties. In fact, they may have forgotten that they owned it. In my mind, this Radisson is a hole. It's a very old property, the place doesn't look like much from the lobby, and the casino is among the grimiest in town. And a tad surly. Located near the beach, but not next to it with a private beach, so you probably won't go. Not a place to go if you plan on being on the beach.

Casino

In the casino, they're giving me glares and heat, even though I'm only betting $3 per hand. Quick heat. Paranoid heat. You always know when you're not welcome in a casino.

LAYOUT Smallish, narrow space, not very clean.

LIMITS Blackjack $3 to $60, roulette $2 to $20.

RULES AND NOTES Free sandwiches, Cuban style. This place is a bit on the seedy side. Card counters NOT welcome.

FOOD AND DRINK Please.

Hotel

Rack rates are $225 plus 11 percent tax. They must be joking. Probably not a whole lot of repeat customers. 146 rooms, 87 suites, all rooms have a separate living area.

Obviously the suites are the main attraction. There's an all-suite tower with nine floors, 87 two-room suites. Big. Separate living room and bedroom, working and dining areas, wet bar, fridge, two TVs, three telephones plus one fax. And a rooftop swimming pool. It's still a hole.

PRACTICALITIES
Hotel Phone Number: reservations 1-800-333-3333,
1-809-721-7300, from the U.S., 1-800-468-8512
Location: 1369 Ashford Avenue, Condado area.

DIAMOND PALACE

Simple as I can put it: The Diamond Palace is a bad crowd. It's not even near the beach.

Casino

In the casino, I buy in for $50 and a lady gives a big whistle. She has six white $1 chips in front of her. Another guy comes by and buys in for $19, all singles.

HOURS Noon to 4 A.M.

LANGUAGE Spanish.

LAYOUT Low and ugly, small.

GAMES Slots, blackjack, roulette, craps, minibaccarat.

LIMITS Blackjack $3 to $200 and $5 to $500, Caribbean stud jackpot $73,000.

FOOD AND DRINK Rooftop restaurant.

THE PEOPLE THERE Locals. Locals and budget travelers.

Hotel

Rack rates, regular room, $135 single, $150 double. Suite $195. 11 percent tax. Checkout noon. 151 rooms, including 33 suites with private balconies. All rooms have in-room safe. Rooftop swimming pool.

 PRACTICALITIES
Hotel Phone Number: 1-787-721-0810, 1-800-468-2014
Location: 55 Condado Avenue. About two blocks from the beach. And not the best beach.

RITZ CARLTON

The Ritz Carlton is new and very fancy but empty, cold, and pretty much devoid of charm. They just cut their rates to attract guests. The casino is nice, but without atmosphere, although they have a nice large projection TV in the bar area, if you're in town on, say, the last night of March Madness. It has an excellent location, beach, and facilities to recommend it, however.

Casino

LAYOUT Very large, big ceilings, marble columns, and a nice bar with a giant screen television. Really giant.

LIMITS This is a pretty high-limit, high-roller type of place. At least, that's what they're trying to attract.

Hotel

The hotel's facilities are excellent, and rooms are new and equipped. Room rates vary wildly. Art hangs throughout the winding lobbies. Luxurious spa.

 PRACTICALITIES
Hotel Phone Number: 1-787-253-1700, 1-800-241-3333.
Location: Isla Verde beach, next door to the El San Juan.

WYNDHAM OLD SAN JUAN

This hotel is the Wyndham *Old* San Juan, not the Wyndham *El* San Juan, and this place is known to most people as simply the Wyndham. This is the hotel you want to be at if you want to be in the old city.

Old San Juan is kind of charming and nice for walking around. I guess that if for some reason I wasn't staying at the El San Juan, then I might want to stay here simply because the neighborhood is so charming to walk around in. But you can also just take a cab over here for a day.

Casino

HOURS 10 A.M.–4 A.M.

LAYOUT The casino is roomy with high ceilings, it appears to be a thoroughly pleasant place to play, very new.

GAMES All the slots from a nickel up, blackjack, craps, roulette, baccarat.

LIMITS $5 to $500.

FOOD AND DRINK Darsena restaurant has a pasta buffet lunch and a Sunday brunch that are begging to be tried out. Pasta buffet, 12 P.M.–3 P.M., don't be late.

Hotel

Wyndham Old San Juan is new and charming on the waterfront of the old city. Light and spacious, with broad stone staircases and marble balconies. No free parking in San Juan hotels, $15 per day for guests. 200 rooms, 40 suites.

 PRACTICALITIES
Hotel Phone Number: 1-788-721-5100, 1-800-996-3426
Location: On Paseo Portuario in Old San Juan, on the water, amid a clutter of winding streets and shops and old buildings.

HYATT DORADO AND CERROMAR

The Cerromar is the kind of place where, although the property is modern and beautiful, you always have the feeling the staff are talking behind your back, and in a lot of cases, right in front of your face, albeit in Spanish.

There's some complicated system at the front security gate by which they try to keep people out. You're just not welcome, you're not. You have to call ahead to their inferior-quality coffee shop to ask about a "reservation" for lunch. Just to get in. Forget about saying you want to gamble.

Absolutely atrocious lunch buffet, $15. They add a 15 percent tip to the bill and then write on the check, "Gratuity not included." Wow.

Two hours of valet parking in the middle of nowhere was $14. You probably think I'm joking. If you do go here, then please throw this book out the window, because there's no reasoning with you.

Casino

The Cerromar Casino is a cheap gambling establishment where the dealer looks at his hole card between his fingers. Limits $5 to $100.

HOURS Noon–3 A.M.

LAYOUT Spacious, quiet.

THE PEOPLE THERE Families who don't want to see anybody else.

Hotel

Whatever. I wouldn't stay here in a million years. But they have a good golf course next door if you're interested.

PRACTICALITIES
Hotel Phone Number: 1-787-796-1234
Location: About thirty minutes to an hour from San Juan, on a private beach.

EMBASSY SUITES HOTEL AND CASINO

Embassy Suites is just minutes from the airport in Isla Verde, but a little walk to the beach. 300 spacious two-room suites, with separate living room and bedroom. Casino, lagoon pool, fitness center, daily complimentary cooked-to-order full breakfast and complimentary 2-hour evening manager's reception. Full business center and meeting space. This place wants the business travelers.

Outback Steakhouse, sort of mid-scale good-quality steak chain from Australia.

PRACTICALITIES
Hotel Phone Number: 1-787-791-0505, 1-800-Embassy
Location: 8000 Tarak Street, Isla Verde.

Entertainment and Nightlife

The Wyndham El San Juan casino and hotel is the nightlife. And there's plenty of it there, every night. There is also a popular five-level disco in the center of town called Area 51, where you have to wait in line forever to get in, and it's just a little bit dangerous. Careful. I would much more heavily recommend the Club Babylon on a Saturday night.

RESTAURANTS

METROPOL TAKE CARE OF YOUR HEART, EAT MORE RICE AND BEANS is the saying which greets you on the front of the menu at Metropol Restaurant. I take it to mean in comparison to the rest of the food on your plate. But if your system can't handle one meal like this, then you should have stayed in St. Louis, because this is why you're here.

Portions are large, but plates return to the kitchen empty. Lunchtime, when almost all of the fifty tables are filled and the hum of clattering forks and rapid-fire Spanish fills the room. Half of the customers don't even look at the menu, I guess they've been coming so long. Service is quick and excellent. Scores of variations on beef, chicken, and fish all accompanied by beans and white rice and astoundingly delicious plantains and garlic-drenched bread. Everything looks delicious. Just get what he's having.

Reasonable. Very few items above $10. Located two doors down from the Hampton Inn, next door to the cockfighting arena, a very short walk from any hotel in Isla Verde.

LUPIS Lupis is just across from the Hampton Inn and next door to the El San Juan, and it's owned by former Yankees fireballer Ed Figueroa, who is there watching over stuff on any given night. It's a good sports bar with truly outstanding $6 hamburgers that are charbroiled and handmade and everything a perfect hamburger should be. They also do the Mexican standards well, have live music, about a dozen TVs, indoor and outdoor and bar seating, and the restaurant is a shrine to the 1977 and 1978 New York Yankees, which needs no explanation.

THE BEACH Isla Verde has the best beach. That's all there is to it. The resort casinos outside of San Juan all have nice secluded beaches to recommend them as well, but then you'll only be there.

OUTSIDE OF TOWN If you want to be anywhere outside of San Juan, it's easy to rent a car to drive around. The rest of the island is nice.

GOLF Bahia Beach is the only eighteen-hole golf course in the San Juan area available for unrestricted play by the general public and tourists. The final three holes run along a two-mile white sand beach. Tee times 1-787-256-5600, or *www.golfbahia.com*, course 1-787-648-7400. Located sixteen miles east of San Juan, very near to the Westin Rio Mar.

Hotel resorts that have golf for guests include the El Conquistador on the east coast about an hour from San Juan. Hyatt Dorado Beach and Hyatt Cerromar in Dorado thirty minutes west of San Juan, the Westin Rio Mar forty-five minutes east of San Juan, and the Wyndham Palmas Del Mar in Humacao about fifty minutes east of San Juan. The El Conquistador looks appealing, but insulated. El Conquistador, 1-787-863-1000.

SHOPPING I didn't see that many great things to buy, but there is some very nice local art in the old city, and Puerto Rico is always a great place to get music.

CHAPTER FOUR

PANAMA CITY, PANAMA

LAY OF THE LAND

The whole world's got people who stand around outside your hotel and want to be your friend, but Panama seems to have more than most. Lots of them congregate just outside the gates to the El Panama Hotel, a motley crew of taxi drivers, pimps, prostitutes, and drug dealers, and most of them are willing to be all four.

◆

NO SE PUEDE TENER ARMAS.
(One is not allowed to have weapons inside the casino.)

◆

Panama City, Panama
GENERAL INFORMATION

YOU'RE NOT IN KANSAS ANYMORE Panama is a good place to find a bank. The United States gave control of the Panama Canal back to Panama at the end of 1999. No one knows what it means, but probably a lot less U.S. servicemen around.

WHERE Panama is located in Central America, below Costa Rica and bordering Colombia to the south. The capital, Panama City, lies at the southern mouth of the Panama Canal.

WHEN Panama puts on a nice Mardi Gras celebration in February or March. It's always humid.

TELEPHONES International phone code for Panama is 507. To dial from the U.S., 011-507 + number.

CURRENCY The dollar is legal tender, accepted everywhere, and quoted in all prices. The only Panamanian money you might see are some quarters and dimes and pennies called Balboas.

ATMS In Panama City, the casinos have ATM machines. The Western Union in Panama City is on the Vía España just north of the hotel El Panama, in the shopping mall there.

BANKS All the banks have branches in Panama City. Citibank provides a familiar and very crowded full service branch immediately in front of the Continental and across the street from the El Panama. If, of course, you don't mind the casual way that the guard waves around his sawed-off hair-trigger shotgun. I'd be interested in knowing the number of accidental maimings by careless seventeen-year-old bank employees. I'm thinking they're not graduates of the Navy SEAL weapons training program.

Panama is a good place to go if you have to find a bank. And my sources tell me, if you've got ten grand or more, you can set up what's called your own "foundation," the details of which are easy, the fee is cheap, and the benefits can be summed up in three words: "completely tax free." And legal, of course. Panama is the new Switzerland when it comes to escaping paying capital gains taxes on income and assets, and just generally making sure the rich get richer. Call the offshore association of Central America, 507-223-3172, e-mail *offshore!@pty.com*, or just go to a bank and mention a foundation.

¿HABLA ESPANOL? Because so many American servicemen were here for so long, English is understood virtually everywhere in Panama City. Most people, however, would still prefer to speak Spanish.

CLIMATE Panama City is very humid—an air conditioner is necessary for your hotel room.

WHAT THEY WEAR You must have a *guayaberas* (typical Panamanian shirt). Trust me. You must have one. And you do get what you pay for, in terms of quality. A top-of-the-line *guayaberas* will last, and it's so comfortable. They breathe, they're lightweight, comfortable, and sharp. Range in price from $8 to $50.

There's not very many people wearing shorts in downtown Panama City. Not very many at all.

INTERNET AOL has local access number. Most hotel phones support modem hookup.

TIPPING IN TOWN Cab drivers expect a tip. Some restaurants have the service included in the bill and some don't.

SAFETY One of my guidebooks mentioned in passing that you might not want to let it be known that you're American because "there exists some anti-American sentiment in Panama." More like they want to shoot you. Or at least take your wallet. Be careful in Panama, friend, you're not in Costa Rica anymore.

Cuidado

The casino manager warned me off going to any local discotheques. *"Necesita mucho cuidado,"* he said. I guess it was pretty easy to tell that I'm not in the Army and I can't hold my own in a fight. Hell, I'm scared of pillow fights, and Panama City is still a bit of the old rough-and-tumble G.I. sailor port raggleweed, and I spent a lot of the time with my hand over my wallet and my heart beating a little too fast. And that was just walking across the street at night.

Demanding the return of your passport from a man carrying a loaded shotgun is in my mind an unattractive and a losing proposition. My advice is to play dumb as long as you can. The situation was this. I'm walking down the street minding my own business, when a bank guard walks all the way from the steps of where he's standing at the bank door with a loaded sawed-off shotgun. He walks all the way to the sidewalk to ask me for my passport. I wasn't even going in the bank. Now I have no proof that he was going to try and scam me, but by all rights a bank guard standing on some front steps should have as much interest in my passport as a raw egg. Anyway, I just played dumb. I told him I didn't have my passport on me, it was at my hotel, and my hotel was around the corner. I stuck to that in the face of the waving gun, because I figure you give up your passport when hell is cold. Once that guy has your passport, there's no telling what it will cost you to get it back. That's another reason you should always carry your passport in a concealed pocket, like an inside shoulder holster. Eventually, he waved me off with a disgusted look. I think he was just trying to make a quick $50.

I'll Walk There Barefoot
TRANSPORTATION ISSUES

LEGAL Americans need a valid passport. Upon arrival at the airport, you will probably have to purchase a visa for $20. You'll also have to pay about a $20 departure tax on the way out. It's a "juice-me" country.

FLIGHTS Taxi from the airport is a fixed rate to any downtown hotel of $25, $14 each for two, $10 each for three or more. Airport taxis are quite nice, mostly brand-new four-wheel-drive land cruisers.

TRANSPORTATION AROUND TOWN Every hotel has their own taxis, the prices of which are typically $5 higher than a taxi that you hail yourself. Hotel taxis are usually of the big old Oldsmobile boat type cars. Metered taxis, while newer, are much smaller Japanese cars.

Taxi drivers are a good source for music information. One of my drivers turned me on to Tony Vega. If you want to get some music and you don't know who to get, hail a local taxi and ask who they're listening to, cab drivers always know about the best music.

WHERE THINGS ARE All the gringos used to have to live within the city limits. The downtown in Panama City is not really a place for walking around. Most people don't. It's more a place for taking a taxi from your hotel to your bank and taking care of business. Everything branches off the long and wide Vía España, which is really too long to be a downtown at all. It goes from one end of the city to the other, and things are sprawled out along it. Some new buildings, but most of the stuff is cheap neon from the sixties and seventies. Nothing is close enough for easy walking except for the small area containing the El Panama Hotel, the Riande Continental, the Marriott, and a lot of banks and exclusive shopping boutiques.

As you go toward the canal, the Vía España turns into Avenida Central. At one point, this is a pedestrian walking street, an excellent place to get a good-quality *guayaberas* at a low price. Ice cream, local food, street vendors, shoe shines for $1, great place to catch some local flavor during the day.

The Money Plays
GAMBLING SETUP—THE QUICK FACTS

CASINOS Besides the slot houses, which say casino on the outside but inside have nothing but slot machines, there are basically two companies running the casinos here in Panama. The Canadian Thunderbird Corporation has got a hold of casinos at the Hotel El Panama, the Grand Soloy, and hotels in David and Colon. A Chilean consortium called Crown Casinos runs casinos in the Riande Continental, Caesar Park, and the Hotel Granada. In my mind, the Chileans run the better casinos, rules and all.

HOURS Vary. The Hotel El Panama casino is open twenty-four hours. Other casinos close at 4 A.M.

ADMITTANCE No entry fee.

AMBIANCE AND AMENITIES Free drinks only for players at management's discretion.

GAMES ON OFFER Blackjack, Canal 21, roulette, craps, horse racing, slots, baccarat, seven-card stud poker, Caribbean poker.

LIMITS $3 to $500.

MONEY Everything is played in dollars.

LEGALITY Casinos are legal and licensed by the government. Winnings are not taxed.

TIPPING POLICIES IN THE CASINO Tips appreciated, but not seen with regularity.

I'll Take the Odds
BREAKING APART THE GAME

BLACKJACK Blackjack rules differ slightly depending on if you play in the Crown casinos (Riande Continental and Granada and Caesar Park) or the Thunderbird casinos (El Panama and the Soloy). At the Thunderbird casinos, you can double down after splitting a pair, but at the Crown casinos you can't. Crown casinos offer late surrender (after the dealer's checked for blackjack), Thunderbird doesn't. At the Crown casinos, the dealer takes a hole card, but at the Thunderbird casinos, the dealer doesn't take a second card until after everyone has acted. Crown casinos definitely have the more American style of blackjack. All the blackjack games in Panama are dealt from six shoes. One card on split aces. Dealer hits on soft seventeen.

ROULETTE Twenty-five cent minimum roulette is an inexpensive way to be a madman. Spread yourself all over the board for $6. For $20 on a roll, go absolutely haywire.

The roulette setups are fairly nice, with tracking screens. American-style roulette, however, so the wheel does have the "00" in addition to the single "0."

CRAPS Only the Crown casinos run craps games, and only in the evening. Try Caesar Park at 8 P.M. or the Riande Continental at 11 P.M.

HORSE RACING If you want to go to the real horse races, the *hippodromo* (Spanish for racetrack), the Presidente Ramón racetrack is about a fifteen-minute cab ride out from the center of town. Racing days are Thursday, Saturday, and Sunday, but Sunday seems to be the best day to go, when they have the featured race for the week. Call 507-217-6060 for post times.

Hippodromo—Thursday 6 P.M., Saturday and Sunday 2 P.M., featured race of the week is on Sundays.

SLOTS At the Crown casinos, they have relatively new slot machines, not really a bad bet as far as slots go. No posted information as to their rate of return, however.

CANAL 21 If I tried to write down all the rules to Canal 21, this book would be at least twice as thick. I will go into the rules a little bit down below, but suffice it to say that it's a little like Costa Rican Rommy only better, it's played at the Granada, the Riande Continental and the Caesar Park, and it's the only game to play in Panama. You'll pull your hair out trying to play blackjack in this town; believe me, I almost did. And lost five C's to boot.

Canal 21 is a blackjack variation, in a sense. At the Crown casinos, however, they spread a blackjack table and a Canal 21 table. I think Canal 21 is much more fun, but that's me. I like new things.

Still in the promotional stages, when I was there they still didn't have all the rules written down yet and there was some disagreement between floormen and dealers at the Granada and the Riande Continental about what the right rules are. This game will succeed however, in my mind, as the locals are well into the game as vastly more exciting than Panama's regular version of blackjack. All rules in Canal 21 are the same as in blackjack, except:

1. A two-card twenty-one pays even money, if you have a two-card twenty-one (a natural) and the dealer gets a regular twenty-one (more than two cards), you get paid. If you both get a natural or if the dealer gets a natural and you have a regular twenty-one, you are eligible for a one-card playoff. Double your bet and each take one card, high card wins. If you tie, then you get paid double, so it seems like you have the best of that, but a queen beats a jack beats a ten, so it's not far from an even gamble.

2. Three of a kind, trio, pays 3–1, but only if you don't bust, and you don't need them in a row. Your hand is still eligible to win or lose besides, so once you get a trio, keep hitting up until twelve but don't risk busting. Same deal with *escalera*, which is three straight flush cards in any suit. Once I had eight cards and about fifteen possible cards to make a rummy hand.

3. Three sevens pays 5–1, three sevens of the same suit pays 20–1.

4. They only use four decks and they cut about half a deck, twenty-six cards, which is awesome compared to the El Panama where they're cutting about three decks of a six-deck shoe in the regular blackjack game. Limits $3 to $100, $5 to $150, or $50 to $500.

5. You can early surrender any hand, including when the dealer has an ace.

6. Like the Casino Colonial in Costa Rica, they offer 2–1 insurance on an ace and 10–1 insurance on a ten, but you're allowed to insure the 10–1 up to half your bet so it can be profitable to keep an ace count. In Costa Rica, they only let you insure up to one tenth your bet. Insurance at the beginning, so you can insure a busted hand.

7. Dealer must hit soft seventeen.

8. You can double down after splitting pairs, but you lose your whole bet and your double if the dealer has a natural, so restrain yourself when he shows an ace or a ten.

Strategy tips: Usually ignore the extra rules and play your strategy the way you play it, except sometimes it's better not to split pairs like sevens into a two, or twos and threes. If the deck is very negative, I think you might be better off not splitting aces into a ten or ace.

HORSE RACING GAME AT THE RIANDE CONTINENTAL There is a nice sit down horse racing game setup at the casino in the Riande Continental. It's a very nice way to while away the time slowly, watch the metal horses actually go around the track and bet from twenty-five cents up to whatever on the winner or the quinella (first and second in either order). Up to about fifteen people can play at once and it's kind of socially fun, and there is thinking involved. On the screen, they tell you about the six horses, from their names to how they've done in their last races, and of course their odds.

Pay special attention to the arrows on the left that tell if they are a horse with early speed or come from behind or middle of the pack. You get a lot of action for $20, and you can get a bunch of action for only $2 as well. There's a new race like every ninety seconds, so you're not sitting around. I hit a bunch of races in a row and managed to win $20 in only fifteen minutes with a $5 investment, so while you're likely to lose slowly, it is possible to get a payout also, and you can bet up to whatever you want.

This horse racing game is a good way to learn a little about the basics of horse racing. The more front running speed there is, the more chance that a come from behind horse will win, because of the faster pace. Think about the rail positions. The early speed wants to get inside unchallenged for the turn and open up a big lead. I could play it all day.

Casinos and Lodging
THE POINT

EL PANAMA HOTEL AND CASINO

You know the locals are gambling because directly opposite the El Panama Hotel Casino is the requisite twenty-four-hour pawn shop. It's called Empanda Nik Grik. Nice. Love the bars, the bulletproof glass, and the cluster of prostitutes hanging around just outside. Not to mention aggressive cab drivers who want to know if you'd like a massage. All in all, it feels a little on the seedy side, somewhere between Amsterdam's red light district and the village of Saigon. Or downtown Atlantic City at 3 A.M. on a Tuesday night.

Casino

HOURS Open twenty-four hours daily. In the wee hours, it becomes packed with Chinese voodoo masters who jabber away and pound the table in disgust when your play doesn't suit their liking.

LANGUAGE Spanish. A little English spoken.

LAYOUT Sign on the door says NO SE PUEDE TENER ARMAS, or *One is not allowed to have weapons inside the casino.* Reassuring. The El Panama Casino feels small and full, but everything's there and they're talking about expanding, so by the time you get there space might not be an issue. The slot machines are the noisy type and you're never more than twelve feet away from the ringing bells. On the whole, it's quite noisy. A tacky Mardi Gras decor is not very pleasant.

GAMES Roulette, blackjack, minibaccarat, slots.

LIMITS $5 to $200, $15 to $500, roulette $0.50 to $25 inside $5 to $500 outside.

RULES AND NOTES On the positive side, the El Panama does have some of the newer multi-game slot machines, where you can choose between two different kinds of poker or video keno. Slots are either twenty-five cents or a nickel. No sightings of gimmick game slots which are now all the rage.

In the blackjack, the dealer doesn't take a hole card until everyone has acted. At the big table, they cut almost half the shoe, three decks out of six, so good luck counting that. Lose only your original bet on a double down hand if the dealer gets blackjack.

AND . . . Watch your money. In one hour, I saw a blackjack not get paid and a roulette dealer try to short me on the count.

There is an ATM machine in the casino that takes all major cards. They give free rooms to one Dominican lady who gambles high, but their comp system is not really developed yet. The casino is not affiliated with the hotel.

FOOD AND DRINK The **Hotel El Panama** coffee shop claims to be twenty-four hours, but I think that's only on weekends, as I saw definite evidence of a closed restaurant about 4 A.M. on a Thursday. Comfortable if a tad mildewy like the rest of the hotel, but the wait staff is very professional and alert even at 4 A.M. when they're bringing you your fried mess and a cup of grease. The **Las Palmas BBQ** is a better bet, poolside every day from 7–11:30 P.M. The grilled meats look pretty fresh.

THE PEOPLE THERE Gringos and Chinese. Lots of American servicemen.

Hotel

For the most well known hotel in the city, the El Panama is a bit rundown and appears to be living off its name. For the standard rate of $140, you could do better. Rooms are large but aging, architecture and lobby are okay. The place has got quite a reputation, when I got into town I couldn't even get a room there, and every other place in town was stone cold empty. Reputation, no other reason.

The hotel is very open and spread out, bright open public spaces with comfortable chairs and fountains.

Room Rates: $140 plus 10 percent. $175 for a room on the executive floor. The executive floor boasts a personal butler, upgraded continental breakfast, soft drinks, and international newspapers, all complimentary.

345 rooms. Honeymoon suite, suites, junior suites, poolside, standard, executive, and handicapped rooms. Lots of different types of rooms which are large, if not a little rundown. Small shopping arcade with a travel agency and a sundries store and two clothing stores with high prices. Full service spa with three indoor lighted tennis courts. Pool and discotheque.

 PRACTICALITIES
Hotel Phone Number: 507-269-5000, reservations 507-223-1660, from the U.S., 1-888-226-3880
Internet Address: *www.elpanama.com*
Email: *reservas@elpanama.com*
Location: Vía España 3. Defines the downtown area, located on the main drag, Vía España, in the cluster of exclusive hotels and the tourist shopping and banks area.

RIANDE CONTINENTAL

I like the hotel Riande Continental. I like that they didn't even blink when I showed up dirty and smelly at 7 A.M. with a poor excuse for why I wanted to check in six hours early, even though my clock had been wrong and I did think it was 3 P.M., but they checked me in with a smile. I like that you have to put your room key in the glass elevator in order to make it rise, that's security. I like that the rooms are comfortable with wood furniture, spacious, and whitewashed clean. I like the fact that the casino downstairs actually has some charm, some space, and friendly dealers. And I like the fact that if you're a guest of the hotel, you're treated right. No preferences, no employees fishing for tips, just good professional service. And I like that.

Casino

HOURS Noon–4 A.M. daily.

LANGUAGE Spanish or English spoken.

LAYOUT Head and shoulders above the casino across the street, space is a big bright spot here. The casino is big, with plenty of space between tables. Most of the slots are sit down. A band plays in the evenings. The casino is new and spotlessly clean.

GAMES Roulette, blackjack, minibaccarat, slots, Canal 21, craps, Caribbean stud.

LIMITS $3 to $500.

RULES AND NOTES In blackjack, the dealer plays with a hole card and the table is outfitted with the same gigs you may have seen at the Mirage in Las Vegas, namely if the dealer has a ten or ace, then he checks for blackjack before the hand continues by means of a small automatic mirror that lights up if he's got an ace or face card. Surrender is allowed, except when the dealer has an ace, which unfortunately is more than 50 percent of the times you want to surrender anyway. This is called late surrender. Early surrender is when you have the option to surrender before the dealer checks for blackjack. Resplitting of aces is allowed. The casino opens at noon, an excellent time for a heads up game, as it fills up by late afternoon.

$2 craps in the evenings.

FOOD AND DRINK The $14.95 nightly poolside buffet is completely pleasant with a nice variety of BBQ meats, salads, and desserts. And the Caribbean band can carry quite a beat for a house band, they rock the night away with the pleasant sounds of the tropics.

Requisite seafood restaurant off the lobby.

THE PEOPLE THERE Pretty dealers and waitresses at the casino. Lots of American servicemen and women are guests of the hotel. Staff is exceptionally friendly.

Hotel

The Riande Continental claims to have one of only two working Wur-
litzer organs in the world. That fact doesn't faze me, but I have to admit I was impressed by its size. That organ is mammoth. It's spread out
over two rooms, and it resonates pretty good when they play it at
5 P.M.

Rooms boast a safe, minibar, hair dryer, prompt twenty-four-hour room
service, 2 P.M. checkout, and the maid comes by at night to turn down
the sheets and see if you want towels. Ask for a room high up. It's got
a nice view of the city. The Riande Continental also has a nice sce-
nic glass elevator and a business center. In the evening, the lazy strains
of Caribbean music might drift up to your room from the pool down
below.

Laundry service is pricey but competent. Same day service. It cost
me $40 to get everything in my bag cleaned and pressed in eight hours.
It was worth it. I kind of had a lot of dirty stuff when I checked in. $7.50
to get a two-piece suit dry-cleaned quick, $3.50 for a *guayaberas* shirt, $1
for underwear. Only $8 to dry clean your tuxedo.

When I called for a reservation, they asked me if I was a U.S. citizen
with the government, which would make me eligible for their special
rate of $68. I said yes. Nobody ever checked, and the $68 rate there was
the best value I found by far in Panama. I think that rate is available to all
U.S. citizens. Maybe. Rack rates are about $100 per night plus 10 percent
tax, still much better value than the El Panama.

240 rooms. Exercise room is not very large, it's just off the pool, but it
does have a few new machines and a television on the wall.

 PRACTICALITIES
**Hotel Phone Number: 507-263-9999, reservations 507-
265-5115, fax: 507-269-4559**
E-mail: *continental@ihpanama.com*
**Location: 8475, Panama 7. Just off the Vía España. Practi-
cally across the street from the El Panama Hotel.**

HOTEL GRANADA

You could actually have a good time at the Hotel Granada. I mean
if you're in the right kind of mood and feel like playing a little Canal 21,
you could actually have a good time there, because the dealers are
mostly nice guys who are the type who will kind of root along for you,
and the floorman is very helpful if you're not fresh on the rules. And if a
few girls from Taiwan sit down who have never played the game before

and are laughing like hell at the Rommy draws, you might have a good time there. I did.

Casino

HOURS 2 P.M.–4 A.M. daily.

LANGUAGE Spanish. A little English spoken.

LAYOUT Not very big, but there's not often a lot of people in there either.

GAMES Roulette, blackjack, minibaccarat, slots, Canal 21, seven-card stud poker.

LIMITS $5 to $200.

RULES AND NOTES They do have the only live poker game in town, but I wouldn't suggest playing in it. It's a limit seven-card stud game with a 3 percent rake, no cap. A limit game with a no cap rake is kind of hard to beat. It's possible, but your ideal lineup would have to be two drunk millionaires, one blind man, and a hell of a lot of luck. And from what I saw, the players weren't that bad and they weren't that rich. The only one with any money on the table was the guy taking the house collection. It's basically the same guys that play every night, the game starts up around 8 or 9 P.M. and doesn't last for more than two or three hours. It can't last longer because the only way to beat the game is to hit-and-run, so what I'll bet my last potatoes happens every night is that one guy wins a few pots quick, quits, and leaves everybody else sitting there with no money and no chance to get it back. They don't have a two-hour rule like in Costa Rica, so hey, if you're really bent on playing poker in Panama, go play the video slot machines. Personally, I don't know why you don't try Canal 21. It's fun, it's not that hard, the dealers will help you, and you're not gonna play it anywhere else. When in Panama.

It's one of those poker games where if you're a tourist and they think you've got a lot of money to lose, they'll go out in the street to try and find guys to play with you. When I got there, they were trying to shake down a local drunk to make five players to start the game. That's when my Spidey sense started tingling. Don't play anything that has to be started up special for you. Stick to what everybody else is playing. There's a reason that they can't keep a poker game going in the town, and it's not because no one will play. The house should know that in the long run they'll get all the money anyway, why they have to take it all in one night is beyond me, but don't be foolish and don't go there looking for a poker game. At least not at the time of this writing.

FOOD AND DRINK The coffee shop is appealing.

THE PEOPLE THERE Mostly locals and Asian tourists. The dealers at the Granada are all men; in fact, all the employees are men with the exception of the cocktail waitresses.

Hotel

The hotel is also run by Riande Group, but it is neither as large nor as elegant as the Riande Continental. Rooms start at $90.

 PRACTICALITIES
Hotel Phone Number: 507-264-4900, 507-263-7477, fax: 507-264-0930
Location: Off the Vía España, but about one quarter mile south of the El Panama and the Riande Continental.

CAESAR PARK

Anyone with more than a passing interest in food should stay at the Caesar Park, because they don't miss a trick. They've got it all down, from the soothing Muzak humming in the spotless public bathrooms to the flowering green plants.

Caesar Park is nice. Wood all around. There's a pleasant shopping mall filled with the aroma of fresh bread from the little bakery where a luscious slice of layer cake or an empanada filled with *jamón y queso* or a chicken breast sandwich on fresh-sliced bread won't set you back more than $5.

Downstairs from the lobby is the outdoor pool, sauna, gym, Jacuzzi, and tropical garden along with the coffee shop, Café Bahía. Not to mention Salty's seafood restaurant and the Italian place and a nice-looking barber shop. And you wouldn't want to miss three o'clock tea time at the Le Trianon Grill, on the fifteenth floor with windows all around and a breathtaking view of the bay.

Casino

HOURS 2 P.M.–4 A.M. daily.

LANGUAGE Spanish. English largely spoken.

LAYOUT The casino is in the same mode as the Riande Continental, spacious with a bar area. All the slots have chairs, mostly seated table slots where you look down onto the slot.

GAMES Roulette, blackjack, minibaccarat, slots, Canal 21, craps, Caribbean stud.

LIMITS During the day limits are $3 to $100 and up; the minimum rises at night.

RULES AND NOTES Blackjack penetration far deeper than El Panama, nearly double. $2 craps in the evenings. Modern reel slots in five cents, ten cents, quarter, and dollar. They always seem to have twenty-five-cent roulette, where you're able to play just one chip at a time on the inside.

FOOD AND DRINK I'd like to shake the hand of the food and restaurant manager. Quality, variety, and creativity.

Salty's seafood restaurant has a giant aquarium for front windows, but don't expect to be eating those fish, they're tropical. Menu shows thought, enthusiasm, and inventiveness, everything sounds good. Tom Yum Kung, spicy Thai prawn soup. Appetizers $6 and entrees $12 to $16. Tues.–Sun., Noon–2:30 P.M. and 6:30–11 P.M.

Crostini Italian restaurant, relaxed and bright wood. Pizzas, personal or large, eighteen different types ranging from $5 to $10, plus the usual array of spaghetti and ravioli dishes.

Café Bahía coffee shop, open twenty-four hours on weekends, weekdays until 1 A.M. Truly original and attractive menu with about fifteen tasty hot sandwich varieties and a nightly buffet with an emphasis on presentation and quality. A huge perk is real Heinz ketchup, even if it does come in little packets. Poolside food service. Entrees about $6.50.

Le Trianon Grill is the class of the joint. An intimate and romantic steak and French-themed restaurant located on the top floor of the hotel, up on the fifteenth, with a nice view of the bay. Dinner Mon.–Sat. 6:30–11 P.M., Proper English Tea served Mon.–Fri. 3–5:30 P.M.

THE PEOPLE THERE Mostly tourists and business folks, of varying nationalities. Americans are plentiful.

Hotel

Owned and run by Westin Hotels and Resorts, the hotel is modern and well appointed. Use of gym is $7 per day extra, but the gym has got the works. Executive floor rooms have coffee maker and coffee, bathrobe, computer hookups, and 6 P.M. checkout. Rack rates are $195 standard or $155 corporate, plus tax. You can't beat anything but the location.

PRACTICALITIES
Hotel Phone Number: 507-270-0477, 507-226-4077, fax: 507-226-4262
Internet Address: *www.caesarpark.com*
E-mail Address: *panbusctr1@caesarpark.com*
Location: It's located in the kind of place where you have to take a taxi or car everywhere you want to go. Nice setting, on the water facing the bay, but it's about ten minutes by cab to the El Panama Hotel and center of town.

PANAMA MARRIOTT HOTEL

The brand new Panama Marriott is a stunner. You walk into all marble. Huge vaulted ceilings over a beautiful lobby. The lobby bar has pleasant art and a giant half circle double staircase leading up to the banquet and convention area. It's impressive.

Casino

No casino, but a casino is planned to open by the end of 2000. The Riande Continental Casino is practically next door.

FOOD AND DRINK The Marriott has a sports bar with lots of big TVs and an emphasis on American sports. Good-looking casual menu. Lots of dining options nearby, this is one of the few neighborhoods you can walk around in.

THE PEOPLE THERE Business travelers.

Hotel

The hotel is brand spanking new with very high standards. 296 rooms, 8 suites, complete with computer hookups, hair dryer and iron and ironing board, in-room safe and minibar, outdoor pool and Jacuzzi, health club has sauna and exercise room. Rates start at about $150 per night plus 10 percent tax.

PRACTICALITIES
**Hotel Phone Number: 507-210-9100, fax: 507-210-9110,
from the U.S., 1-800-228-9290**
**Location: Calle 52 and Ricardo Arias. In a perfect loca-
tion off the Vía España just behind the Riande Continental and very close to the El Panama Hotel and a branch of
every bank in the world. Nice neighborhood, for Panama
City.**

Entertainment and Nightlife

The El Panama Hotel has a happening little samba and rumba place called the Coco Club. Dance floor is rocking at 3 A.M. The Josephine's group runs three night/strip clubs in the center of town. Upscale gentleman's clubs, they are all around the corner from each other, in easy walking distance of the Riande Continental or El Panama or Marriott.

Josephine's, phone 507-223-0035. Wednesday and Saturday open bar with $20 cover, no cover $12 per drink other nights. 9 P.M.–4 A.M. Mon.–Sat. Josephine's Gold, phone 507-263-6890. Elite, phone 507-264-9527.

Happyland is across the parking lot from the El Panama. It's a bit sleazier than the Josephine's outlets but normal drink prices, pretty enough girls, and the option of a $45 massage in the back make it a reasonable spot.

THE CANAL AND SIGHTSEEING Don't be misled. Besides the Panama Canal, there are no tourist sites in Panama City. The old city is the older part of the city. The ruins are a pile of stones. The tourist attractions are the banks and the shopping. Casco Viejo is the old part of Panama City that has the presidential palace and the theater and a few fancy restaurants. There really isn't that much to see.

Go to the canal instead. After all, if nothing else, it is the Panama Canal. Though I have to admit the best and most interesting view I got of the Panama Canal was from the air, as I was flying away.

OUTSIDE OF TOWN Coronado resort is a cheap twelve-minute flight from Panama City. It is a luxurious resort with huge rooms and everything else, including a casino, tennis courts, and an eighteen-hole golf course by George and Tom Fazio. 240-4444 for info or fax 240-4899.

FOOD AND BEVERAGES The Panamanian beer is named Atlas. It's somewhere in the Schlitz or Old Milwaukee camp. It's not good. Costa Rican beer, Bavaria, is far better than its Panamanian counterpart.

An inexpensive wine in Panama and in Costa Rica is Concha y Toro, from Chile, which I found to be surprisingly good.

Directly across from the Riande Continental, just cross the street when you walk out the front door, is a twenty-four-hour cafeteria with cheap prices and reasonable food, like if you're drunk and need something filling and cheap. Jimmy's restaurant, it's called, opens in the evenings and stays open all night. Fine quality and dirt cheap. Fresh charbroiled steak about $5 with baked potato and salad. In the evenings, you can get a hefty steak charbroiled in front of your eyes on the hopping charcoal embers. Later on, like after midnight, get whatever you want from the cafeteria-style counter inside. The roast chicken is nightly a fair piece of meat for $1.50. As far as I can tell, they're open all night, closing only in those dreaded daylight hours when normal people are out and about. Located across the front door from the Riande Continental but not across the Vía España. You can see a bunch of outdoor wooden tables and glass through to the cafeteria counter and more tables inside.

Niko's is a twenty-four-hour Greek joint just off the Via de España right next door to the supermarket. You can't miss it. Gyros, hot and cold sandwiches to order, and a long cafeteria counter that is popular with locals.

OTHER STUFF

LONGER STAYS For longer stays, try the Las Vegas hotel suites, which although contrary to its name does not have a casino, but provides studio and suites with living/dining/kitchenettes, and will give discounts for long stays. Phone 507-269-0722, fax 507-223-0047, *www.hotelvegas.com*.

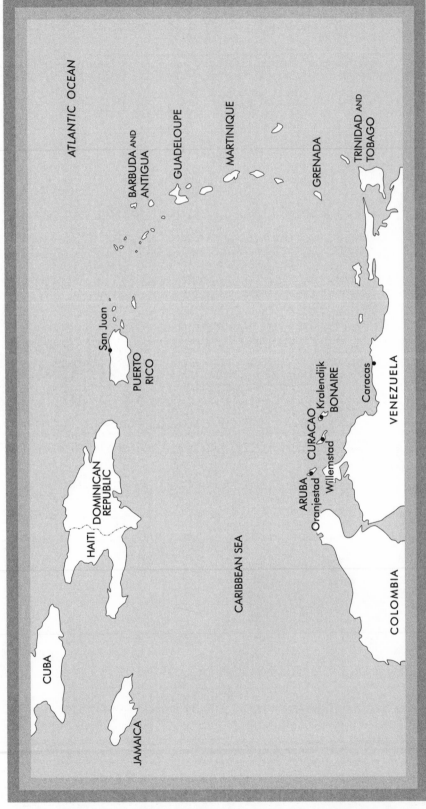

ABC ISLANDS, NETHERLANDS ANTILLES

CHAPTER FIVE

ARUBA

LAY OF THE LAND

Aruba's one of those islands that's really geared toward the tourist. You can't help but stumble across a million of those guides like *Experience Aruba, Aruba Nights, What's Hot Aruba*, and *Aruba Gourmet Guide*. All the food and shopping options will be there for you. It's easy.

♦

The man from Texas had to make a rainbow. He was the table captain, sitting in the third base seat and giving bad advice to everyone—whether they liked it or not—about what they should do with their hands. He was betting $25 most of the time, but sometimes he'd up his bet to $55, two green and a red, and sometimes he'd play two hands at once. It was at one time during a particular digression while commanding the entire table's attention with talk of his skill and knowledge of blackjack, when he realized that he had two $62 bets out on the circles, consisting of two red, two green, and two white chips each, and if he put two black chips there under each bet then he would have "a rainbow." So he pulled out a roll of hundreds and peeled off four. Now he gets a pair of eights for his first hand, a dreaded sixteen, so he peels off $300 more from his roll and splits them, getting a seventeen and a fifteen into the dealer's three. On his second hand he has a ten, so he peels off $300 more and doubles down and gets an eight for eighteen. The dealer makes twenty and takes $1,200 in bets and his thick roll of hundreds can't even hold a rubber band anymore. Blackjack can be dangerous in Aruba.

You got the beach, and you got the gambling. Don't pretend there's anything else.

Aruba
GENERAL INFORMATION

YOU'RE NOT IN KANSAS ANYMORE Aruba is a small island well developed for tourism. A gem of sun and fun for the traveler who doesn't want to be anywhere too foreign, but still wants something completely different. It's always beautiful in Aruba. Water comes from a desalination plant.

WHERE Aruba is the westernmost of the three Netherlands Antilles Islands, which all lie about fifty miles off of the north coast of Venezuela. Aruba is the most developed of the three islands for tourism, and it was also the first island to have an oil-processing plant in the area. That was the boom time. Time is one hour ahead of New York except during Daylight Savings when the time is the same (spring to fall).

WHEN The spread in room rate prices between Aruba's high and low season is like 300 percent at most hotels. The VERY high season is between December 19 and January 3. The high season is from January 4 to March 1, and the sort of high season is from March 2 to April 30. The low season is from May 1 to December 18. Nice hotel bargains then. It's not like the weather in Aruba is any different. It's just that no one comes from America during that time.

TELEPHONES From the U.S., 011-297-8 + number.

CURRENCY Owing to someone's bright idea, the Aruban florin is different than both the Dutch florin (guilder) and the Netherlands Antilles florin. Go the hell figure. Exchange at Afl 1.77 = $1. U.S. dollars are readily accepted everywhere. My advice is: Don't even think about the florins. ATMs are mostly at the banks. Casinos are for credit card or cash.

SAFETY Aruba is not a high-crime island, nor a dangerous one. Any person taking reasonable care will feel comfortable at all times.

WHAT THEY WEAR Dress is very casual, all over the island. The Stellaris Casino at the Marriott Hotel is probably the most elegant gaming place, fashion-wise.

I'll Walk There Barefoot
TRANSPORTATION ISSUES

LEGAL U.S. citizens need either a passport or a birth certificate or a naturalization permit to enter.

FLIGHTS Aruba is a long way, but it's not expensive to get there. Check Sunday travel or the Internet for good rates. Package deals are okay for Aruba, because you're not gonna get a great deal if you don't get it before you get down there.

AIRPORT Queen Beatrix International Airport is in Oranjestad, the capital. Actually, the whole island is in Oranjestad, as far as I can tell. It's not that big an island. The airport is about ten minutes from the center of town and fifteen minutes from Palm Beach, driving slow on the one main road.

WHERE THINGS ARE The Palm Beach area is the only place where you'll have both a good beach and nice casinos, so I would highly recommend staying there or close to it. The downtown is for shopping and food.

TRANSPORTATION AROUND TOWN Pumps are in liters, gas is a little more expensive than in the U.S., attendants pump. It's not a bad idea to rent a car in Aruba. That way you can visit a lot of the different casinos and restaurants. Taxis are a pricey option all over.

The Money Plays
GAMBLING SETUP—THE QUICK FACTS

CASINOS The casinos are all privately owned and licensed by the government.

HOURS Because of some unknown deal with the government, Crystal Casino is open around the clock. All the other casinos close at 4 A.M. The Holiday Inn poker game goes until it ends, no matter how late it is.

ADMITTANCE Gambling age is eighteen. ID sometimes required. Dress is very casual, except later at night when dress is semicasual.

AMBIANCE AND AMENITIES Drinks are free for players.

GAMES ON OFFER Caribbean stud poker, blackjack, roulette, craps, baccarat, slot machines, live poker, sports and race books, bingo.

LIMITS $5 to $2000, more on request.

MONEY Games are mostly played in dollars. Aruban florin is played at some casinos with an exchange value of $1 = 1.77 Afl.

LEGALITY Aruba is very safe and very legal.

TIPPING POLICIES IN THE CASINO Dealers share all tips.

AND . . . There are a lot of Americans vacationing in Aruba.

I'll Take the Odds
BREAKING APART THE GAME

CRAPS They know how to play craps in Aruba. They definitely know how to play over at the Marriott, where a bunch of wise guys down from America will give the table electric energy and make sure the stickman is on his toes. Double odds is standard all around town.

BINGO Bingo is mostly played at the Royal Cabana Casino. They have a big showroom for the bingo games, they're huge, and I'm sure that means it's fun, fast, and you get paid big if you win, and you can win big. That's the only place I'd go. That's the niche they've carved for themselves, the bingo home of the island. Try getting a parking space at that place on bingo night. I couldn't even park next door at the Outback Steakhouse.

CARIBBEAN STUD POKER Caribbean stud was "born and raised" in Aruba. That's where they invented it, supposedly, although I've heard it was actually a poker player named David Sklansky. It doesn't mean you're gonna win or lose more there, although the jackpots in Aruba are generally bigger, and they bear paying attention to. But if you like the game, maybe you'll feel an affinity for the history of it by playing it in the Holiday Inn casino, where they have the wall of champions, people with big smiles, royal flushes, and new cars and lots of money.

A friendly everybody-can-win brochure describes the game as "not only easy, it pays off with a frequency not often seen in other games . . ." I don't know what this means. Maybe it pays off, but most of the time you're putting up three bets and getting back one. I don't know. Call me crazy. I know it's a pleasant way to spend your time. Just make sure that if you hit, you're gonna get a big jackpot, that's all I've got to say. It would suck to get struck by lightning and not have been betting on the event.

ROULETTE Most of the places around town have a $25 maximum on any number. I find this a tad restrictive. They don't want anyone to get too high a payout at any one time. Brother, if I'm ever standing somewhere betting on the number sixteen and it comes up five times in a row, I certainly want to have the option to get a little more than $25 on it for that sixth roll.

BLACKJACK The only variation in the blackjack rules on the island is that in some places the dealer hits on soft seventeen (ace and six), and in other places the dealer sticks on the hand. You would much rather have the dealer stick with the hand. Double on any two cards. Six-deck shoes. Limits $5 or $10 minimum, up to a few thousand. The house edge on this game is −0.4 percent.

BACCARAT The big baccarat players go either to the Wyndham or to the Crystal Casino. That's where they go.

Poker in Aruba

The man from Texas leans over to me and asks, have you ever been in a game as good as this? Actually, I had been thinking about leaving. It's three-thirty in the morning and we're sitting in the poker area of the Holiday Inn's Excelsior Casino on the beach in Aruba, an island off the coast of Venezuela, and as I am theoretically playing in the 10–20 Hold'em game in closest proximity to the equator and the only one within an even legitimate striking distance, that fact alone makes this game a little interesting.

It's not the action I'm complaining about. Of the six of us playing, five are in every hand. It's not that I'm worried about the stakes or the play. The game is well run, drinks are free, and 10–20 Hold'em seems like a reasonable limit given the hour and the clientele.

No, what is worrying me is the rake, and I'm talking about the $15 that are being dropped out of every pot into the giant hole in the dealer's corner, and it brings forth a question that has plagued poker players time and again. At what point can a game not be beat in the long run?

We've all heard of the extremes. My favorite story is about the old Stardust chop game, where the dealers were instructed to just "take as much as you can," and legend says it was not uncommon to win a pot that had less money than you put in it!

The house rake will exist as long as there are poker games, and one of the reasons Las Vegas has and probably will continue to thrive as poker capital of the world is because in general, the house rakes are lower there than they are anywhere else in the world, and so poker players are able to survive for longer periods of time without getting ground into the dust, as it is said casino percentages will do to you.

Now, I had heard there was a game down there. I had heard there was a game down there from my friend Morty, who had gone with his girlfriend a few years ago because he had no job and he had a little bit of money and he had heard the two words together which will grab the attention of any twenty-something mad gambler's mind—beach and poker. And in the days of the Wild West and Los Angeles Hold'em, Morty the bookmaker went down to Aruba with his girlfriend and managed to pay for a two-month vacation with winnings from the poker table. He seemed to feel the game could be beat, and I mean who wouldn't, with an apartment and a blender and days on the beach and afternoons with the daiquiris and the piña coladas and evenings with comfortable clothes in the Holiday Inn poker room.

But I was down there four tourist-crazy years later, and I was cursing the fact that I couldn't find a hotel room for under $200, so I rented a car at the airport and figured I'd just wing it and first check out reports of the poker game. That's how I found myself at three-thirty in the morning sitting at one of the biggest poker tables I'd ever seen, seats for eleven, playing 10–20 Hold'em with a friendly crew of characters that included the American owner of the casino, who had unbuttoned his suit coat and was casually sipping a martini over his stacks of chips.

When I got into the game around midnight, the table was full, eleven hardy souls manufacturing giant pots on the green felt. But now the night is waning, we're down to six, and try as I might to watch the game, hard as I try to settle in and take stock of the players, watch the flow of the game and who's betting and who's calling, my mind starts drifting to the rake and my eyes rivet to the drop hole, where the dealer collects a stack of chips every hand and drops them into nothingness, the vast unreturned resources of the casino.

And I'm thinking this. I'm thinking $15 a hand. I'm thinking thirty hands an hour. I'm thinking $450 is being taken an hour from a six-handed 10–20 table upon which there is $3,000 in chips. In six hours, the game will be completely broke.

On the other hand, I'm thinking that if I get dealt a pair of kings in this spot, I'm liable to win a lot of money.

Without getting too deep into heavy mathematics, for I am no mathematician, is the game beatable? Should I get up from the table, suck up the $200 room rate and get some sleep? Or should I play on into the night, try and win some more dough from a glazed eyed crew while fading and dodging the rake, the monster steam shovel with the killer claw?

Casinos and Lodging
THE POINT

ARUBA MARRIOTT RESORT AND CASINO

Probably the best hotel of the lot, the Marriott is on the end of Palm Beach row, and it's brand-new, big, and beautiful. Maybe it's not so crowded. They do get the craps players, though.

Marriott's the kind of place where they'll have one $5 blackjack table crammed to the gills with two people waiting to get on it besides, one $25 table with one guy playing, and a $100 minimum table completely empty but with a dealer standing and waiting, and they won't open up a second $5 table, just keep the dead spread. They protect their high limit players.

Casino

HOURS Noon–4 A.M.

LANGUAGE Mostly English.

LAYOUT The Stellaris Casino is large, with a wood bar. A pretty good band plays daily except Wednesdays until 1 A.M. and weekends until 2 A.M. up in an alcove just over the casino. They play just what you feel like hearing.

GAMES Craps, blackjack, Caribbean stud, slots, roulette.

LIMITS Table games, $5 to $2,000.

RULES AND NOTES In blackjack, dealer stands on soft seventeen. The dealers shuffle their own shoes, but they're fast. Penetration is lukewarm to poor. Dollar roulette chips, $5 minimum. $10 minimum on craps with double odds.

FOOD AND DRINK All the dining options befitting a luxury beach resort.

THE PEOPLE THERE Lots of American tourists, but also a smattering of Dutch and Latin Americans.

Hotel

The lobby in the Marriott is four levels high. They spared no expense when they built the thing. 413 rooms and four restaurants, this high-rise hotel also boasts a stunning private pool with lots of lounge chairs and water volleyball. Rates vary drastically depending on the season. Standard room, $135 to $400, ocean view $40 extra. Executive king room or junior suite, $210 to $600. Rates don't include 17.66 percent tax and service charge. Maximum four persons per room.

 PRACTICALITIES
Hotel Phone Number: 297-86-9000, 1-800-223-6388 from the U.S.
Location: On the end of Palm Beach row, just north of the Holiday Inn, on L. G. Smith Boulevard.

AND . . . Adjacent to the hotel is Marriott's Aruba Ocean Club, which has 218 rooms and one- and two-bedroom villas. All villas have ocean views, TVs, VCRs, full kitchen, separate living and dining areas, and accommodate up to eight people.

Special amenities include pool, three spas, children's pool, full access to Marriott facilities and casino. One-bedroom villas are $160 to $450, not including tax. Two-bedroom villas are $225 to $650, not including tax. Reservations and info at 1-800-VILLAS-9.

HOLIDAY INN HOTEL AND CASINO

When Larry Flynt wants to play in a private poker game with a $200,000 buy-in, he comes to the Holiday Inn. Because they let him play upstairs in his private room and then he comes downstairs to play $10,000 a hand blackjack. So the Holiday Inn Casino is no stranger to serious gambling. But the hotel does suffer from that cheap beach motel feeling. And the rates are anything but cheap.

Casino

The Excelsior Casino.

HOURS Slots, 10 A.M.–4 A.M., table games and sports book, 1 P.M.

LANGUAGE Mostly English.

LAYOUT The Excelsior Casino, or whatever it's named as the casino name keeps changing, is spacious enough, with separate areas for table games, slots, poker, and sports book, but I wouldn't call it elegant. It probably suffers from the fact that it's part of the Holiday Inn Hotel. It has been recently renovated, however, and the casino ownership is not shy about putting money in to improve facilities. The casino is American owned, by a family that is also involved in options trading in Chicago.

GAMES Roulette, blackjack, poker, race and sports betting, craps, Caribbean stud.

LIMITS Blackjack $10 to $300, roulette $5 to $25, minimum sports bet $20, minimum horse race bet $2 on exactas and doubles.

RULES AND NOTES In blackjack, the dealer stands on soft seventeen. Dealer checks for blackjack immediately if he has an ace or a face card. The home of Caribbean stud, and there's usually a big jackpot. The sports book is quite spacious, but takes only local action (no phone or Internet accounts) on most every game being played in America that day. Plenty of seats and an extensive selection of American horse tracks with live simulcasting.

The poker room is in a nice space with five tables. Games start as soon as they have enough players, typically after dinner. The games are allowed to run after the rest of the casino has closed, and sandwiches and drinks are usually available to players. It's conceivable for weekend games to go around the clock. Limits are either $5 to $10, $10 to $20, $20 to $40, or higher on request. Game is usually Texas Hold'em, occasionally seven-card stud. There is a steady core of local players supplemented by a never-ending supply of American and Venezuelan tourists that keep the game thriving despite the high rake.

FOOD AND DRINK Hotel deli and liquor shop has cold Budweiser and Gallo Chablis, among others. Hotel has a few restaurants. Room service menu is very substandard.

THE PEOPLE THERE A lot of Americans. Apparently the poker tables are quite popular with Venezuelans, who come over at every opportunity.

Hotel

The Holiday Inn looks like a Holiday Inn, with a big open lobby. The rooms are very standard but they all have balconies. The beach is perfect, but public and a tad crowded. Room rates start at $175, and frankly, you could do better. 600 rooms.

 PRACTICALITIES
Hotel Phone Number: 297-86-3600
Casino Phone Number: 297-86-7777
Location: North part of the Palm Beach area, next to the Aruba Marriott. Just off of L. G. Smith Boulevard.

WYNDHAM HOTEL AND CASINO

The Wyndham is a hotel with the three "ahs." Honesty, opportunity, and atmosphere. It's a nice hotel, it's a new hotel, it's a big hotel. The Casablanca Casino, just think of it.

Casino

HOURS Noon–4 A.M.

LANGUAGE English, Spanish, or Dutch.

LAYOUT The Casablanca Casino is a casino with class. Cool air pumps through on a hot day. Beautiful cane and wicker chairs next to spanking new slot machines. The place feels Caribbean and gambler friendly. There's a separate high roller and baccarat area, as well as a sheltered bar with video poker and comfortable tables.

GAMES Blackjack, baccarat, roulette, Caribbean stud, slots.

LIMITS $5 to $500.

RULES AND NOTES Blackjack, dealer stands on soft seventeen and checks hole card for blackjack. Roulette, fifty-cent chips, $2 to $25. Nice MVP players card for slot players, cash back, or gifts.

FOOD AND DRINK Above-average restaurant selection for the area. Both the Italian and the Asian joints look top-notch. You can ask for a snack while you're playing, a small sandwich or something.

THE PEOPLE THERE High-roller area attracts some Asian locals. Hotel is mixed tourists, but quite friendly and comfortable. Staff is very pleasant.

Hotel

444 rooms. Nice high-rise with pool and beach and shopping arcade. Standard rates begin at $200 + 17 percent, fair value for the island.

 PRACTICALITIES
Hotel Phone Number: 297-86-4466
Casino Phone Number: 297-86-2283
Location: On the beach, at the southernmost part of the Palm Beach strip.

ROYAL CABANA CASINO

As one of the only stand alone casinos in town, the Royal Cabana has had to carve out its niche on the island. And they have. They have the bingo, they have the female impersonator revue show, they have the best buffet in town, they have the Iguana Lounge nightclub, and, of course, they have the walk-in humidor cigar shop.

Casino

HOURS Slots open 11 A.M., table games 6 P.M.–4 A.M. seven days a week.

LANGUAGE English, Dutch, or Spanish.

LAYOUT This stand alone casino is huge and round. At times, it is the busiest casino on the island. It's tough to even get a parking spot, jammed to the gills next door to Outback Steakhouse. The casino gets quite crowded and noisy, even though it is large with tremendous ceilings in the table game space.

GAMES Caribbean stud, blackjack, roulette, bingo, slots, baccarat.

LIMITS $5 to $500.

RULES AND NOTES Bingo is a hot ticket held in the massive showroom where they also have a popular female impersonator's revue. This is the largest-stakes bingo in town.

Sundays 4 P.M., 10 games, free drinks and snacks, $11 for 8 cards.
Wednesdays 8 P.M., 7 games, free drinks and snacks, $6 for 4 cards.
Fridays 8 P.M., same as Wednesdays
Saturdays 8 P.M., 8 games, $10 for 8 cards

Caribbean stud jackpot is a healthy $100,000. Dealer hits on soft seventeen in blackjack. They have screens for the roulette, so you can keep track of all the numbers, one of the only places on the island.

FOOD AND DRINK The $11.95 all-you-can-eat dinner buffet daily until 11 P.M. promises good quality and value. There is a dinner package available with the revue show, which is every day at 9 or 10 P.M. There is also a more formal restaurant that becomes the Iguana Lounge happening nightclub after 11 P.M. Gauchos is a nice walk-in humidor cigar store that is open from 6 P.M.–2 A.M.

THE PEOPLE THERE This is one of the casinos of choice for local gamblers. Most tourists usually find their way there at one time or another, however, either for the show or the good buffet or the bingo.

Hotel

No hotel.

PRACTICALITIES
Casino Phone Number: 297-87-7000
Internet Address: *www.royalcabana.com*
Location: J. E. Irausquin Boulevard, 250. Between town and Palm Beach area, just a little south of the Palm Beach strip.

ALLEGRO HOTEL AND ROYAL PALM CASINO

Like I usually do in a casino, when I got to the Allegro I pulled out my notebook and jotted down a few things to remember. After a few minutes I was accosted by a security guard who demanded to know what I was writing. When I told him that I was reviewing the casino, he said that I wasn't allowed to write any notes. Wouldn't you call that puzzling?

Formerly the Americana, the Allegro Hotel is rather grand-looking. You drive into a well-tended garden with grass and trees and flowers. The Royal Palm Casino, however, well let's just say I'd rather have two teeth pulled. Because that's what they must make it feel like if you manage to win any money in there.

Casino

HOURS Noon–4 A.M.

LANGUAGE Some English.

LAYOUT The Royal Palm Casino is not impressive, although the space is adequate, and a cordoned off high roller area could be nice but doesn't look as if it sees much use. There is a nice wall mural of poker and dogs.

GAMES Blackjack, roulette, craps, Caribbean stud, slots.

LIMITS $5 to $500.

RULES AND NOTES Roulette, fifty-cent chips and $2 minimum. The slot machines are old. The casino is empty at 8 P.M. In blackjack, the dealer hits on soft seventeen.

FOOD AND DRINK If you have to eat.

THE PEOPLE THERE Are not very friendly.

Hotel
419 rooms, you can do better for the price.

 PRACTICALITIES
Hotel Phone Number: 297-86-4500
Casino Phone Number: 297-86-0690
Location: In the middle of the Palm Beach area.

SONESTA HOTEL AND CRYSTAL CASINO
This is simply the downtown casino. It is the busiest casino in town and also the only gambling establishment on the island open twenty-four hours. The only drawback to this hotel is that you are not on the beach, but of course there is a more than adequate swimming pool and the shopping and restaurants are all right there if that's what you'd like to be near to.

Casino
HOURS Twenty-four hours a day, seven days a week.

LANGUAGE Pretty much everything. English is spoken.

LAYOUT Crystal Casino is big, lots of square feet around. But it's usually crowded and noisy out on the extensive main floor. There is a private salon for the big gamblers. The casino can be entered from the main street, where you walk up a flight of steps and past a security guard to get into the casino.

GAMES Baccarat, blackjack, roulette, Caribbean stud, slots, race book.

LIMITS $2 to $500, higher limits in the Salon Privee.

RULES AND NOTES Posted sign that casino may not redeem your chips if you take them outside of the casino. The race book is clearly the class one of the island. Very nice TV setup, à la the Mirage in Las Vegas, with twelve screens that can become three big or twelve small ones. Here, they Xerox the *Daily Racing Form* and give it to you for free. Beat that.

The tracks covered and simulcasted include Gulfstream, Sportsman's, Turf Paradise, Hollywood, Maywood, Philadelphia Park, Balmoral, Aqueduct, Bay Meadows, Santa Anita, Sam Houston, Turfway, Hialeah, and Golden Gate, plus the occasional race from Dubai. So a horse player can feel comfortable about finding a day's worth of action.

In the blackjack, the dealer hits soft seventeen. The dealer doesn't take his second card here until after the action is done. Nice place for roulette, with screens and a $2 minimum.

FOOD AND DRINK There are a lot of restaurants in the immediate area, plus some fast-food options.

THE PEOPLE THERE This casino is very popular with the serious local gamblers, including a strong Asian population.

Hotel

298 rooms. Rates start at around $200.

PRACTICALITIES
Hotel Phone Number: 297-83-6000
Location: In Oranjestad, across from Seaport Village, between the airport and Palm Beach.

Entertainment and Nightlife

Havana Night Club is the most happening music and dance spot in town. The cab drivers know it. Monday night is tourist night, Wednesday is ladies night, Friday and Saturday are just plain awesome. All kinds of music. Open very late.

The Iguana Lounge is open from 11 P.M. to 4 A.M. at the Royal Cabana Casino.

FOOD That's all everybody does is eat, there's a lot of restaurants because there's not a whole lot else to do. There's tons of those free dining guides that list every restaurant in town. The nice hotels have some nice restaurants. There's basically every possible option on the island many times, from gourmet to ethnic to fast food to in between.

Since Aruba is a Dutch Island, you can get lots of lovely little Dutch foodstuffs from a late-night cart across from the Sonesta Hotel. Croquettes or the like won't set you back more than a few florins.

DIVING Diving for wrecks, plenty of old freighters, tugboats, and the 400-foot long-scuttled Antilla wreck, sixty feet down. Most hotels are associated with a diving outfit. Dives for absolute beginners to experts, but the real diving is next door in Bonaire.

GOLF There is an eighteen-hole Robert Trent Jones–designed golf course at Tierra Del Sol. Telephone 297-86-0978. Nick Price shot a club record sixty-seven there in 1998 in a match against Payne Stewart, who shot a sixty-nine. Price took $100,000.

SHOPPING Shopping is subpar. The best place to walk around and look for stuff is unquestionably the area around the seaport and the Sonesta Hotel. It gets busy at night.

BONAIRE

LAY OF THE LAND

What kind of place is the Plaza Bonaire Casino? It's the kind of place where nobody wins. It's the kind of place where a gaggle of teenage boys on a high school trip down from Missouri pull out their $20 bills and order rum and Cokes and are just happy that they're drinking and gambling underage, and have no idea how to even double down much less a thought that these are the worst blackjack rules on the Seven Seas.

◆

A guy has just gotta set his foot down sometimes. Sometimes you've just had enough of the tourist prices and you aren't gonna budge until you get a corporate rate and you have been up all night and you have no shame left, none at all, and you don't care if you have to go through every manager in the hotel, including the big boss, because the worst that can happen is you get thrown out on your ass, but not before you make a huge scene with everyone, and at least that's gonna make you feel better. Hotel managers oughta be on the lookout for travelers who have gone over the breaking point, because there ain't no stopping them. After staying up all night gambling, I had hiked from the airport with my four bags, but got lost and ended up sloshing through the mud in the full heat, so you can understand that I was in one of those rare frames of mind that when they refuse you a corporate rate, you're just automatically asking to see the manager. Oh, did I revel in the event of one manager calling me a liar in the lobby. Great time to raise my voice. She went running.

I'm now writing from a grand suite. Corporate rate.

Bonaire
GENERAL INFORMATION

YOU'RE NOT IN KANSAS ANYMORE The middle of the three Netherlands Antilles Islands, Bonaire is known as one of the great scuba diving sites in the world, and it is still relatively unspoiled. Nine out of ten tourists there are thinking about diving. Pretty beaches are the norm.

WHERE Bonaire is fifty miles north of Venezuela, 30 miles east of Curaçao, and 1,720 miles from New York. The island is comfortably outside the hurricane belt. The sun even shines when it rains.

WHEN The tourist season is similar to Aruba.

TELEPHONES From the U.S., 011-599 + number.

CURRENCY NA florin is similar in value to the Dutch guilder. Dollars will get you everywhere. Credit cards are widely accepted on the island.

I'll Walk There Barefoot
TRANSPORTATION ISSUES

LEGAL Americans need a passport.

FLIGHTS Flamingo Airport in Kralendijk, the capital of Bonaire, does have international flights. However, most flights go through either Aruba or Curaçao.

AIRPORT The airport's a different story. Everyone's waiting in line, sweating in the stuffiness, while two ladies sit behind air-conditioned glass and do their best to make them wait longer. Get to the beach as fast as you can.

The Money Plays
GAMBLING SETUP—THE QUICK FACTS

CASINOS There are only two casinos on Bonaire. Privately owned and government licensed.

HOURS 6 P.M.–4 A.M., table games from 8 P.M.

ADMITTANCE Gambling age is eighteen, but ID is rarely checked for hotel guests.

AMBIANCE AND AMENITIES The attraction is the island, not the gambling amenities.

GAMES ON OFFER Blackjack, second-chance poker, roulette, slots, Caribbean stud.

LIMITS $5 to $500.

MONEY Play is in dollars. The NA florin is also accepted.

LEGALITY Gambling on the island is legal and safe, although it's not safe for the health of your bankroll.

TIPPING POLICIES IN THE CASINO Tip if you want. Go right ahead.

I'll Take the Odds
BREAKING APART THE GAME

SECOND-CHANCE POKER They spread a game here called second-chance poker. You get dealt five cards after putting up your first bet. Change one card by doubling your bet. The difference between this game and Caribbean stud is that you get to draw a card, but the dealer still needs to make ace-king high to qualify your hand for any payout above 1–1. Payouts are as follows:

one pair 1–1
two pairs 2–1
three of a kind 3–1
straight 4–1
flush 5–1
full house 7–1
four of a kind 20–1
straight flush 50–1
royal flush 100–1

It'll cost you $1 extra per hand to take a chance at the jackpot, which is fixed at $20,000. Fixing that kind of jackpot at $20,000 is like an insult. I mean, you're not gonna hit it anyway, and if you do, you're getting paid like 2 percent of what you should be. I wonder where the rest of the money is. Bet limits $5 to $300.

BLACKJACK I split my aces, and when one of the aces got another ace, I asked to resplit them. "Oh no, sir," said the dealer. "Split aces only get one card. Those are international rules." "Oh yeah?" I said. "Which nations are we talking about?" "If you say so, sir," he said.

In Costa Rica, you can take as many cards as you want on split aces. In Curaçao, if you split aces and get another ace, you can resplit them. And in Argentina, if you split aces and get a face card you get paid 3–2. Bonaire doesn't have the international rules to blackjack. What these are: These are the worst rules to blackjack.

Casinos and Lodging
THE POINT

Unlike Aruba, a visitor looking for a cheaper room will do all right by showing up without a reservation, as there are lots of small places in town that cater to the scuba equivalent of surfboard bum.

PLAZA RESORT

The Bonaire Plaza Resort is five stars, and it's definitely five stars. Owned by the Dutch Van der Valk consortium, it's the kind of place where you're taking everything with you, from the soaps to the shampoos to the little candles they put in the rooms, because it's all so much better than the stuff you're using at home. Luxurious in a beachy way. Rooms are spacious, cool, and sterile clean with tile floors and either a huge terrace or a massive balcony. The smallest room they have is a junior suite, and it ain't small, two queen beds with a full four seater glass dining table with four cane chairs and a sofa and refrigerator, coffee machine, and the works. This place is for people who want to dive and who want to be pampered. The grand suites have a separate toilet and shower room, with that funny-looking bidet thing that no American has a prayer of figuring out.

The happiest thing at the Plaza Resort is the guests—to a one, they've got that stupefied glow of relaxed contentment—clearly the staff is doing something right. Everywhere you look, beautiful bushes are blooming purple, pink, and orange. Sedate Caribbean music sets the mood in the shaded open air. The restaurant is within watermelon seed spitting distance of the swimming pool. Salads on plates as big as manhole covers shine with luscious goodies that can't have been picked before yesterday. Want a glass of ice water? Have a pitcher. Want to spend three hours lingering over lunch or just sitting there catching the constant breezes that rustle past the shade and gently shake the trees? No problem. It's your hotel, and you're the guest. You do as you please.

Completely private.

Completely relaxed.

Completely spread out. All of the rooms are on two floors, when you look out all you see are trees, flowers, and sunshine.

The only problem with the place is the casino. Gambling is apparently not thought to be as big a draw as scuba diving. Maybe they're right. This is the kind of casino that caters to 40 percent American tourists and doesn't even have a craps table, the kind of place where their second-chance Caribbean stud jackpot is fixed at $20,000, the kind of place where nobody wins—I mean I didn't see anybody win. The kind of place that even the gambling addicted locals would stay away from because it's just ripping your money down a sewer and you got a better chance of playing the local numbers when they pay 500–1 on a three digit proposition that's 999–1. The kind of place where the dealers are instructed to deal as fast as humanly possible, not for the benefit of the players, but because they'll take people's money faster and absolutely nobody can think at that pace. The dealers go so fast that you can barely even get your bet out there, much less see what they've got. This is a small-time casino, with no evidence of serious gambling. The games aren't crooked, but they sure are skewed against you.

Casino

HOURS 6 P.M.–4 A.M., table games from 8 P.M.

LANGUAGE English or Dutch.

LAYOUT Pleasant with nice high ceilings, but the rug is about twelve years old. What does it matter what it looks like? Where else are you going to go after dinner?

GAMES Blackjack, Caribbean stud, second-chance poker, roulette, slots.

LIMITS $5 to $300 or $25 to $500.

RULES AND NOTES In the blackjack, if you play alone you must play two hands. Lose all to a natural if you double down. No resplitting aces, split other pairs twice. Ace-jack spades pays 2–1 (big whoop). Penetration is a horrible 35 percent (they cut 3½ decks out!).

No craps table. With all those Americans around, no craps table? It's because in craps, the odds aren't enough in their favor.

American style roulette, no screens. $1 min.–$25 inside, $10–$200 outside. Nice assortment of slots—video line slots, five cents, twenty-five cents and one guilder. Nobody wins. And all the dealers know it. You can see it on their faces as they stand there and take the chips. Nobody wins.

Drinks come in little plastic cups. Don't want to spend money on a dishwasher? $10 in free casino chips for hotel guests.

FOOD AND DRINK The food at the hotel is all fresh and competent, if not spectacularly memorable or adventurous. Caribbean Point restaurant for breakfast buffet and fancy European dinner, Banana Tree restaurant is casual food next to the swimming pool, Tipsy Seagull is crappy fried fish.

Very good breakfast in bed, which you can actually eat on your glass dining table. The complete breakfasts come with quite an assortment of bread, rolls, cheese, meats, and spreads. The king breakfast has champagne, orange juice, fresh fruit, smoked salmon, omelet, and bacon for $27. Everything else is very reasonable, you can really get that energy going. Full menu delivered at whatever time you request the night before.

THE PEOPLE THERE 27 percent of guests are American tourists. Staff is mostly Dutch.

Hotel

Plaza Resort is Van der Valk's only five-star property. It is one of the top luxury scuba diving resorts in the world, as Bonaire has some of the world's best diving sites. Hotel has 64 junior suites, 64 grand suites, 24 one-bedroom villas, and 24 two-bedroom villas. Suites are spacious and air-conditioned, with refrigerators. Grand suites have a separate toilet from the bathroom. Villas have all the above plus a living room and full-size kitchen. Standard rates begin at $220 per night, plus 22 percent tax and service charges. There are safety boxes in the room, but you gotta pay $3 a day to use one. What does this mean? If you don't pay $3 a day extra, the maids are allowed to steal your valuables? Hotel has fitness center and photo shop. Complaints are a surprising dearth of hot water, the electricity has been known to go out, and the wakeup call is only an incessant beeping.

After I went over her head, the desk clerk made what I thought was an obvious point of making me carry my own bags to my room. Who ever heard of a five-star joint where you take your own bags to the room?

PRACTICALITIES
Hotel Phone Number: 599-7-2500
Internet Address: *www.plazaresortbonaire.com,*
www.interknowledge.com/bonaire/plaza/index.html
E-mail: *info@plazaresortbonaire.com, plaza@bonairenet.com*
Location: J. A. Abraham Boulevard 80, Kralendijk. Basically across the street from the airport, but I wouldn't recommend walking there. Ten minutes from the center of town.

Entertainment and Nightlife

There's not a whole lot going on.

DIVING Sand Dollars and Captain Don's are the largest and most respected dive operations on the island.

CHAPTER SEVEN

CURAÇAO

LAY OF THE LAND

How much is an ocean view worth? How much is it worth to have the beautiful pink of the setting sun glowing into the plate-glass window of your room, stretched out over the ocean and onto the crystal beach and when you step out onto your balcony and survey the cove, the ocean, the palm trees, and the lovely ripples on the water, the only sound you can hear is the occasional song of some Caribbean bird, and besides that, nothing. How much is that worth, you ask? Well, for $20 less you can have a view of the parking lot.

◆

The thing about Curaçao is that it can't decide if it's an all-around vacation island or primarily a package resort. I'd say a good 75 percent of the visitors are on an all-inclusive plan, nuts and bolts from airfare to dessert. The other 25 percent are getting ripped off by high prices caused by low volume. Taxis cost $20 to go anywhere, dinner out is gonna be at least $60 a person, and the hotel rates are more than triple what the package guests are paying. Yet it's a shame because there are some fine dining spots and entertainment options on the island. Take the Casino Curaçao Resort, for example. Here's a hotel that's got a perfect spot on the island on a private beach. Two of the restaurants are fantastic, a seafood joint called Pirates Cove, and an Indonesian restaurant named Garuda that specializes in a rijstaffel (Indonesian smorgasbord with a Dutch twist) with all the trimmings. But nine out of ten guests are Canadians who wear the wristbands that signify all inclusive, so they have all their meals in the main dining room. And the restaurants are empty. Well, almost empty, they survive on two or three paying customers a night, fools like me who don't have dinner included in their plan. So prices they charge are higher, far higher than they ought to be, and the result is a disparity that is grinding the island's tourist industry to a halt.

They really did me up right. I mean, at that point I had already been staying there ten days, and by that time I had just gotten my teeth into their cash and they took my bill, my whole bill, and just lopped the room rate in half and cut a good $800 off my hotel bill. Just 'cause I gave them a good gamble.

Willemstad, Curaçao
GENERAL INFORMATION

YOU'RE NOT IN KANSAS ANYMORE Curaçao's claim to fame is its natural harbor, which means the island surrounds a huge natural sheltered cove. That's why it's the seventh-busiest port in the world.

Willemstad, the capital, is a charming Dutchlike port separated in two by a pontoon bridge which opens to the sides when a cruise ship comes into port. It is the kind of town that once you've been there for an afternoon, you have a tough time finding a reason to go back. It's kind of lame, actually.

WHERE Curaçao is the easternmost of the three Netherlands Antilles Islands, thirty-five miles north of Venezuela in the Caribbean Sea. Atlantic Standard Time.

WHEN It's always nice there, hotel rates are cheaper in the summer, however.

CURRENCY The Netherlands Antilles guilder is different than the Dutch guilder. Rate at writing was $1=1.8 NA guilders. Bank notes are 5, 10, 25 ($14), 50 ($28), 100 ($56), and 250 ($140) guilders. Exchange rates are subject to frequent change.

There aren't any ATMs in casinos, but you can get cash off your credit cards. ATMs are at banks in town and at the world trade center, there are a lot of banks in town.

CLIMATE Temperatures average eighty-two degrees year round. It's pretty perfect weather.

KON TA KU BIDA? (HOW'S LIFE?) The official language is Dutch. The native language of Curaçao is Papiamento, however, which is a mixture of Spanish, Portuguese, Dutch, English, French, and some African tongue. Most natives speak four languages: Papiamento, Dutch, Spanish, and English. How's that?

English is widely spoken, and you will encounter no problems if that's your only tongue.

TELEPHONES The country code for Curaçao is 599 + 9.

I'll Walk There Barefoot
TRANSPORTATION ISSUES

LEGAL U.S. citizens must have a valid passport. $10 departure tax?

FLIGHTS You can get to Curaçao from anywhere. You really can. Great flights from New York or the ultracheap charters from Toronto. I wouldn't wholly recommend, however, flying there via Caracas.

Everybody kept asking me why my ticket was so cheap. "Well, I guess no one wants to fly to Caracas," I said. They announced that all passengers for my flight should proceed to the white van. There was no white van, only a white two-door Volkswagen, which drove me and another passenger out to the plane. I had seat number 2. Not 2a, not 2d. Seat 2. This is the type of plane you fly to an insurrection. There were five of us plus the stewardess, who came around with fifty-cent bingo cards midflight and we played in Spanish. You know, instead of duty free.

Canada 2000 is a travel agent that runs charters from Toronto. **Travel Liberty** is a travel agency that runs charters from New York.

WHERE THINGS ARE The airport is on the north side of the island, Willemstad is just across on the south side of the island situated around the huge natural harbor. The CCR is on a bay about two miles west of town. The Sonesta is right next door. Most of the other hotels are in town, right near where the cruise ships dock. The Holiday Beach Hotel is kind of by itself. It lies between the town and the CCR. Closer to town. The beach there isn't as nice because it's more open and public and doesn't feel quite as private and safe as up in Piscadera Bay. The Sonesta has the nicest beach of all of the hotels I've seen, and the pool is not for kids. It's for bikinis.

TRANSPORTATION AROUND TOWN Taxis are fixed fares, but they're expensive. Fares are for one to four people from 6 A.M.–11 P.M. Fifth person is 25 percent extra. After 11 P.M. is 25 percent extra. Airport to Sonesta, $14. Airport to Holiday Beach, $15. CCR to town, $14.

The Money Plays
GAMBLING SETUP—THE QUICK FACTS

CASINOS Casinos are privately owned and government licensed.

HOURS All casinos close at 4 A.M.

ADMITTANCE Gaming age is eighteen. Dress is casual, except at the Sonesta at night.

AMBIANCE AND AMENITIES Drinks are usually free for players.

GAMES ON OFFER Craps, blackjack, roulette, slots, sports betting, Caribbean stud, bingo.

LIMITS $2 to $500, higher limits may be available by request at the Casino Curaçao Resort.

MONEY Casinos allow play in either Netherlands Antilles florins or dollars.

LEGALITY Casinos are legal, winnings are not taxed.

TIPPING POLICIES IN THE CASINO Tips are appreciated, dealers share tips.

AND . . . The Casino Curaçao Resort feels to have the best security setup. They've got the big guardhouse and barrier so no one gets onto the premises without a reason. It just feels safe, that's all. I mean, if you're holding a lot of cash. The Sonesta's not bad either.

I'll Take the Odds
BREAKING APART THE GAME

BLACKJACK At the Casino Curaçao Resort, they allow you the option of doubling down on either two or three cards. This is in addition to early surrender. Six-deck shoes with good penetration. The combination of these factors make this a very advantageous game for the player. With perfect strategy, you may find it difficult to lose. With just a good knowledge of blackjack, your wins may be far bigger than normal. In any event, it's a very nice blackjack game. Quick vig is +0.28 percent.

Other casinos on the island have blackjack, but not the exact combination of rules that makes the Casino Curaçao Resort a blackjack player's heaven. Don't be misled.

Under the heading of gentlemanly things to do. If someone's playing heads up against the dealer, wait until he loses a hand before coming in, or the end of the shoe. It means something. The boys from Wisconsin did it, and frankly it's appreciated.

Adventures in Card Counting

The food's bad, the beach smells like oil, and if you can find a room for less than $100 a night, then you must be sleeping in a tent. Yet here I am, and what for? For 21 percent. You heard it right. For less than one fifth of a percentage point, I've braved customs in Caracas, a boring Canadian charter group, and coffee that's only a dark gray and has the potency of lily-livered toilet water. Curaçao is nothing more than a small island just off the coast of South America, but it has a secret claim to fame, a happening in one obscure casino on the northwest side of the island that 90 percent of visitors don't even find their way to, and the other 10 percent just pass on through by accident while checking out the bingo game. Yet this event, this situation, is such that if word got out, it would be enough to make hordes of people drop everything that they're doing and descend on the place like a pack of dirty red ants on a piece of cheese. Yes. Because I'm sitting in a blackjack game that is positive off the top.

Positive off the top. Four magic words that you could go your whole life without ever hearing once. And as you may have just experienced, these words don't really mean much unless you know something about blackjack.

Actually, you have to know a whole lot about blackjack, but maybe I can help to explain.

Blackjack is an anomaly among casino games, because it's the only game found in casinos where the odds are not fixed. In fact, they change every hand. This is because cards are dealt from a number of decks (the shoe) until they are gone, and depending on which cards are left in the shoe and which cards have already been dealt, playing strategies and the odds waver, they bounce, they seesaw with differences. Now in your typical Las Vegas blackjack game, when the game begins, when all the cards are remaining in the shoe, if you play perfectly, you have about a 49.5 percent chance of winning the hand. Just under even money.

What a card counter does is: A card counter always knows what the odds are. And if the odds change, if the odds change to the point where the player has more than a 50 percent chance of winning the next hand, then the card counter raises his bet. He raises his bet a lot. You see, he's been betting the minimum bet every time, he's always been betting $5 when the odds were against him, and now that the odds are in his favor he's ready to bet $100 on the hand. Or maybe more. This is the essence of card counting.

Something should be cleared up, and it should be cleared up right now. Card counting is not cheating. It's not. It's just playing the game well. And casinos don't like that. Card counting uses no tricks, no devices, no illegal methods. A card counter never does anything that's against the rules. It is merely playing the game with skill. But it is a fact that someone who knows how to play blackjack with skill can beat a casino in the long run, and casinos are allowed to bar any person from playing in their casino they want, for no reason other than they don't want their action.

The movie *Rainman* probably formed the extent of my knowledge about card counting until I took it up seriously. And *Rainman* was not accurate. I had heard that the game of blackjack was beatable. I had heard that the game of blackjack was beatable by geniuses, men with Ph.D.s in mathematics from Harvard and autistic freaks who could memorize the order of six decks of cards. What I set out to find is if the game of blackjack is beatable by a normal person, a person with no exceptional skills other than time to practice and a willingness to study.

And the first place I turned for help was to the Gamblers Book Club, for they are the source. Tucked away in Las Vegas, the store is nothing short of a holy site for those in the know (see Las Vegas chapter, Breaking Apart the Game). Peter Ruchman is the blackjack guru and computer expert whose advice I naturally sought out in regards to my blackjack potential. Ponytail Peter has been barred from more casinos than a two-bit pickpocket. He says, "The first time, I was like, 'Oh no!' Now, it's just another casino." He could certainly steer me in the right direction.

"It's hard," he said, "it takes a lot of practice and memorization." He looked at me skeptically when I said that I was prepared to read and practice for two hours a day on my computer for two months before even trying in a casino. But he said that it might then be achievable.

He gave me two books and a software package and sent me on my way with this piece of advice. "Read the book over and over," he said, "until you get it." Well, he was right. No one's going to get this the first time.

I had two books, I think Peter went for the classics. One of them was *Playing Blackjack as a Business* by Lawrence Revere, the late blackjack pioneer who amassed one amazing amount of blackjack knowledge and an accessible method to learn. You have to put the time in.

Basically, the game of blackjack has been put through a computer. The game of blackjack has been put through a computer countless times from every conceivable angle and situation and reduced to a series of numbers and percentages. And one of the things that has been found is that every different numbered card affects two things in a unique way when it is removed, or dealt, from the deck. It changes the overall odds between the player and the house, and it changes the perfect strategy play a slight percentage. The reason mathematical geniuses do better at counting cards has to do with accuracy. The percentages we're talking about are so slight, and so exact, that the closer you can come to adding and subtracting the exact numbers as the computer, the more accurately you will know what the odds are.

In general, face cards are good for the player and small cards, those numbered two through seven, are bad for the player and good for the house. The more high cards there are in proportion to low cards remaining in the deck, the better the overall odds are for the player. That's why it doesn't matter if it's one deck or eight decks, two decks or six. A card counter doesn't have to remember all the cards. Counting cards is merely keeping track of a ratio of large cards to small cards as they unfold from the shuffled decks (shoe).

If the ratio between large cards and small cards gets skewed to a large enough extent, the overall odds for the player will actually be better than the overall odds for the house. This doesn't mean a card counter will automatically win the next bet. Merely that the odds are in his favor, 1 or 2 percentage points, which means he might now win 51 times out of 100 hands instead of 49. That's not much. But it's enough to build a skyscraper on in the long run, ask any casino owner that.

It is at this time that the card counter increases his bet, because by betting the minimum when the odds are against you and then betting the maximum when the odds are in your favor you can expect to come out ahead in the long run. That is the first part of card counting. The first part of card counting is in the betting. That is how the card counter expects to win at blackjack. He must identify those situations where the odds are in his favor and bet accordingly. And he must likewise be able to identify those situations where the odds are not in his favor and also bet accordingly.

The other half of card counting is proper strategy play. This is also hard. This takes practice. This takes memorization. As the ratio of big cards to little cards changes, so do the proper strategy decisions. For example, depending on what that ratio is, sometimes you would hit your thirteen when the dealer shows a two and sometimes you would stand with it and let the dealer try and bust. The proper strategy play depends on what that ratio is. Card players call that ratio "the count." To make things even more confusing there are two counts, related by a mathematical formula. The "running count" is the ratio of big cards to small cards that have come out of the shoe, and the "true count" is the ratio of big cards to small cards that are remaining in the shoe.

In the case of the example above, perfect blackjack strategy would say to stand if the true count is zero or above, and hit if the true count is below zero. In order to ensure proper strategy decisions in every situation, a card counter must memorize a strategy chart. There's no getting around it. A strategy chart contains every possible two-card combination for the player against every possible up card for the dealer, and the proper percentage plays you make depending on the count. There's a different strategy chart for every different set of blackjack rules as well, which adds up to a whole lot of memorization. These decisions have been figured out by computer, each situation run millions of times to see which plays garner the best odds for the player.

It's important to note that these two practices—proper strategy and proper betting—go hand in hand. This is because the percentages being dealt with in blackjack are so minute. Consider this. Standard Vegas blackjack rules using a six-deck shoe, give the house about ½ percent off the top of the deck. But that's only with perfect strategy play. Improper play, and if you play without having the right chart memorized then improper play is unavoidable, can increase the house advantage to 5 percent or more. In good conditions, a card counter might start to increase his bet when he has only a 1 percent advantage, so you can see how improper play at blackjack can completely wipe out any advantage that the deck may have given.

And that is one reason why card counting, although possible, is harder than a lump of coal. One mistake and you give the house their advantage back. Knowing the count is useless without knowing the strategy plays to implement. Knowing perfect blackjack strategy is not effective without knowing the count to apply. Everything must be practiced until it is second nature. And everything must be done without alerting the casino to your objective, because once they suspect you, once they suspect that you can beat them at their own game, the jig is up.

How does a casino know when a person is counting cards? Usually by the variation in their bets. Anytime a person is sitting at a table for two hours, betting $5 a hand, and all of a sudden the person wants to bet $100 per hand for five hands in a row near the end of the shoe, a casino might identify this person as a card counter. If they're paranoid, they'll convict you anytime that you raise your bet near the end of a shoe. And they are paranoid in Las Vegas.

Back to Curaçao. What makes Curaçao different is the rules and what they mean. All around the world, from casino to casino and from country to country, the exact rules to blackjack differ. Some casinos play blackjack with six decks and some casinos play with four. Some casinos let you surrender your hand for half the bet at any time, and some casinos only let you surrender if the dealer doesn't show an ace. Some casinos let you double down on any two cards, and some casinos only let you double down on ten or eleven. Each of these rule variations, each of these minute rule changes have an effect on the overall odds. And believe it or not, the composition of blackjack rules at the Casino Curaçao Resort in Las Vegas are structured in such a way that with perfect strategy play, the odds are in the player's favor right from the start. Right off the top of the deck, positive off the top.

Now it's not much. Only about one fifth of a percentage point. But enough to lay down everything and travel halfway around the world. Believe me.

Why? Because when a blackjack game is positive off the top of the deck, it means that you can bet big from the first hand. In a traditional Vegas blackjack game, the odds will only move in favor of the player about one out of every three shoes, and then only for a few hands, usually at the end of the shoe when there are not many cards left to be dealt. In Curaçao, however, the odds are with the player for the bulk of the time, and always at the beginning of the shoe. There's almost no way to spot a card counter except by the fact that he will win a ton of money, because instead of sitting there and betting small in the beginning, his first bet is the maximum. And then he just looks like a high roller.

Now on one hand, anybody can learn it. And on the other hand, it takes a lot of practice. A lot of practice. The first thing you have to do is to find a counting system. There are a lot of different counting systems of varying complexity, and the principle behind all of them is that the human mind is not a computer and cannot remember every card that comes out of the deck. The principle behind all of them is to come as close to the exact ratio of large cards to small cards left in the deck in as simple a manner as the mind can handle quickly and without any errors. And as the counting systems vary in complexity, they also vary in exactitude or accuracy.

How does a person keep track of the count without memorizing all the cards? The count reflects a balance of low cards to high cards. Before any cards have been dealt, the balance is even, there is the same number of big and small cards in the deck, and the count is zero. Every card that comes out of the shoe has a value, and this value is added onto the count respectively.

For example, in my basic counting system, face cards have a value of −2 and threes, fours, fives, and sixes have a value of +2. So if the first three cards out of the shoe are a ten and three in my hand and a jack up for the dealer, those cards have a value together of −2 (−2 [ten], +2 [three], −2 [jack]). Add this number to my beginning running count of zero and the new running count is −2. Now I must make a mathematical conversion to change the running count, which reflects the cards that have come from the deck, into the true count, which reflects the cards left in the deck. Applying the true count to my strategy chart would yield advice telling me to hit my hand, take a card. If I then hit and got a queen (−2) and busted, that would change the running count to −4. And I've lost the hand. Onto the next one, running count at −4. It's only one running number that the counter has to remember, not individual cards. It just takes practice, that's all.

It takes two things to beat the game of blackjack. It takes perfect strategy play in every situation, and it requires one to bet high when the count is positive (odds in your favor) and to bet low when the count is negative (odds are against you). Oh yeah. You also need a little luck. A computer could do these things. But can a person?

Casinos and Lodging
THE POINT

CASINO CURAÇAO RESORT

The Casino Curaçao Resort is the preferred casino of the local high rollers, although you will find $500 maximums next door at the Sonesta. But if you want to really bet big, the CCR will surely make exceptions for you. One night around 1 A.M., a Venezuelan chieftain comes in with a small entourage and wants a private roulette table. It's provided, and he and his flunky proceed to cover the table with $25 and $100 chips on every spin, betting about two to three thousand per roll. They were well over the house limit, but the Corsican casino manager showed no signs of being ruffled, except maybe he smoked his unfiltered cigarettes a tad more rapidly. The duo hit a bunch of numbers in a row and cashed out winners of more than $19,000, which was paid in cash with nary a whimper. Now, that's a casino. All the manager did was smile, give them an armed escort to their car, and say, "Come back again." I'm sure they will.

Located on a private beach with a cove a five-minute cab ride from downtown and directly next door to the Hotel Sonesta, the CCR probably provides your best bet for a pleasant vacation. Most of the guests are Canadians on the all-inclusive plan, and with the price they're paying, you can't beat the deal. $750 for seven nights, including round-trip airfare from Toronto, it doesn't get any better. Walk-in guests can expect to pay between $100 and $130 for a large and modern room with airconditioning, TV, a balcony with a gorgeous ocean view that lights up pink at sunset time, and breakfast included. Not bad if you bring your own fun or want a romantic spot. The only problem with the CCR is that if the wind is blowing the wrong way you get the smell from the oil refineries, which is not really what you want to be smelling at the beach. The hotel is presently being taken over and converted by Sheraton, and with the location they've got, expect facilities to be even better.

If you give some gamble, the CCR casino staff will treat you right. The casino manager is a good bloke from France who previously ran casinos in Africa, and he's strangely not out of place in Curaçao. The CCR is easily the tightest ship in the business as far as a casino goes. When the big gamblers come in from Venezuela, when a man comes in with his younger companion and his girlfriend, a high-class prostitute, and they want to play with all black $100 chips on the roulette table and spread out about $3,000 a roll covering one third of the board, they're playing at the CCR. And the manager's gonna stick one of those tall black dealers in the game with those big hands who can speak Dutch, English, Spanish, and Papiamento and multiply seventeen times seventy-five so fast it didn't happen and never misses a payout or a bet or an odd and keeps that wheel cooking around the table about one spin every twenty or thirty seconds, or as soon as they're ready. Now, that's gambling. And then pay out $24,000 in cash and give the guy a guard to walk him to his car. Interesting place, that CCR. What it goes to show you is that the quality of a casino has as much to do with the philosophy of its management as anything else. And when I tell you that these guys are willing to give you a fair gamble, just check out their blackjack section.

Casino

HOURS The casino is open from 11 A.M.–4 A.M. daily, table games from 1 P.M.

LANGUAGE English, Dutch, Papiamento, and Spanish.

LAYOUT Clean, but nowhere near elegant or classy, the casino relies on its no-nonsense reputation as a gambling joint and its liberal game rules to attract players. Gamblers go where the money's at. It's a large room, with separate sections for bingo and slots, and it's cool and quiet during the day. During the week, the action doesn't pick up until after midnight, when a bunch of local high rollers are prone to showing up and betting the table maximum at whatever game is of their choosing.

Bigger than a grapefruit but smaller than a bread box, the casino is spacey enough to accommodate a crowd and still have a seat for you, though it's not nearly as large as the cavernous Holiday Beach Casino.

You get to the casino by walking on a covered wooden walkway from the open air lobby and past the seafood place, so it's separate from the hotel in the sense that you're not gonna walk into it by accident but it's right there. I like that. And you can't see anything from the lobby, and I like that. Sort of demure, it is.

GAMES Blackjack, roulette, Caribbean stud, craps (only on weekends after 11 P.M.), slots, and a very popular bingo parlor.

LIMITS $5 to $300, higher by request.

RULES AND NOTES Lots of bingo, it's probably the prime bingo game on the island, separate bingo room with about ten big tables, the entry is always cheap, you can play a full session for like 40 florins, which is about $25, and get cocktails, snacks, door prizes and you can win $1,000 or so, I think, plus there's all kinds of jackpots.

Friday night at seven is the big bingo time.

The casino really heats up after 1 A.M., late night at the Curaçao Casino when the local high rollers come in.

They are starting up a good player's club, with red, green, and black cards depending on your level of play, room rates discounted to free food. Call ahead to Lucio Monte to make a reservation. They'll take care of you.

CHEAP LIMITS $5 to $300, slots five cents up to $1, standard reel machines.

HI LIMITS Pretty darn big, if you have the money and know how to ask.

FOOD AND DRINK All the food in the main dining room is a good thing as long as you're not paying for it. By that I mean that 80 percent of the guests are on the complete plan with everything included, and the prices off the menu are a little steep. Much better value at the Beach Grill or next door at the real kitchen of the Sonesta. The seafood restaurant at the CCR has also gotten very good marks and the Indonesian place looks very appealing. Basically, you'll get a good meal all over that place, but it's hard to go cheap. In fact, the only place to really go cheap is the snack bar in the casino. You can do some damage over there. Chicken legs are only about a buck, as are decent sausages, Dutch patty things with beef or cheese, croquettes, those are the ones or a nice container of popcorn.

The casino has a decent snack bar, one of the only places in town where you can put something in your stomach for less than a double saw-buck ($20). Chicken drumsticks are good, and they have hot dogs, popcorn, or meat-filled pastries, as well as grilled cheese sandwiches, all in the $1 to $3 range. On weekends, they also pass around a tray of chicken nuggets after midnight. Drinks are free, and the servers are surprisingly good about approaching you on their own initiative to see if you care for something.

Coconut Bay Beach Club and Restaurant, kitchen open daily noon until 10 P.M., Saturday and Sunday, 11 A.M.–11 P.M. This grill is on the beach, and it's a nice place to sit. Coconuts mixed grill for 25 florins, may very well be the best deal on the island. You get every different kind of fresh grilled meat with vegetables and baked potato and some nice bread. Yes.

The Calypso Terrace is the restaurant kind of all over the ground-floor lobby dining room which has two levels, one a little raised and one down at the beach and swimming pool level. The menu changes every night and is always themed buffet. The breakfast buffet is pretty good for a hearty morning eat.

Garuda is the Indonesian Restaurant. Lunch Tuesday–Friday, dinner Tuesday–Sunday. **Pirates** is the seafood place right next door to the casino. Lunch and dinner daily.

The room service menu is a little overpriced. $20 for the entrees, $7–$10 for the salads. 7 A.M.–10 P.M.

THE PEOPLE THERE Run by an ever-present Corsican with a charming French accent, the casino exudes an honest reputation where serious gambling is encouraged. They are only too happy to pay winners in cold American cash.

Clientele is a good mix of tourists and locals, although on the whole the locals are the bigger bettors, as most of the tourists are budget-minded $5 players on the inclusive plan.

The dealers are professional and friendly, the managers know the rules and the games. The dealers can all add and multiply like calculators.

Hotel

CCR is on its own private beach, on Piscadera Bay. The beach is nice, the swimming and sunning area nice, it's just that oil refinery smell, depending on how the wind is blowing. The hotel is on a beautiful property located away from town facing west into a beautiful bay. Nice beach.

Recently taken over by Sheraton and due to undergo renovations to be completed by 2000. Glass elevator looking out over the water, rooms are very large and have AC and big balconies complete with table and chairs. Watch the pink sunset from your room or from the bar. English is widely spoken. Free bus service twice a day back and forth into town.

The hotel is under conversion to a Grand Sheraton, which will probably be nice when they finish it. But the heart of the place is the casino management and if you like to gamble, it's a pretty good place, no matter if they've renovated or not.

Room rate? Well, when I got there I gave my song and dance, the whole song and dance, and the lady gave me a pleasantly bemused smile through my whole spiel and knocked the room rate down about $20, to about $99 a night, net. And then every time she saw me she asked me how the writing was going, smiling again. They're nice there. But the standard room rate is $115 plus 18 percent, which includes a very lavish breakfast buffet. But you have to get a room facing the ocean. Or else you might as well be in Kansas again.

Facilities include 181 rooms, 15 suites, AC, private balconies, and remote-control TVs with HBO. Nice tennis courts with night lights, volleyball net, swimming pool mostly for kids, drugstore for sundries, and a barber salon. Front desk can make golf reservations at Wilhelminalaan, a nine-hole course.

Seascape diving is on site dive out fit that does everything from beginner course to master dives.

Tennis courts are free in the day, at night light costs $5 a half hour, rackets are $5 to rent.

PRACTICALITIES
Hotel Phone Number: 599-9-462-5000, fax: 599-9-462-5846
Casino Phone Number: 599-9-462-5000
Internet Address: *www.ccresort.com*
E-mail: *curesort@cura.net*
Location: John F. Kennedy Boulevard, on a private beach next to the Sonesta. Five-minute ride or twenty-minute walk to town.

OTRABANDA HOTEL AND CASINO

I don't like the atmosphere in the Otrabanda Hotel or Casino. The casino feels small, not much room between the tables and if you're at a full blackjack table, there's frankly not enough room to sit down. The atmosphere is hostile, the casino is ugly and uncomfortable, and I'd go elsewhere and that's that. Try the Porto Paseo down the road.

Casino

HOURS 2 P.M.–2 A.M.

LANGUAGE Spanish, Dutch, Papiamento, and some English.

LAYOUT Small but clean, frigid air piping through, not much elbow room.

GAMES Blackjack, roulette, slots, Caribbean stud.

LIMITS $2 to $150.

RULES AND NOTES In blackjack, one card on split aces, no surrender. Dealer stands on soft seventeen. Penetration is poor, they cut a full 2.5 decks out of 6. Blackjack is very popular with locals here because of bonuses that require no bonus bet. If you get 678 suited, it's worth 2x your bet, 777 pays 2x, seven-card twenty-one pays 2x, 222-three suited pays $150, 333-two suited pays $150, A2345 suited pays $500, but that ain't gonna happen. Probably, you won't get any of them.

In roulette, the casino is equipped with the automatic chip rackers that speed the game up a lot. Nice crisp new chips. Very inexpensive roulette with twenty-five-cent minimum—$10 on the inside and $2 to $150 on the outside. Players must buy their own drinks. Watch your chips when cashing in, Otrabanda has a bad feeling to it.

FOOD AND DRINK Rooftop restaurant has an interesting menu and a nice view.

THE PEOPLE THERE Popular casino with locals, as it's in town.

Hotel

Rates range from $85 to $115, including taxes and breakfast. Swimming pool, no beach.

PRACTICALITIES
Hotel Phone Number: 599-9-462-7400
Casino Phone Number: 599-9-462-7058
Location: In town, very near to where the cruise ships dock in the center of Willemstad. Fifteen minutes from the airport.

SONESTA HOTEL AND CASINO

The Sonesta is clearly the class of the island. The beach is secluded and stunning, the atmosphere is regal. Soft yellows, bright whites, lots of trees, and cool breezes.

Fridays are the big night at the Sonesta Hotel and Casino, when they have a free buffet and live music, plus a raffle with a $300 cash first prize and a second prize of $100 gift certificate to the fanciest restaurant on the island. The staff is friendly, especially the craps dealers led by Rodney, the flaming stickman who sings and swoons with the music. It's a nice craps team they got over at the Sonesta.

Rodney knows all the lingo and loves to use it. "The point is four, sir, hit the four and close the door! Yo eleven yo, pay the line we're doing fine, ten ten do it again, thank you sir, all the action is appreciated, sir!" It's the best craps game on the island, the only drawback being the restriction of single odds. But you ain't gonna find better unless you hike to Aruba.

One time I'm shooting with a Venezuelan fellow along with two guys from Syracuse, and every time the Venezuelan needed a nine, he'd yell out in a thick accent, "Forty-five, Jesse Jackson, c'mon Jesse Jackson!" (He meant to say Jesse James, a four-five is called a Jesse James, which just goes to show you that puns don't travel well.)

Casino

HOURS Slots, 10 A.M. to 4 A.M. Table games from 2 P.M.

LANGUAGE English, Dutch, Spanish, or Papiamento.

LAYOUT Very new and elegant casino, nice space with class facilities, you could dress up. It's not cramped but not large, a bit noisy on Fridays. Friday nights it's jammed, the rest of the time is fair to middling, depending on who's at the hotel.

GAMES One craps table, six blackjack tables, four Caribbean stud, and two or three roulette setups, slots.

LIMITS $5 to $500.

RULES AND NOTES $500 maximum is the largest posted limit you'll find on the island. In blackjack, no surrender, split aces get one card. The blackjack rules at the Casino Curaçao Resort next door are far better. Only casino in town where you cash out your own chips instead of taking a check to the window. Five-cent slots can while away the heat of the day, plus all the old video poker twenty-five cents and the usual reel machines.

Drinks are free, but the waiters must be summoned and they are downright surly if not tipped every drink. But the craps dealers will get him for you by ringing a little bell they have for just that purpose, if you're gonna play craps the atmosphere more than makes up for everything else. The bathroom in the lobby is large and smells delicious, like Juicy Fruit gum.

FOOD AND DRINK Emerald Grille is a real steak house with a nice classic menu. Open from 6–11 P.M. U.S. beef comes in six different cuts, $20–$30. Tartar, shrimp cocktail, Caesar salad, everything you'd expect to find at a premium American steak house, but it don't come cheap. Intimate lighting and seating.

Lunch at the poolside bar, a hot dog or some chicken sates, will cost you at least $10, but they kind of got you because where else are you gonna go. Also Portofino Italian restaurant, and Palm Café.

THE PEOPLE THERE The casino is well run, and they won't scream if you win. The craps dealers are hands down the best on the island, everyone else is friendly enough and qualified, but not quite as good caliber as next door at the Casino Curaçao Resort. Clientele is mostly tourists. The Sonesta is the only place where you might not see all package tour tourists, and consequently they tend to be a little better heeled, a little bigger gambling, a little more party and drinking, and not as much family.

Not many singles running around, the island is more of a couples place, nor is there a ton of entertainment besides the beautiful pool, the ocean, and the fine tropical breezes. There are plenty of young couples, honeymooners, and foursomes who've brought their own fun.

Hotel

Hotel is the swankiest joint on the island, prices start about $150. The pool and private beach are first-rate, with all the trimmings. AAA four-diamond hotel with 1,000 meter white sand beach. There's a free form pool with swim-up bar, tennis courts, fitness center, and all rooms have deck chair balconies. Rack rates are $255 winter, $180 summer. Fitness center, rooms all have deck chair balconies and are large and modern.

 PRACTICALITIES
Hotel Phone Number: 599-9-736-8800, fax: 599-9-462-7502, from the U.S., 1-800-SONESTA
Internet Address: *www.iseeyou.com/sonesta*
E-mail: *soncure@ibm.net*
Location: Next door to the Casino Curaçao Resort on its own private white sand beach. Twenty-minute walk or five-minute ride to town.

PORTO PASEO HOTEL AND CASINO

Located directly across from the cruise ship docking pier, the Porto Paseo caters mostly to cruise-ship people who have about five hours in port and want to gamble. The casino is crisply clean, cool, and pleasant. The floor people are very friendly, helpful, and speak all languages. This is where I'd play if I came off the cruise ship. Drinks are free for players.

The hotel is not large, rooms are spread out back around and near a nice swimming pool, which is completely hidden from the road. Rooms are comfortable and fairly large and new with AC and a refrigerator. But it's not a beach location and there's no view.

Casino

HOURS Noon–4 A.M.

LANGUAGE English, Spanish, Dutch, Papiamento.

LAYOUT Very clean.

GAMES Blackjack, roulette, Caribbean stud, slots.

LIMITS $5 to $300.

RULES AND NOTES There's always a man around there who catches your eye and taps his nose. I think he sells cocaine to the people on the cruise ships. Well, that's where he is. There's also a guy who walks through town and stands in front of the Hotel Van de Velde, and he's always talking like he knows you.

THE PEOPLE THERE Mostly cruise-ship layovers.

Hotel

Hotel has 50 rooms, 1 two-bedroom suite, 2 apartments. Pool has lounge chairs. Rack rates including breakfast, tax, and service, which means the 20 percent extra is all included. $95, $110, $125/double, triple, quadruple.

 PRACTICALITIES
Hotel Phone Number: 599-9-462-7878, fax: 599-9-462-7969
Casino Phone Number: 599-9-462-7007
E-mail: *ppaseo@cura.net*
Location: de Rouvilleweg #47. In town, directly opposite where the cruise ship docks. A little up the road from the Otrabanda.

SAN MARCOS HOTEL AND CASINO

The San Marcos is for locals and some South American tourists. They are not particularly kind or friendly to gringos, but you can play there. The floor lady did everything but spit on me when I went over to read the rules.

The place is just dirty dirty and that's all there is to it. Dirt on the floor, dirt on the machines, dirt on all the people in there, and forget about using the bathroom unless you've been in a stall in Washington Square Park. On the other hand, the San Marcos has the best selection of slot machines on the island.

Casino

LANGUAGE Papiamento, Spanish, Dutch, English.

LAYOUT Do they sweep up the empty coin wrappers? It looks like Belmont Park on Derby day after the sixth race.

GAMES Lots of slots, blackjack, roulette, Caribbean stud.

LIMITS $3 to $200.

RULES AND NOTES Surprisingly good slot selection for a filthy hole in the wall, including a bunch of brand-new nine-line video five-reels that are one cent per credit. So you can do some damage very cheap. Anywhere from a penny up to ninety cents per spin. Also five-cent machines of the same type.

FOOD AND DRINK No.

THE PEOPLE THERE Almost exclusively locals with a smattering of South American tourists.

Hotel

You should get your head checked if you're thinking of staying here.

 PRACTICALITIES
Casino Phone Number: 599-9-461-6628
Location: In town, you have to cross the pontoon bridge or ferry to get there.

HOLIDAY BEACH HOTEL AND CASINO

The Holiday Beach is mostly a family place. It's big, it has that large open beach motel feel about it, and it has good services. My complaint is that it's so open as to make me feel a tad insecure. I like the Casino Curaçao Resort and the Sonesta better, where I know for sure that no one is wandering around who's not a guest. The Holiday Beach is in the process of setting up the first public sports book on the island, in a large corner of their casino.

Casino

HOURS Daily, 11 A.M.–4 A.M.

LANGUAGE English, Spanish, Dutch, Papiamento.

LAYOUT The largest casino in town, space-wise, the casino has an enormous sitdown slot area, as well as a sports book, snack bar, and lots of table games.

GAMES Sports betting, blackjack, Caribbean stud, roulette, slots, poker.

LIMITS $5 to $300.

RULES AND NOTES Live entertainment Friday and Saturday nights. Happy hour Sunday–Thursday 6–7:30 P.M., Friday 7–9 and Saturday 8–10. Best video arcade in town is here. There is a poker room, technically. Supposedly there's a group of locals who have a game every few weeks. But I went there or called every day for a week, and no game ever got started. Maybe in the future.

FOOD AND DRINK The on-site twenty-four-hour Denny's is the culinary saving grace of the entire island. A great eating option on the island. Really. Food is fresh and well prepared. Hamburger with a salad is so good I could go for one right now. Ristorante Giorgio serves informal Italian.

THE PEOPLE THERE When I was there I encountered three New York wise guys out of Miami putting in ninety-six phone lines for a neighborhood sports book. You don't need ninety-six phone lines for a neighborhood sports book. This might be a heavy office.

Hotel

Hotel offers 200 rooms with "private balcony" and a big dive center. Rack rates are $150 winter, $110 summer, plus 20 percent taxes.

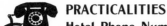

PRACTICALITIES
Hotel Phone Number: 599-9-462-5400, fax: 599-9-462-4397, 1-800-223-9815 from the U.S.
Internet Address: *www.hol-beach.com*
E-mail: *holbeach@cura.net*
Location: On the beach, just outside of town. About a five-minute walk to the town center.

PLAZA HOTEL CURAÇAO

Plaza Hotel Curaçao is owned by the Dutch Van der Valk group, and this hotel primarily caters to Dutch package and charter groups. There's no beach, but there is a swimming pool, Old World decor, and the strangest restaurant menu I have ever come across. Ever. Lamb sweetbreads with snails and blue cheese, or scallops with tomato marmalade and cream of iceberg lettuce soup. This may be from a chef who was banished to Curaçao.

Casino

HOURS Noon–4 A.M.

LANGUAGE Dutch, some English.

LAYOUT The Plaza Casino at the Van der Valk smells a bit musty, a bit like urine. It's decidedly an unpopular place, empty.

GAMES Slots, blackjack, roulette, Caribbean stud.

LIMITS $3 to $250.

RULES AND NOTES There's an interesting five-seat video poker machine where you play against the dealer. You can see two of his cards and draw and raise if you want. It's a little like Caribbean stud, as in if you get one pair you get your money back. Two old ladies play the game with dish rags and Kleenexes covering up their video screens, for luck, they mutter in Papiamento as I sit down to play. The game is a total chop game. Just accept that anything that takes up that much floor space rakes a minimum of 25 percent. Just my thought.

FOOD AND DRINK Free plastic cups of Pepsi in the casino. Le Tournesol penthouse restaurant is open Tuesday–Sunday 7–11 P.M. Bring a sense of adventure and a Maalox.

THE PEOPLE THERE Mostly Dutch tourists.

Hotel

High-rise hotel, rack rates $150 winter, $105 summer, including tax and service (20 percent).

PRACTICALITIES
Hotel Phone Number: 599-9-461-2500
E-mail: *Vdvalk@ibm.net*
Location: In town, just across the pontoon bridge.

Entertainment and Nightlife

There's not a huge nightlife in Curaçao. There are some live music bars, outside of the hotels. There's also a movie theater with seven cinemas. Phone 599-9-465-1000.

THE COACH SPORTS BAR has got the most atmosphere in town, some of the best food, and no fooling around sports, which is kind of good in the Caribbean. Daily dinner specials include Monday all-you-can-eat ribs, Wednesday Pabellon Criollo special and Friday happy hour 5–7 P.M.

On a big-screen TV, they show all the NBA games or ML baseball games, European soccer, American football, the NCAA tournament, and most importantly, all the pay-per-view boxing matches.

The food there isn't just good bar food. It's great big, delicious, char-grilled bar food, juicy steaks with thick-cut fries, burgers or fish or specials or bar appetizers and salads and you should go with an appetite and a giant thirst. Order your eight-ounce Amstel by the dozen. Located on Rooseveltweg 50 (Desi's Mall). Just get a cab. Phone 599-9-869-7180. Hours Sun.–Thurs., 5 P.M.–1 A.M., Fri. and Sat. 5 P.M.–2 A.M.

Ringside Seats

My stomach lining got torn out a long time ago. So bear with me, for I am only a fool, a poor gambler at the whims of fate. You don't believe in fate. Well, I do. In fact, I think it serves every gambler well if he's on the lookout for it, if he lets it into his life, reads the bones in the circle and the tea leaves in the dregs of the saucer. The gambler, like the traveler, must not be set in his ways. He must think on the fly, change when the time is right, and press his advantage in the heat of the battle. You think I spin yarns, that I am full of hot air, but I can show you how fate will lead the gambler on a string, a carrot ahead of the nose of the mule.

I went to bed the night of March 12 the same as every other self-aware male in the world, with two thoughts on my mind. The line, and where I would watch the fight the next night. Actually, I had kind of given up on watching the fight, but no matter where I was, the prospect of the first real heavyweight matchup in Lord knows how many years had me sizing it up with real appreciation.

I was in Curaçao, for God's sake, trying to beat some rinky dink black-jack game fifty miles off the coast of Venezuela, and I figured I had about as much chance of seeing that fight as Lennox Lewis was gonna have of knocking out my man, the great Holyfield. But that wasn't gonna stop me from sending in the cheese, I didn't think.

The fight was only on pay per view and I was gonna settle for round by round reports from HBO and the Internet. But the line, the line was a different story. I mean, this was the first heavyweight championship bout of some merit since I almost could remember and the line was reflecting it. The champ Holyfield was a slight, but not a big favorite over the towering British giant, Jamaican Brit Lennox Lewis. I knew I could get action in Danish kroner on the Internet via my Australian bookmaker, and the 1.8 return they were offering on the champ was damn attractive indeed.

Nowhere, it turns out, is too far away for the draw of the boxing heavy-weight championship of the world. One guy from the charter group named Canadian Dave who was a boxer himself and knew everything about every-body, he managed to find out that the best sports bar on the island was showing the game on big-screen pay per view, and he reserved a table for five with ringside seats. Five men, who left the wives back at the hotel, crammed in with a million screaming natives in a sports bar in Curaçao, and everyone but me pulling for the underdog. Phillippe said that maybe be-cause we weren't ringside we saw it differently, but I saw the nine-ounce Amstels, the sixteen-foot TV with a reserved table directly in front, the first real steak sandwich with steak fries I'd seen in a while, all the shit on the walls like a real sports bar, the satellite TV, the nice menu, black label Scotch and orange juice, distilled water, and I saw the riot that ensued when they called the fight a draw. I got my money back from the Australian bookmaker, but I was also happy to make it home alive. At least that night.

Let's face it. Traveling can wear on your sense of well-being. I wake up at 5 A.M. in a Quality hotel somewhere near the Miami airport with a ticket that goes to Curaçao via Caracas in five days and I have no earthly idea as to where I might be come nightfall. I mean I've heard good things about Curaçao, but Venezuela supposedly passed legislation to legalize mainland gambling last year and begs to be checked out. My ticket was issued by American Airlines, but my flights are to be on Servivensa and Antillean Airlines, so how I get from point A to point B is anyone's guess. Furthermore, I have a $200 voucher for a ticket on Lacsa, the Central American carrier, so a few days in Nicaragua is a definite possibility.

FOOD AND DRINKS Polar beer from Venezuela in the eight-ounce container, one thing the Venezuelans have not learned is beans about beer. A lot of the beers down here come in eight-ounce bottles. It's a bit weird. As the bartender at Coconuts Grill put it, "Here in Curaçao, everything's small except the prices."

You're really in trouble if you get hungry in town, KFC may be your only food option, or the central market if you're hardy.

Domino's Pizza delivers all over to all the hotels. It is Domino's, but hey, you know if you need it. The chicken wings are pretty good.

SHOPPING Because of all the cruise ships that pile in daily, Curaçao has all the shopping for people who just need something to do after being cooped up on a boat. Electronics, souvenir, jewelry, the prices aren't that special. Sleepy town, the requisite Caribbean band strikes up when the cruise ship docks.

 GOLF Nine-hole golf course is open to visitors at Curaçao Golf and Squash Club. Two squash courts open 8 A.M.–6 P.M.

DIVING Though not as pristine as Bonaire, there is good diving to be had on Curaçao, and plenty of people come down for just that purpose. The bigger hotels all have dive outfits associated with them, usually they come right and pick you up at your beach.

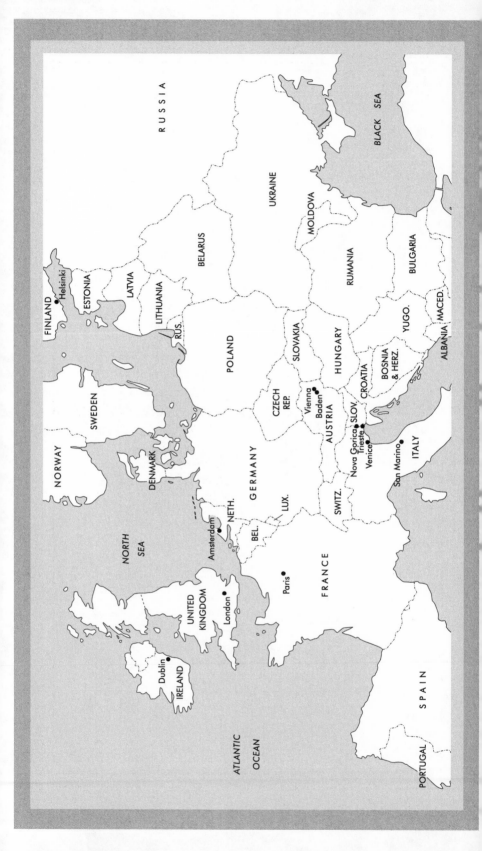

THE EUROPEAN TOUR

Gambling in Europe

When you mention gambling in Europe, nine out of ten Americans start talking about Monte Carlo. Even if they have never been there. And frankly, I say big deal. I mean big deal. What's so great about pretension? It never did anything for me. Hey, if you got a lot of money, I mean a lot of money, and you want to spend $65 for an ice cream soda and have people turn their nose up at you anyway, be my guest. In my experience, there ain't nobody going to Monte Carlo twice. No regular people, anyway. They say it's a playground for the rich? Let them have it. As a gambler and as a traveler, I like value and I like culture. I don't need a tourist trap. And that's what Monte Carlo is, in my opinion.

Monte Carlo is like going to your high school prom. It's for people who usually wear a track suit every day, but for once in their life they dress up fancy because they're supposed to, and then inside the casino is all the people you usually see in track suits trying to act different. It's a load of malarkey.

For me, gambling in Europe is about time, place, and people. Who needs to go to Monte Carlo with a bunch of Americans and be a bunch of Americans in Monte Carlo?

It's like, people go to Europe and they go to Monte Carlo to gamble because they're supposed to. Like losing your money there has some honor to it. Well, let me tell you something. They got slot machines in Monte Carlo now. In the old days, it may have been princes and kings playing chemin de fer, but now they got slot machines there just like the Circus Circus in Las Vegas and they think about making money per square foot just like the MGM Grand and they bring in tourist buses and spit 'em out on that grand piazza, and who needs it? That ain't Europe, in my opinion.

Gambling in Europe is about camaraderie. Gambling in Europe is about playing games like gentlemen and then laughing about it afterward at the bar, win or lose. Gambling in Europe is about old locales, tradition, and culture, yes, but it's not in Monte Carlo. Gambling in Europe is about going where the Europeans go. Let them show you how to do it because they know how to have fun. And they know how to gamble.

There's a reason that every spot I review in this chapter is a spot on the European Poker Player's tour, and it's not just because I'm a poker player. Hell, you don't have to be a poker player to enjoy them. You don't even have to ever play poker while you're there. They have all the other games, too. It's just that that's where it's happening. That's where people are gambling. European poker players are not your typical bunch of American degenerate hustlers who grew up trying to take money from a bunch of floozies. European poker players are people who come from a long tradition of gambling, a tradition of honor, respect, and a code of ethics. And European poker players are the nicest bunch of sick roulette, blackjack, sports betting, and mad drinking buddies you would ever care to run across. And they're willing to be friendly to you. They're willing to be your friend and talk about new days and old, and they've got money. They ain't coming up to you on the side and asking to borrow or talk about how they got beat in that big pot by some asshole who raised with no hand. They're happy to have the action, and they know how to keep everything in its place.

You see, it has to do with the evolution of gambling in Europe. You have to realize that that's what makes European gambling different from American gambling, in essence. It's the evolution of it. It's a fact that in Europe, gambling is as old as the kings and queens. As old as the royal courts. In old Europe, people didn't gamble to make money. They gambled because they had money. It was looked upon as a mark of distinction that you had the money to gamble with, and it was looked upon as a sign of respect that you could win or lose with an impassive equanimity because you could. And it still is. Among the European gamblers, the real gamblers, you don't get looked upon with respect because you win or lose, respect is based on how you win or lose. And I think that's worth being around. Because there's nothing I hate worse than a bad loser. Except a bad winner. And that's a culture that's worth being a part of. Because if you can't accept it as a game, as a game that can have two outcomes, then you should stay in America, you should keep to Las

Vegas, because in Las Vegas it doesn't matter how you win, just that you win. In Europe, *how* you do it is everything.

Nick the Greek Dandalos, quite possibly the most storied gambler of all time, was European in his attitude. He was famous for saying, "The next best thing to playing and winning is playing and losing. The main thing is to play." And I never understood that, those words always rang hollow to me, until I got to Europe and started hanging out with people who had been in the business their whole lives but didn't let it affect them. Good people in a bad business, people who could bring their values, their own values, to what they do and make it honorable. Because they are honorable, they are honorable at the table and away from the table, and when they're around your wife and when you call them on the phone, when you eat dinner with them or beat them in a pot that you can't even jump over with a last card draw out. They say, "Nice hand," and that's all. Don't move a whisker. Curse the dealer? Never. Why? No gentleman would do that.

Take Liam Flood. He's the man who runs the Irish Open, a tournament held every Easter weekend in Dublin. A bookmaker for most of his life, a legal bookmaker, now retired. Asked one time if he had concerns about the evils of gambling, he said, "Well, considering that my father was a bookmaker for his whole life and his father was a bookmaker before him, from that point of view I'm not really concerned about the evils of gambling." And what he means, what he means is that these men, these men who I learned from, they were men of honor, men to be respected, fair men. And so, no, I don't hold the view that to gamble means that you have to lose your integrity, to give up your honor. And you don't. And maybe more Americans should learn that.

Maybe more Americans should learn that gambling is not necessarily an evil in itself. It can be evil, don't get me wrong. It can be evil and destructive, mean and cruel, and it can make men into animals, reduce them to naked beasts baring their teeth and ripping for blood. But it doesn't have to be. Respect yourself. And if you respect yourself, and if you've got the money to gamble, then come to Europe. Come to Europe and pick a stop on the tour and come for the entertainment, for the fun, for the culture, the camaraderie, and the experience. I'll see you there.

THE EUROPEAN POKER TOUR

EPPA The European Poker Player's Association is becoming a moving force in European gambling. Established in 1995 as a fledgling group of European poker players faced with enormous poker expansion but also very varying rules and rakes, the EPPA was set up to deal with the concerns of traveling poker players, who over the course of the year spend two weeks in Helsinki, four weeks in Paris, four weeks in Vienna, a week in Baden, Slovenia, Amsterdam, and countless weeks at sites around the U.K., Ireland, and deepest Germany. These players follow what has now become the European Tour of poker, but lacking sponsorships the only difference between an athletic tour such as the Tennis ATP.

What the EPPA now offers, in partnership with many casinos and card rooms around Europe, is a scheduled tour of gambling sites over the course of a year. While virtually all of the casinos and card rooms participating in the European Poker Tour feature poker and gambling as a year-round activity, it is during these tournament times, when rooms are reduced and buffets are laid on along with parties and sight-seeing trips and some of the most unbelievable action to hit the heavens is spread, that these locales become ideal for anyone in search of a gambling vacation.

What makes poker different in Europe? What makes gambling different in Europe. To me, first it's the camaraderie. Because most people are traveling, because most people are staying in the same hotels, and because most people have seen each other before, people hang out. When you're done playing poker, it is more than customary to belly-up to the bar and drink until the wee hours of morning. It's what you do. And if you've never seen anyone before, don't worry. European poker players are surprisingly friendly. I say surprisingly, because if you've only gambled in Las Vegas, then you haven't properly been introduced to what gentlemanly gambling is all about. Where no one ever throws cards or says a nasty word to the dealer, and if someone does, it's the players who speak out, the players who know it's wrong. Most players in Europe, the ones who play a lot, adhere to strict codes of conduct as to their behavior in a casino, and this has much to do with the history of gambling in Europe as anything else.

The thing you have to realize about these poker tournaments is that the casinos spend a ton of money on them. Unlike in America, where casinos will run tournaments during slow periods and look at them as moneymakers, casinos and card rooms in Europe look at these tournaments as ways of advertising. Holland Casinos in Amsterdam pours a ton of money into their tournament, including all the money to train the dealers up into tip-top shape by letting them deal to dead spreads for three months a year. And the food and drinks they pour on. And the laser light show when the finals takes place. They can't be making a dime on that thing, but they just pour it on, and the place is packed, and the tournaments are just great.

You see, to go to those tournaments it isn't even like you have to really be a player, because there's a cheap tournament every day, like $100 or $200, and those tournaments are great to play in, because the payouts are huge and the tournaments are always sold out and half the time the person who wins, it's their first time playing in a tournament. Now there are a lot of good players who win a lot of the tournaments also, but it's not like in America, because there's a lot of loose money on the tournament table. There's a lot of loose money, and anybody has an opportunity to pick up a little luck and turn $200 into $30,000 in one afternoon.

And then you don't have to play the cash games. Because what with the drinking after the tournament and the blackjack and roulette all around, it's more fun sometimes just to play a few tournaments and that's it, and then just have a blast the rest of the time. And then you know exactly what it will cost you.

Helsinki pours on a sightseeing trip and Christmas party, Baden has gourmet food twenty-four hours a day with a menu that changes every six hours. The Irish Open takes all players to the biggest horse race of the year, and the tournament director in Amsterdam can't stop buying free drinks for everyone in sight. Slovenia gives away rare pieces of artwork to tournament winners, and the Concord plays an event that is the identical to the World Series of Poker in Las Vegas, but for one fifth the price. Yes, it's gambling. But you have never had so much fun.

The current European Poker Tour not only offers stops year-round on the mainland, but there is a ranking system for EPPA members, whereby points are earned according to tournaments placed in and prize money won in a competition for a yearly free roll tournament, where the prizes get bigger every year.

EPPA RANKING EVENTS, EUROPEAN TOUR 2000

Mar. 1—12	Paris, Aviation Club	Euro Finals of Poker
Mar. 14—28	Vienna, Concord Casino	Vienna Spring Festival, including the European World Series of Poker Trial
Easter Weekend	Dublin, Merrion Square Club	Irish Open
May 24—28	Slovenia, Hit Casino Park	Torneo di Poker
June 12—18	Helsinki, Casino Ray	Midnight Sun Tournament
Sept. 15—24	Paris, Aviation Club	Autumn Tournament
Sept. 26—Oct. 4	Vienna, Concord Casino	Austrian Classics
Oct. 5—7	Baden, Casinos Austria	Poker European Masters
Oct. 24—Nov. 1	Moscow, Cosmos Casino	Moscow International Poker Festival
Nov. 5—12	Amsterdam, Holland Casino	Master Classics of Poker
Dec. 12—17	Helsinki, Casino Ray	Helsinki Freezeout

While there are about forty events on the calendar for the European Tour 2000, only ten to fifteen of these events are EPPA ranking events, and these ranking events are the biggest ones and by far the best gambling events to attend.

The dates of these ranking events may change by a few days or so from year to year, but they are all held essentially the same time every year. The chart on page 177 shows the events I consider premier. Visit the EPPA Web site for all the updated event dates, at *http://eppa.bigfoot.com*.

The Money Plays
GAMBLING SETUP—THE QUICK FACTS

CASINOS There are now many casinos in Europe, ranging from state-run operations to private concerns. Their chief concern is elegance. Casinos Austria operates twelve casinos in Austria, of which Casino Baden is perhaps the most elegant. There are several private poker rooms in Vienna, the largest and most long-standing being the twenty-four-hour Concord Casino. In Holland, the government owns and operates a chain of Holland Casinos, the nicest and most popular of which is located in Amsterdam. The Casino Ray in Helsinki is state owned. The Aviation Club in Paris, the Merrion Club in Dublin, and the Hit Casino in Slovenia are all privately owned concerns.

HOURS Gambling is primarily a nighttime activity. Casinos are mostly open from about 3 P.M. until 3 A.M. The Concord Card Casino in Vienna is twenty-four hours year-round.

ADMITTANCE You must be eighteen years old to enter the casinos. There is a dress code in virtually all casinos in Europe. Jacket and tie required at some places. Not as formal as the El San Juan, but hey, it's colder than Puerto Rico as well.

Many casinos in Europe have entrance fees, typically around $5. While not much money, it does tend to raise an American's hackles to pay to get into a casino. Fortunately, during any stops on the European Poker Player's Association Tour (see page 175), this entrance fee is typically suspended during tournament time. Often, nicer hotels will have free casino entrance cards for their guests.

You'll need your passport to get in at practically every casino in Europe.

AMBIANCE AND AMENITIES Many casinos are beautifully housed in Old World palaces. Casino Baden is particularly elegant.

GAMES ON OFFER Poker, blackjack, roulette, craps, slots, baccarat, red dog, sic bo.

LIMITS Table games, $5 up to about $5,000.

MONEY All games are played in the local currency. Most casinos will allow you to change dollars and then reconvert them with no fee for a period of twenty-four hours. All casinos have money-changing facilities, but if you want the best rate, go to the American Express office.

LEGALITY Everything is very safe and very legal.

TIPPING POLICIES IN THE CASINO Dealers expect tips. In fact, they're used to getting very big tips, but just tip what you think is fair and understand that as gambling is looked upon with slightly different eyes in Europe, the dealers expect bigger tips from gamblers than their American counterparts. In Europe, it's expected that you have money if you want to gamble.

AND . . . ON THE SQUARE Everything is on the square.

I'll Take the Odds
BREAKING APART THE GAME

BLACKJACK They've got shuffling machines in the blackjack games throughout Europe. Personally, I think it takes the fun out of the game, and I know it takes a lot of the potential skill out. Basically, the cards are continually shuffled every hand, so you are always getting random cards out of the deck. I think this makes it harder to get a streak going, but that would not be a theory backed up by mathematical fact. Because of competition, these machines will not soon be popular in America, and that's a good thing.

ROULETTE European roulette wheels have one zero, and Europe is the original home of roulette, and they play it the right way here, with soft plastic chips and large markers which can be pushed across the felt by a long wooden stick held by a man sitting in a high chair.

CRAPS Eh. You're not in Vegas anymore. The name for it here is European Seven Eleven. All the standard bets can be found here, with a few changes. First, you can't back up your bet at true odds. Secondly, if you lay the six or eight, it only pays odds of even money as opposed to 7–6 in Las Vegas or the true odds of 6–5. All the other bets are standard, except there is no come. They'll take bets from $5 equivalent up to about $3,500. That's pretty big.

CHAPTER EIGHT

BADEN AND VIENNA, AUSTRIA

Baden, Austria

The sweets of Europe. Okay, Baden is expensive. But it's as close to a gambling orgy as you're ever going to get. I mean it is twenty-four hours a day of free gourmet food and drinks and a packed casino with every type of gambling known to man. In an Old World European palace spa town in the crisp October air. Now, where else are you going to find that?

It's the Poker European Masters Final. Through a plentiful haze of Cuban cigars, a parade of the stars to Queen's "We Are the Champions." Glasses of champagne in hand, the competitors on a single-file march to the silver bucket for the seat draws. Lothar Landauer, the most successful player in the history of the tournament, is sporting his tote bookie visor like an eagle-eyed accountant. Crowds and tables, the ceiling in all elegance, a fresco from the seventeenth century that blows away Steve Wynn and his breasted wall mural ladies from the 1990s, as usual. Europe's been around for a while.

POKER EUROPEAN MASTERS AT BADEN

Now in its eleventh year, the Poker European Masters has become one of the premier poker tourneys in the world. Aside from the fact that the limits go up very fast, the prize payouts are huge, and for as little as a 3,000 schilling buy-in, you can walk away with a first prize of over 2 million ATS. It's a lot of money, a prize pool of over 7 million schillings.

The tournament is typically run over three days, Thursday night through Saturday night, although we were drinking long into the mid-morning Sunday, and people were still playing as well.

The way it works is this. From Thursday through Saturday, three qualifying tournaments are played. These tournaments are only played down to the final twenty-four players, each of whom qualifies for the grand final on Saturday night. The tournament is 3,000 schilling buy-in with optional re-buy and add on of 3,000 schillings each. If you qualify on Thursday, you will have paid no more than your initial buy-in plus optionals. What an opportunity, for a tournament that paid almost a quarter of a million dollars to first place in 1999. The seventy-two-player final is played on Saturday night, for all the money. Limits go up quick, so you'll need more than your share of luck to take the prize. First qualifying tournament is held Thursday at 7 P.M., the second is held Friday at 3 P.M., and the last chance qualifying tournament is held Saturday at 1 P.M. The final starts immediately following, about 7:30 Saturday evening. You must have played in the first two qualifying tournaments in order to play in the last-chance tourney. First place gets 36 percent of the prize pool.

During the Poker European Masters, Casino Baden becomes a veritable action hotbed. The rakes are high, but most of the games are pot limit, and when you consider how much money is on the table and you are liable to win, the rake is not too high, and it's still worth traveling halfway around the world for. They spread over forty cash tables, most of which go around the clock. Up to seven- or eight-pot-limit Omaha games going with a 5,000, 10,000, or 20,000 schilling buy-in. These are some action games. In addition, pot-limit Hold'em, seven-card stud, and a variety of limit games. The rake in the pot-limit Omaha is 250 schillings per half hour, about $40 per hour. But they do have individual stopwatches at each table for the dealer to control the time, so you are never paying time when there's a problem, when they have to call over a floorman and stop the game or bring new cards in or anything. You're not paying for that, and so you get a full thirty minutes of play for your money. It is a high rake, though, and the European Poker Player's Association may be involved in getting a lower rake in the future.

The tournament is usually sold out, despite the fact that there are many many seats. Pre-registering is a must, call the casino direct at 43-0-2252-44496 and put the VIP package of $400 on your credit card.

And in addition to the poker, you can play everything else. The casino is packed to bursting all the time.

Baden, Austria
GENERAL INFORMATION

YOU'RE NOT IN KANSAS ANYMORE Technically called Baden bei Wien, Baden is an old spa town, located in the woods about twenty miles from Vienna. People have been going there for hundreds of years to bathe in the restorative powers of its hot springs, stroll in the parks and the woods, delight in Austrian pastries and nature and massage. The whole town is very walkable.

WHERE Baden is easily accessible by tram from central Vienna or transfer from the airport. Austria is nestled in Europe, bordered by Germany and Switzerland and Italy and the Czech Republic. It is a safe and orderly country to travel to. Things are very well run.

WHEN The Poker European Masters is held at the beginning of October every year. This is a wonderful time to visit Baden, as the autumn weather is just turning crisp. The Concord Casino in Vienna usually runs a big tournament in the two weeks before the Poker European Masters, and they provide good accommodation rates for players at a hotel next to a tram stop in the town and a free twenty-four-hour shuttle to and from the casino.

I'll Walk There Barefoot
TRANSPORTATION ISSUES

LEGAL Americans need only a valid passport to be stamped for a stay of up to three months. Then again, sometimes they don't even stamp your passport.

FLIGHTS Airport: You will come to Baden via Vienna. The easiest thing to do is to go to Wien Mitte, the city air center, either by inexpensive bus from the airport or via the U-Bahn to Landstrasse, #3 and #4 go there. From there you change to the S-Bahn, S1 goes to Baden, about a thirty-minute ride. It's cheap, you're on public transportation. Don't forget to stamp your ticket on the U-Bahn and S-Bahn.

Vienna is a major international city, and easy to get to. Alternatively, if you fly in to Zurich or Germany, it's not much of a train ride to get to Vienna. And European trains are nice, you're usually traveling in comfort.

Or you can pay the nice people at Mondial Travel of Baden, who do a fair job at not an unreasonable price. They'll make all your reservations including flights for about a 25 percent premium over what it would cost to do it all yourself. For the Poker European Masters, they will pick you up and return you between the airport in Vienna and your hotel in Baden, so they are an easy way to take care of all the details if you are just flying in and out. If, however, you intend to stay a little extra and see Vienna and check out the Concord, Baden is not too difficult on the hoof. Just a few phone calls, that's all.

Mondial Travel. Phone: 43-2252-44242-30. Fax: 43-2252-44776. E-mail: *wunderl@mondial.at*. They also get a lot of the good accommodation across from the casino booked up early. Choices include the Grandhotel Sauerhof, the Parkhotel, the Hotel Gutenbrunn, and the Hotel Admiral am Kurpark. These are all exceptional facilities. The Sauerhof is the best and most elegant, about eight minutes' walk from the casino. They all run about $100 to $150 per night, cheaper for a single.

INFO Lots of Baden information for the visitor can be found at Baden's official website, at *www.tiscover.com/baden-bei-wien*.

Casinos and Lodging
THE POINT

CASINO BADEN

Casino
HOURS During the Poker European Masters, action round the clock. Normal hours are 3 P.M. until closing, around 3 A.M.

LANGUAGE German. Enough English spoken so that you will be fine.

LAYOUT The main building that houses the Casino Baden is three hundred years old if it's a day, and it is magnificent. There is a pool and fountains in front that look stately and romantic when lighted at night. You wouldn't want to enter this place dressed in anything but your best. At least not the first time.

The casino is spread out over three levels. Big, sweeping circular staircases carry you up, or there are elevators as well. Everything is grand, from the lobbies to the entranceways on every floor, from the chandeliers to the ceilings.

FOOD AND DRINK The way the tournament works is that you pay about $400 for a tournament VIP pass. All right, this is a lot. But it entitles you to unlimited food and drink for the entire four days of the tournament, and they absolutely pull out all the stops. It's like a cruise ship, only better. You just raise your hand and get what you want. Anything off the menu, any drink at the bar. Whether you're playing or just standing around, or sitting in the restaurant area. And the menu changes every six hours. Plus they have a live buffet three times a day, the kind of buffet where stuff is bubbling and roasting and scrumptiously spread and graciously served. Fine wine, all the alcohol you could want, brandy or cognac or whiskey. Beer in tall thin steins, of many varieties.

The catering is done by a gourmet catering company, Do and Co., and wow. Check out some of these menus, all nicely written and printed up for you to peruse. Or take with you for memories. I tried to have everything at least once, but it took a fixed resolution to never stop eating. Each menu, every six hours in the casino, featured a different type of cuisine.

One afternoon for starters, you could choose between mozzarella tricolor salad, smoked salmon, or onion soup. You could follow that up with entrecote à la bordelaise, grilled salmon, or homemade pasta with mushrooms. Dessert was mousse and cakes.

Six hours later, the menu was Asian. Starters of crispy chicken salad, or Thai minced beef salad with mint, or Thai fish soup with prawns. Main courses were chicken and shrimp sate, Hong Kong steak, and Thai rice. Baked figs, fruit salad, or fresh strawberries followed.

The American menu featured shrimp cocktail, spinach salad with ewe's cheese, and pumpkin soup. Follow that with grilled tuna, Uruguayan beef, or spaghetti with pumpkin. Finished off by chocolate cake and sour cream and strawberry torte. May I just pause for a second to applaud the merits of Uruguayan beef.

Buffet breakfasts with ham and eggs cooked to order, every juice, roll, cheese, cereal, and croissant that you could imagine. Viennese sausage around the clock, goulash soup, tortellini with spinach and parmesan, Spanish fish soup, petit fours, chili con carne, turkey on the spit, won ton soup, and seafood salad. It's insane.

And the drinking. Despite the heavy nonstop action, you will have to find some time for drinking, and most people there do. There's a large bar area to hang out in, and it can get pretty wild. In a civilized manner, of course.

Hotel

No hotel at the casino.

OTHER HOTELS

During most of the year, Casinos Austria offers casino VIP packages in conjunction with some leading hotels in Austria that are located near casinos. These packages include two nights stay in a double room. Breakfast buffet or breakfast in room. Bottle of champagne and fruit basket. Transfers to casino, if not in walking distance. Gaming chips for 300 ATS per person. Late check out.

Prices at the Grandhotel Sauerhof, which is a premier destination, start at $200 per person, $150 at the Parkhotel Baden. For information, call 43-1-581-0611, fax 43-1-586-1752, Hotels and Casinos Austria. They also have some lovely casino packages in spots other than Baden, like skiing in Innsbruck, or tennis and golf in Kitzbuhel.

Hotel Gutenbrunn is old world, charming, and kitschy. Rooms numbered 06 are perfectly placed in the corner with two sets of windows that catch all the sun. Views from 406 are quite literally breathtaking. Funny furniture. Located on Pelzgasse 22, phone 02252-48171, $80 to $100 per night. *www.tiscover.com/hotel.gutenbrunn.*

Parkhotel Baden. Practically across the street from the casino. Phone 43-0-2252-44386.

Grandhotel Sauerhof. An exceptional place. Could be the nicest in town. Located on Weilburstrasse 11, Phone (0) 2252-42251.

PRACTICALITIES
Casino Phone Number: 43-2252-444-96, poker hot line extension 256
E-mail: *pokerem.ba@casinos.at*
Internet Address: *www.pokerem.com, www.casinos.at*
Location: Next to the Kurpark in the town of Baden, you can't miss it.

Entertainment and Nightlife

Club Babylon. Remember those two words. Let me tell you about this brothel called **Club Babylon**. I know a guy who went to this brothel while he was in Baden, and liked it so much that four weeks later he flew all the way back to Europe to go to the brothel. "It's incredible," he said. "Like none other in the world." I've heard of other people who liked it there too. Just make it known you want to go to Club Babylon, and you'll get there. Everybody else does. It's easily accessible by taxi or car from Baden or Vienna.

 WINE You are right in the heart of some prime wine country. Get something called the Heurigenkalender, which is a schedule of which wineries around town are having tastings of their new wine. It runs freely, and it's delicious. Or call 02252-45640, the Heurigentelefon.

GOLF There are four or five golf courses in the area around Baden. The Hotel Admiral am Kurpark, the Parkhotel Baden, and the Grandhotel Sauerhof all offer special golf packages. Inquire when making reservation. Or you can go yourself.

Golf and Country Club Brunn 0-2236-33711, eighteen holes, twenty kilometers from Baden, 550 to 650 schillings.

Golf Club Enzesfeld 0-2256-81272-1, eighteen holes, eight kilometers from Baden, 500 to 750 schillings.

Golf and Sportclub Fontana 0-2253-606-401, eighteen holes, five kilometers from Baden, Championship Golf Course, 1,000 to 1,300 schillings.

AUSTRIAN TELEVISION It's their prerogative, but an Elvis movie dubbed into German? Now I've seen it all.

Vienna, Austria

THE CONCORD CARD CASINO

By my accounting, the Concord Card Casino was the first location in mainland Europe to offer legal poker. Anyway, it was certainly the first place with real live twenty-four-hour poker games going at every limit. That was in 1993. They are still the premier limit poker room in Europe. The Concord is not located in the center of town, but it is easily accessible by bus or streetcar. During tournament weeks at the Concord, players are shuttled for free back and forth from the hotel, which has a nice sauna and cheap poker rates and a happening bar.

They also have a sports book, on the run betting for all big-screen soccer games, plus American sports. The kitchen is decent. Cream spinach plus a potato rosti plus a fried egg is a sleeper choice, Austrian brain food.

In the spring, the Concord runs an annual World Series of Poker Trial. This event is identical to the World Series held every May in Las Vegas, a no-limit Hold'em contest over four days, except the buy-in in Vienna is less than $2,000, as opposed to $10,000 in Vegas. This tournament is a thrill to play and offers big prize payouts. While in Vienna, don't forget to check out the opera house. With all the action, you may find it hard to make time, but try.

Most of the games here are limit, with rakes much lower than those found at Casinos Austria. The dealers here are the best in Europe, hands down. The poker room manager, Thomas Kremser, has learned the business from the bottom up. He's a star, and the room reflects it. The card room is located on Geiselbergstrasse 9, Vienna 1110. Phone 43-1-749-0136. E-mail *event@ccc.co.at* or *www.ccc.co.at*. They also run the week-long Austrian Classics during the days leading up to the Poker European Masters in Baden, and a lot of people make both of these events a wonderful two-week gambling vacation.

As far as accommodation goes in Vienna, the casino will be happy to set you up at a hotel with a poker rate. Just call or e-mail them. The hotel that they set you up at will not be in the center of town, but much cheaper and easily accessible to town via Vienna public transportation, which is excellent. If you want to stay in the center of town, you're on your own.

 PRACTICALITIES
Casino Phone Number: 43-1-749-0136
E-mail: *event@ccc.co.at*
Internet Address: *www.ccc.co.at*
Location: On the outskirts of Vienna, Geiselbergstrasse 9, Vienna 1110. Accessible by tram #6 from the West Bahnhof, the train station in the west part of the city. Get off at the Geiselbergstrasse stop.

AMSTERDAM

LAY OF THE LAND

I do the same thing every time I'm in Amsterdam. I leave my hotel in the morning and I start walking. And in the late afternoon I arrive back to my hotel, having spent hours wandering around completely lost. And it was always wonderful.

♦

I'm standing at the bar with Twitchell, a man of great respect. Actually, he's the one standing, as I'm leaning against the bar railing for support, cool brass in a half circle. With the way Twitchell has been pouring the tall thin steins of beer down my throat, I can use the support. The tournament is down to only a few players and the big cash games have broken up, so most of us are congregated in the bar area, making it a serious business of letting our hair down. Amsterdam is a people town.

HOLLAND CASINO

They do wonderful things with those dealers there in Amsterdam. I mean, considering they only deal poker like that one week a year, they do amazing things with those poker dealers. They have them all in there for months before the tournament, training and dealing at practice tables, and when it gets to tournaments and live-action games, they really know what they are doing.

The Master Classics of Poker was the first major tournament on mainland Europe, it's still going and bigger every year. Held during the second week of November every year, the casino, the staff, everyone goes all out. What a spectacle. Six tournaments with buy-ins ranging from $100 to $200, plus the Master Classics final, which goes over two days and costs 5,000 guilders (approximately $2,500) to play, and pays over $100,000 first prize.

The casino helps with hotel reservations, making it easy to visit one of the most beautiful cities in the world. The Holland Casino also features full gambling at a range of games, in a classy atmosphere.

Would you like an example of how much they try to please the players? Up until 1999, it was not legal to play the poker game called Omaha in the Netherlands. A law proposing its legality was tied up somewhere in the government bureaucracy. When the poker players showed up in November 1999, they wanted to play Omaha. And in the twenty-four hours between the first and second day after the poker players arrived in town, the head of the poker room managed to get Omaha legalized. He was on the phone, waking up government ministers all night, he said. That was just to make the players happy.

Casino

HOURS 1 P.M.–3 A.M. daily.

LANGUAGE Dutch, English, German, everybody speaks everything in this country.

LAYOUT The casino is very nice. On two floors, with all the slots downstairs. The large upstairs room is circular, with a bar and restaurant ringing the casino halfway around. The table games are lovely, box men sitting in high chairs. High ceilings and a piano player. It's sometimes tough to find a place to sit, it's so busy, but they do have plenty of eating tables.

GAMES French roulette (one zero), blackjack, punto banco, poker, Pai-Gow, Caribbean stud, slots, red dog, and the big wheel.

LIMITS It's a pretty high limit place. Table games usually have a 25-florins minimum.

RULES AND NOTES Every person who plays in the tournament gets a nice full-color shot of themselves at the table to take home. It's a nice touch, so dress up like you're ready to play some cards.

Most of the cash poker games are played pot limit. They also spread limit games here, but I wouldn't play in them. The rake is too high. During most of the year, Holland Casino is a bad place to play poker, because of the high rake, which is 5 percent up to 40 guilders. That's high for a limit game. During the tournament, however, the rake is lowered and the games are pot limit.

FOOD AND DRINK The restaurant on the ground floor, while expensive, is out of this world. Nothing but raves coming out of that place. But the casino restaurant does a fair job at that. I would generally not recommend the buffets, but the food off the menu is well prepared, excellent ingredients and good eating.

Hotel

No hotel. See Accommodation, below.

PRACTICALITIES
Casino Phone Number: 31-0-20-521-1111,
Master Classics hot line 31-0-20-521-1102
Internet Address: *www.hollandcasino.nl*
Location: On the Leidseplein, a beautiful square in the center of town. Take Tram 1, 2, or 5 to the Leidseplein.

ACCOMMODATION

Amsterdam used to be a twenty-four-hour town, but now there's a law that requires most things to close at 3 A.M. So you're basically going to need a hotel room. And it can be tough to get a good hotel room in Amsterdam.

Amsterdam is far and away the most difficult city in Europe when it comes to accommodations. It is at once cheap and overpriced, impossible to navigate, based upon this very simple fact. The typical Dutch hotel has eleven rooms, one of which is fantastic, and the rest range from above average to fair to middling. You have no idea what you're getting unless you been there before.

The problem with accommodations in Amsterdam has something to do with the fact that it's a very old city. It's a very old city and most of the hotels are located in old buildings, small and beautiful. Your typical hotel has one or two rooms that are big and beautiful. Then it has several average rooms, and then many rooms in odd corners and at odd angles to the narrow staircases that run up and down practically every building in town.

The larger chain hotels have small rooms, and at the smaller hotels, the big rooms are hard to get. Personally, I'd much rather stay in a small hotel in Amsterdam, because that's what it's all about. Larger hotels run well over $200 per night, but it's possible to get a good room in a family hotel for only about 150 florins (approximately $75). Less than that and you're looking at serious budget places.

While it is very hard to recommend a hotel in Amsterdam, one exception is the **Hotel de Filosoof.** Every room is different here, but they are all individually furnished and decorated by the owners in the motif of a different philosopher. Some of the rooms are fantastic, large with glass porches. Try the Wittgenstein room, for example. The neighborhood that this hotel is located in is nothing short of lovely, just off the park and Overtoom. About a ten-minute walk to the casino, but that's like the nicest part of the day.

Hotel de Filosoof, Anna Vondelstraat 6, phone 31-0-20-6833013, *www.xs4all.nl/~filosoof.* Rooms here are among the most reasonable in town, 155 florins for something you'll never forget. Take train #1 from Central Station.

If you do stay at the Hotel de Filosoof, grab a take-a-way from **Khorat Top Thai,** around the corner. Classic Thai food, stupendous, located at C. Huygenstraat 64, phone 020-683-1297, there's some serious papaya salad and Pad Thai noodles here.

The Waterfront Hotel is small, but it has a nice location on the Singel Canal. Every bed is a waterbed, but there's not much in the rooms besides a giant waterbed and a TV. Singel 458, phone 020-623-9775, ask for a room with a window facing the street, the room on the top floor is the one you're seeking. About $80 per night.

Hotel Arrive falls into the serious budget category, but it's friendly and safe. Toilet and shower are in the hallway, but you only have to pay about 75 florins ($35).

Located on Haarlemmerstraat 65–67, phone 020-622-1439.

The hotels that the casino will hook you up with are nice, but pricey. **Amsterdam Marriott,** phone 31–20-607-5555. **American Hotel,** phone 31-20-624-5322. **Golden Tulip Hotel,** phone 31-20-671-7474. **The Parkhotel,** phone 31-20-671-7474. None of these hotels is more than a five-minute walk from the casino, and all are full-service hotels with every amenity. Except the rooms are kind of small. When you call for a reservation, make sure you mention that you are playing in the Master Classics tournament and want the casino discount rate. It's still pricey.

If you really want atmosphere, try the five-star **Hotel Pulitzer,** a hotel comprised of twenty-four seventeenth-century connecting canal houses. 224 different rooms with traditional furniture, $200 to $300 per night. Prinsengracht 315-31, phone 31-20-523-5235.

FOOD

Don't leave town without going to an Indonesian restaurant and getting a *rijstaffel,* which is apparently Indonesian for a lot of everything. You usually need two people to get one of these down.

Kantjil and Tiger, Spuistraat 291, Spui stop trams #1, 2, 5. $20 will get you a *rijstaffel* at one of the most popular places in town with the locals.

This place is one of the latest-opening restaurants in town, packed on the weekends with people coming out of bars. Long wooden tables.

MARIJUANA

It is legal to smoke marijuana in Amsterdam. It's legal. But you don't smoke on the street. Pot smoking is restricted to coffee shops. Anything called a coffee shop in Amsterdam is a place where you can sit and smoke pot. Most of them have pretty good coffee as well, and many serve alcohol.

Marijuana is available in two forms: grass and hashish. Amsterdam is primarily a grass town, in my mind. Despite the availability of lots of hashish, Amsterdam is a grass town because you're not gonna see pot like that anywhere else. And most Americans don't know how to smoke hashish, which requires a little preparation. You can't just stick a piece of hashish in a pipe and smoke it, like you can do with grass.

Pot growing is a connoisseur's art, and there are many horticulturists in the Netherlands who have devoted much time and research to this pursuit. The different names of pot you see represent different varieties of marijuana. They all look, taste, and act upon your mind slightly differently. Some marijuana is very strong. Recommended varieties include White Russian, White Widow, Orange Bud, Edelweiss, and many more. Beware of the Flying Dutchman.

All the marijuana is what it says it is, and is regulated by the government.

You can either buy the weed at the coffee shop and roll your own joint, or most coffee shops have prerolled joints for sale. In Europe, most people mix the pot with tobacco, so if you know that you don't want tobacco, just buy the straight grass joints. Many coffee shops also have water bongs for you to use, if you want. These are easy and clean to smoke out of, just ask.

In general, marijuana can be fun, but be careful. Smoking too much marijuana is no fun at all and can result in vomiting, nausea, dizziness, paranoia, and rapid heartbeat, often all at the same time. Know your limits, and if you don't, go slow.

The nice thing about smoking marijuana in Amsterdam is that it's normal. It's normal to sit and have a coffee and a joint, in a brightly lit atmosphere with pleasant music and conversation, if you want it. It's neither dirty or looked down upon. You'll only arouse people's ire if you smoke it outside, or if you smoke too much and get yourself in real trouble.

Just ask the person behind the counter for the menu. One half to one gram of pot is fine for one joint and one person. More than that, and it's a lot to smoke. The only rule to coffee shops is that you must order something to drink. I guess they want to keep you hydrated. Besides that, it's more than all right to buy pot one place and smoke it somewhere else.

Never attempt to leave Amsterdam with any pot at all. You will end up in jail.

One of the fun things about smoking pot in Amsterdam is going to a lot of different coffee shops. Different coffee shops have different clienteles, different atmospheres, different amenities. Do you like techno music or classical? Do you want to play pool or watch sports? Drink or go on the Internet? They're all over, just look for the sign: COFFEE SHOP.

The coffee shop closest to Holland Casino is the original **Bulldog Coffeeshop**, located on the Leidseplein. There are two bars here, an upstairs bar and a downstairs coffee shop. It's nicer to sit upstairs, even though the drinks are expensive. You can buy your pot downstairs and then go into the upstairs bar to sit and smoke. The Bulldog is open 9 A.M.–1 A.M., try their prerolled pure grass joints (no tobacco), not a bad deal at four for 25 florins ($12).

Besides that, just walk around and you'll find them. The only one to stay out of is the Grasshopper, and many places in the red light district that prey on tourists.

AND . . . Amsterdam is a stupendous book town. Bookworms will love to browse through the eclectic collections of the dusty booksellers that wind through the canals.

Amsterdam is easy to get around in, but buy a map. Also get yourself a strip card, a fifteen-clip tram ticket that will let you wheel around wherever you want to go. It's about $5. Trams are safe, and dead easy to ride.

Don't miss the giant chess games that take place daily in the big square just outside the Holland Casino.

Dean says to me, "Dutch people never complain about the rain. So why do I always buy an umbrella the last day I'm here?"

CHAPTER TEN

PARIS, HELSINKI, SLOVENIA, AND DUBLIN

Paris

THE AVIATION CLUB

Paris is the only place where someone might not like you because you're American. They're much too polite to be rude to you, but I have honestly met very few Frenchmen who have an affinity for Americans. Unless, of course, you speak French. If you speak French, by all means go to Paris.

The Aviation Club is one of the nice places to play in Europe. The host and owner of the club is Frenchman Bruno Fitoussi. Games usually start at six or eight in the evening, until 6 A.M. Everything at the Aviation Club is stellar, from its location on the Avenue des Champs-Élysées—yes, that's right—to the expensively elegant furnishings, to the gourmet dining room, where players retire punctually at ten o'clock when all the games stop and all the chips are left on the table. They retire as a unit to the hundred or so seat dining room where they feast on an elegant five-course meal, followed by brandy and cigars. And then, they return to the tables and continue the games. All of the poker games here are played pot limit. You can also find plenty of backgammon here, backgammon tournaments on Thursday and Saturday nights.

There are, however, a few knocks about this place. If you haven't been personally invited by Bruno, the host, you may find that you are treated somewhat less than special.

It's a fine and a fun place to play, you just have to watch out for yourself, that's all. Some grumbles among seasoned players that the club is mostly interested in your money.

Speaking of money, the club will change your foreign currency to francs in order to play. The rate is far less than you'd get at a bank, but when you change your money they bundle it with a paper clip and write your name on it, saying that they will save the receipt and you can reconvert your francs back at the same rate at the end of the tournament week. What I found, however, is that they only save those receipts for one night. After twenty-four hours it is more than likely that your receipt will have been "lost." So unless you plan on changing your money back into dollars at the end of each night of your stay, go to a bank.

In short, the Aviation Club is too nice a place not to come, but I would stick to the tournament times. First of all, this is because the tournaments are excellent value for the money. Second, the influx of overseas players, in my mind, contributes immensely to the overall atmosphere of the club.

Premier times to come are during their Four Seasons Tournaments, a week each in spring, summer, fall, and winter.

You have to be a member to play here, but it's not difficult. Just call before you come, and then bring your passport. The attire at the Aviation Club is rather formal, men should wear a jacket and tie.

Casino

HOURS Every day from 2 P.M. until 6 A.M., Saturday night open until 9 A.M.

PARLEZ-VOUS FRANÇAIS? The language is French. English spoken.

GAMES ON OFFER Poker, backgammon, baccarat, and blackjack.

LAYOUT Elegant space, with many separate rooms. Lounge, tournament room, cash game room, two dining rooms, bar, backgammon room, and lounge. You'll be comfortable.

FOOD AND DRINK Nothing short of gourmet. Don't miss the sit-down dinner at 10 P.M. which features all the wine you can drink and several courses, including the all-important cheese course. It's delicious, and so much fun to eat leisurely with your fellow players and know that you're not missing any of the action. The set menu is very reasonably priced, as well.

After midnight, you can order Asian food from the kitchen. The Vietnamese *pho* soup is excellent.

Hotel

There are several reasonable hotels within a short walking distance of the Aviation Club. They can help you with a reservation. I can recommend the Hotel Lord Byron.

Hotel Arc Élysées, 45 Rue de Washington, 33-1-4563-6933, $100.

Paris Marriott, 70 Avenue des Champs-Élysées, 33-1-5393-5500, $300.

Hotel Balzac, 6 Rue Balzac, 33-1-4561-9722, $200.

Hotel Chateaubriand, 6 Rue Chateaubriand, 33-1-4076-0050, $150.

Hotel Lord Byron, 5 Rue Chateaubriand, 33-1-4359-8998, $100.

 PRACTICALITIES
Casino Phone Number: 33-1-4562-2688, fax: 33-1-4289-2181

Internet Address: *eppa.bigfoot.com/ACF* or *www.european-poker.com/ACF*

Location: Aviation Club de France, located on 104 Avenue des Champs-Élysées, right on the main drag. You have to walk up a flight of steps, through a glass door on the street.

Helsinki

CASINO RAY

I'm loving the saunas in Helsinki. I'm loving the saunas, and the reindeer sandwiches, and the exhibition of antique slot machines that they have in the classy third-floor casino at Casino Ray. Finn poker players are polite, gentlemanly, and they know how to drink. And I mean drink. Haven't you ever wondered where the expression the Crazy Finn came from? A nice bunch of guys, really.

And the casino does it up during their two tournament weeks, they are really good hosts up there and you will enjoy it in the cold as much as you will enjoy it in the midnight sun. Free breakfasts and Poker Christmas Party, which is reportedly one hell of a bash. Jyrki Sinisalo is the poker manager, a friendly guy who does a good job. The casino is in the hotel, and it's a nice enough hotel. The rooms are not that big, but the sauna is excellent. Nice town to walk around in, especially if you like old books. The only universal knock about Finland is the food. The country just can't seem to get it right in the culinary department.

Call in advance of coming to guarantee your hotel room and place in the tournaments. Helsinki is seven hours ahead of Eastern Standard Time. Or just go to their Web site.

Casino

HOURS Daily from noon until 4 A.M.

LANGUAGE Finnish, but don't worry. English is widely spoken. Strangely enough, the only language in the world that Finnish is remotely similar to is Hungarian. Go figure.

LAYOUT Casino is on the second floor of the hotel. It's a nice space, considering the fact that it is one large windowless room.

GAMES ON OFFER Poker, slots, blackjack, roulette.

FOOD AND DRINK Eh. Portions are small, but haven't you always wanted to try smoked reindeer?

Hotel

The casino is located inside the Hotel Ramada Presidentti. Call the casino for reservations, or call the hotel and mention the poker rate. About $140 for a double room, nothing special. Don't miss the sauna.

 PRACTICALITIES
Casino Phone Number: 358-9-680-800, fax: 358-9-694-2922
Internet Address: *www.casino.ray.fi*
Location: Casino Ray, Helsinki, in the center of town. Etelainen Rautatiekatu 4. Try and say that ten times fast.

Nova Gorica, Slovenia

HIT HOTEL CASINO PARK

First of all, Slovenia is not a war-ridden country. There hasn't been a war there for a long time, and the city of Nova Gorica is beautiful. The war stuff is happening south and east of Slovenia in those other Balkans. Nova Gorica is only about an hour from Venice in Italy, and four hours drive from Vienna. Consequently, the casino gets more than its fair share of mad Italian playboy gamblers. The nearest airports are either Trieste or Venice, and the casino is more than happy to help you arrange transportation. In addition, starting in the year 2000, the tournament will be preceded by an Adriatic gambling cruise, leaving from Venice. Visit the EPPA website for details at *http://eppa.bigfoot.com*, as a gambling cruise followed up by a few days in Italy and topped off with a week in Slovenia is not a bad vacation. Actually, it would be hard to do better.

The casino is lavish, and they go all out to service visiting player gamblers. During the tournament one year, some British players called and said that as their plane was delayed from England, they weren't sure if they would make it in time for the tournament start. The poker director calmly waited to start the tournament until they had arrived. Now, that's service.

All the games are on offer here, and the daily poker tournaments are a highlight of the tournament time. The friendly and helpful poker manager is Stasko Stibilj. By contacting the casino, you can have all of your travel arrangements taken care of for you. The casino is called the Hit Hotel Casino Park, and it is located inside the Park Hotel complex.

 PRACTICALITIES
Casino Phone Number: Sala Poker at 386-65-126-2341, ask for Stasko. Fax: 386-65-28-470
Accommodations Phone Number: Call Hittours International at 386-65-28-202, fax: 386-65-28-204
E-mail: *stasko@hit.si*
Internet Address: *www.hit.si*
Location: Delpinova 5, Nova Gorica, Slovenia. Thirty minutes from Trieste and just over an hour from Venice.

Dublin

THE MERRION CLUB

Ah, who wouldn't want to visit Dublin in the springtime? Ireland is the first place in Europe where Texas Hold'em was introduced, via Irish gambling legend Terry Rogers, who made fame in the seventies and eighties by booking the World Series of Poker and being the first man to successfully do so. The Irish Open is run by his protégé, a gambling legend in his own right, Liam Flood, whose reputation for honesty and hospitality is enough to guarantee the quality of the Irish Open solely on those merits. But the Irish have been known to have a bit of fun.

The Irish Open is held every Easter weekend in Dublin, Thursday thru Sunday. Besides stellar hospitality, free full buffets every day, cash games and satellites, and Irish crystal trophies for tournament winners, the tournament hosts arrange for all visiting players to attend the horse races. It's a party, Irish style.

Casino

The tournament is held at the Merrion Club, downtown Dublin.

HOURS Gaming tables daily from 3 P.M. until 8 A.M.

LANGUAGE Irish (some English spoken).

Hotel

Lots of hotels within walking distance of the club. Call Liam Flood for assistance reservations. To name a few:

Buswell's Molesworth Street, 353-1-676-4013, $100.
Davenport Merrion Square, 353-1-607-3860, $160.
Harcourt, Harcourt Street, 353-1-478-3677, $70.
Merrion Hotel, 353-1-603-0600, $250.

 PRACTICALITIES
Casino Phone Number: 353-1-628-6246. Ask for tournament director Liam Flood.
Location: 81 Merrion Square, Dublin 2, Ireland.

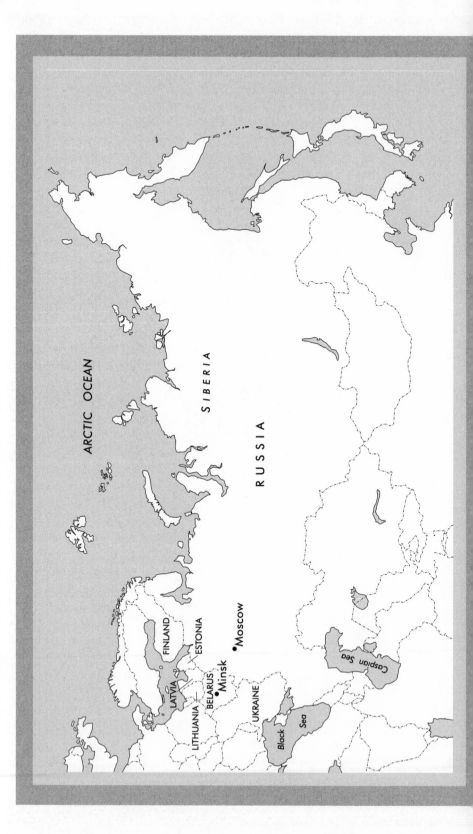

THE EASTERN BLOC

PART

4

CHAPTER ELEVEN

MOSCOW, RUSSIA

LAY OF THE LAND

Walking out of customs in the Moscow Airport and into the pitch-black Siberian winter, I only wanted one thing: a man in a suit holding a sign with my name on it. I got my wish.

A series of points and arm sweeps led us to a car, a Russian Bona, somewhere between a 1972 Volvo and an '84 Datsun, which sputtered to life in the below-living temperature of the Moscow airport outdoor parking lot. Part of driving in Moscow, I soon found out, is to scare the piss out of the person in the passenger seat.

Four men in a car. Two men have guns. One man has $100,000 wrapped in black plastic. I have a notebook, a pen, and my Russian bear hat. We're driving through the streets of Moscow and leaning on the horn. The burly Russian chauffeur has a Madonna tape stuck in the deck and "Crazy for You" is playing. He looks at me. "Crazy for you," he says. He means, of course, life. Life is crazy for you. He should know.

Hair on your ass. That's what I call Moscow. Not dangerous exactly. Just get a little hair on your ass, as the Luma Kid likes to say. I have to tell you, it's my kind of town.

Moscow, Russia
GENERAL INFORMATION

YOU'RE NOT IN KANSAS ANYMORE There's no Iron Curtain anymore, but if there was, Moscow would still be behind it. As far as gambling goes, however, the only comparison for Moscow today is Las Vegas in the 1940s. It's wild, there's a lot of money around, and you have to be very smart to get ahold of it. And careful.

WHERE Moscow is the capital of Russia, located in eastern Europe but western Russia. The city is large, easy to travel in, and quite exotic. In a Russian sort of way.

WHEN The Russians like to gamble. A lot of Russians like to gamble, and there is no best season for gambling, per se. But if this poker tournament continues, and there is no reason why it shouldn't, then the Casino Cosmos is clearly the place to be come the end of October.

CLIMATE Cold is not an appropriate word for the way Moscow gets in the winter. You will not be making a moral choice about whether or not to wear fur, you will reach for it as an absolute necessity, for that's the only way to stay warm in Russia. A fur hat does wonders for your overall body temperature when outdoors, with a good fur coat you could probably sleep outside. Or at least with the window open.

TELEPHONES Some of the hotels have international pay phones that take credit cards. Even though it may be expensive, you'll be happier with a cell phone in Moscow. That's what everybody else uses. Bring a cell phone. Mostly, Russia is not the easiest place to make contact with the rest of the world. In Moscow, my European cell phone worked like a charm, even if it was a tad expensive.

CURRENCY Rubles are used for everything Russian. Dollars are used for business, and everything else. Leaving Russia with rubles is like buying expensive wallpaper. The ruble is a wildly fluctuating currency. At the time of my visit, $1 = 27 rubles.

MONEY Moscow is a dual currency society, with two separate lives. There are dollars, and there are rubles. And some things are priced in dollars and some are priced in rubles.

Getting Money out of the Country: You are not allowed to carry out more money than you bring in. That's the law, and it bodes ill for your potential gambling winnings. The quick answer is: Go shopping.

I do, however, know people who have circumvented this law with success. And as I have I recently read that in the neighborhood of several hundred million dollars is funneled out of Russia illegally every month, it appears that more than a few people have circumvented this law more than once.

Many people attempt to carry the money out without declaring it. Mandy, who's done it many times with varying degrees of success in amounts ranging up to about $100,000 at a time, gives the following advice. "Don't have it on your person, for they may pat you down everywhere, including your crotch. Roll it up in a suit or shirt and have it in your carry-on luggage, as they may open your bag and rifle through it, but they probably won't unroll and unwrap it."

Apparently the casino manager can give you a special form that declares that you won the money in a casino and can now carry it out of the country. My gut instinct is that this is a bad idea, because the first thing that this does is to alert the customs officer that you have a gigantic wad of cash in your suitcase.

Transferring the money out is probably your best option. The poker room can help to arrange money transfers to your foreign bank for only about a 3 percent service charge. This is fair and it works. There are also branches of many international banks around town. Not all banks will transfer money for you, but if your bank is there, you may be in luck.

One fellow I'm with, the German fuckin' wonder, is standing in a bank on his last day in Moscow arguing about $1,000. He finds a bank that appears willing to put $25,000 in his bank account in another country for $26,000, and he says, "Too much." The man's other option is to carry it out through customs and hope they don't stop him, and I'm sitting there, saying, "I'd pay, I'd pay, I mean we're in fuckin' Moscow." In the end he carried it out and reports are he made it back safely.

I also know people who have mailed their money out. They go to the American Express office and buy Travelers Cheques and mail them out of the country. If the checks are lost, then they can report them as lost to American Express. I have known some people who buy checks, and then rip them up and flush them down the toilet. Then they can definitely report them as lost to American Express when they get home.

ATMS Some of the casinos have ATM machines that take most ATM card varieties, and credit cards. These machines seem to be working fairly, and you can get money in dollars or rubles.

YAH NYEH GUHVARYU (MNOGAH) PAH-ROOSKEE (I don't speak Russian) English is an okay language to get by on in most of Moscow. However, when hailing a private cab, don't expect the driver to speak a word of English. Be prepared to point on a map or have the address written down, in Russian. Price is negotiated by finger counting.

SAFETY Moscow isn't as dangerous as it sounds. You can travel all over with absolute freedom, though at night there's no reason not to have a driver who doubles as an armed bodyguard. No reason at all. Because in Moscow you can get someone who speaks a little English and knows the town and has a car and a gun all for about $10 an hour. But you don't need it. You can walk out of the Hotel Cosmos at 2 A.M. and stand in the street and hail down a passing car and get a ride anywhere in town for 200 rubles, providing you can communicate to the driver where you are going. It makes good sense to never get in a car that already has more than one person in it.

As far as guns go, there don't seem to be a lot of random hijackings. The people with guns are the ones in business, and they have more important concerns than you. The people driving around with guns are not concerned with you. They're just trying to keep from getting robbed or killed themselves. But you see, they're in business. If you're not in business in Moscow, you don't have to worry. You don't have to worry at all.

As a tourist, the thing you really have to worry about is getting stopped by a policeman and being asked for your passport and visa, which you must have. Regardless, it is usually just a question of how much it will cost you, discreetly: $20 or $50 is a lot of money in this spot.

Three in the morning, a random part of Moscow—very random—and our taxi driver is stopping to ask two men standing on a corner next to a liquor shop for directions. He has no idea where we're going. I think it might be his first time in Moscow. In nine out of ten towns in the world, you'd be thinking about getting rolled and robbed around this time. Three in the morning. Deserted streets, stopped car, and three men with you and your buddy having a lot of cash. But in Russia, it's just not like that. They think they're ripping you off, thinking that $8 that you offered them is so much money that they would drive you to China to get it. They ain't gonna rob you. Moscow is funny like that.

WHAT THEY WEAR Glittering long-legged blondes in designer everything. Straight out of a designer mall. Not exactly tasteful, but everything is the most expensive. If you're there in winter, the country is leather and fur, and I figure you might as well go to Moscow in winter because that's what the damn country is all about.

You will need a hat and warm socks, but don't worry. You can get yourself a black Russian bear hat on the Kremlin steps for about $10, $20 if you look really cold. If you get a good guide when you go to the Kremlin, he'll tell you a story about when Napoleon invaded Moscow. Napoleon had prepared for everything. But he had not prepared for the Moscow winter. And after six weeks he took his army and he left, he just couldn't take it. They left everything there, including their cannons. It was just too cold. That's why the animal rights movement doesn't really cut it in this town. You need fur to stay warm. And if you walk the streets and ride the Metros, you see that everybody wears a fur coat and a fur hat. Everybody has one, just to stay warm. And those Metros are about four hundred feet underground, way down there, and it's usually warm down there and the Russians, they sit all packed together in those tubes and they never unbutton their coats or remove their fur hats, and they never sweat. It's amazing, really.

TIPPING IN TOWN The town is wide open. You must use money to get what you want. Tip when appropriate, and tip well when appropriate. I always feel that if you are tipping someone who you will be seeing again, tip them extremely well the first time.

INTERNET Good luck. Good luck getting on the Internet. You could have a laptop computer that plugs into a cellular phone, but if you bring a laptop computer in or out of the country, they may confiscate it or all of your software. The Radisson Slavjanskaya allows guests to connect to their Internet server for ten cents per minute. Go there if you're desperate.

I'll Walk There Barefoot
TRANSPORTATION ISSUES

LEGAL Everyone visiting Russia needs a visa. Unless you're from Hungary, like my friend Tibor. He says Russia has a "long and friendly" relationship with Hungarians. With a smile. If you're American, getting a visa to Moscow involves a little bit more than going to the embassy and paying cash. Although in some countries, this might do the trick. You need an official invitation, and these are not so difficult to get, as this would accompany a room reservation. You can get an official invitation either from a casino or a hotel. Your purpose for going is pleasure and tourism. Once you get your invitation, then you can go about the process of getting a visa.

CIBT, Inc., 25 W. 43rd Street, Suite 1420, New York, NY 10036. Phone

1-800-925-2428, 1-212-575-2811. They will organize your visa only or visa and flights. $40 service fee. This is what you want, rather than having to go to the Russian Embassy in America, where they might take you for a defector. This agency has received very good reports. Other than that, call around. If you are not in America, just take your official invitation to the local Russian Embassy.

FLIGHTS I've heard Aeroflot, the Russian airline, is quite good and actually has new planes, contrary to what you would think. I'm still not flying them yet, though. They wanted to spruce up their image so they had an official smile day, where every employee and stewardess had to smile all the time. The obvious question is: What happened the next day?

AIRPORT I got there to experience the airport in all its beauty. Night, in the dead of winter. Not a smile to be found.

Female customs officer sets a new standard in sternness. Smiling is not going to help you here. Just make sure your papers are in order. This is not the country to be arriving in without an up-to-date visa and passport.

The customs forms: One of the tricks they try in Moscow is to get you to not fill in a customs form. This would be a mistake. There's always two lines. One long line with a red light that is for people with something to declare. And one green line with one person standing there that is for nothing to declare. If you travel through the green line on your way in, then you won't get a customs form at all, and then you're in danger of getting very screwed on your way out. Trust me, you have something to declare. Yourself, for instance.

Pick up a few extra customs forms on your way in. Just in case. Just in case that when you're leaving Moscow it's not the day a customs official has run around and picked up all the English customs forms and thrown them in the wastebasket so there's nothing left but Russian customs forms and then you'll fill it in wrong and have to pay. Just one of the scams they got going at the airport.

The most important declaration you make on your entrance into Russia is the one about how much money you are carrying with you. Make sure to declare every dollar you have! Because the official law is that you are not allowed to carry out any more than you bring in. So if you don't have a stamped entry form with some money declared on it, they can reasonably confiscate everything you've got on your way out.

Item 3.1 on the customs declarations reads: "National and other currency in cash, currency valuables, articles made of precious stones in any form or condition. Yes or No." Mark "Yes." And then in the chart under it, write how much money you have on you in words and numbers and currency. You must also record your mobile phone and laptop computer.

A note about laptop computers. There are people who travel with laptop computers in and out of Russia successfully. But you should know the risks. They have a problem with software piracy, so it is a possibility that they could erase or confiscate any software you have. And it's not a stretch of the imagination that they would threaten to confiscate your computer or empty your hard drive. As with anywhere else in Russia, if you remain calm and discreetly offer money, then your problem will eventually be solved in your favor. But I wouldn't travel there with a laptop unless it was a necessity, and I'd make sure everything was backed up and insured before I left.

Moscow duty-free is a joke—they're not charging you duty, but they charge you what they call a tax for being stuck in a small place with no other options. Moscow Airport is a different country than the rest of Moscow. At least that's the main place where you will still meet up with bureaucracy in all its stifling forms. Don't lose heart, just get through it.

Never walk through the green fast track—never ever go through the fast track. Always declare.

STREETS They run all over the place. You'll need a map.

WHERE THINGS ARE Lots of interesting things are found in and around Red Square, including the Kremlin. The American Express office is on a big street called Sadova Kuvrinska, #9. That sounds just the way it looks. It's a big street.

TRANSPORTATION AROUND TOWN In the daytime, the Metro is the easiest and most colorful way to travel about, and you can get anywhere for 4 rubles, about sixteen cents. Stand in line the first time you go in the Metro and buy a ticket for 50 rubles or so. You swipe your ticket through the turnstile when you enter the Metro station, and it subtracts 4 rubles off your card. The same way it works in New York. That way you won't have to stand in line at the ticket window every time you go through the Metro. The ticket lines can get quite long.

The nice thing about riding the Metro is you get to hang with the Russians, and the Metro is very clean, safe, and orderly. You'll get lost a few times, as there isn't really anything in English. It's all about reading maps and pictograms. Anyway, it's fun to ride around and see all the people in their fur coats and hats.

The Metro system has about ten interconnecting lines, each of which is a different color and name. One of the lines is a circle line, and all the other lines look like spokes on that wheel. It's not that hard, you just need a little patience.

The other way to get around town is by private taxi. If you get a taxi from the front desk of the hotel, you'll pay a bundle. If you are staying at the Cosmos and playing in the poker room, they can get you a driver with a car at a very reasonable price. And don't forget the armed body-guard option.

It is also quite easy and by all reports very safe to just hail down a car as a taxi. Basically, in Moscow, every car is a taxi. For everyone. There are very few marked taxis in Moscow. Everyone is riding around and happy to pick someone up because then they have money for gas, it seems. Sit in the back, because it's an insult to put on your seat belt.

The taxi price from the Casino Cosmos to and from the airport is about $40, which is fair considering it's at least a forty-minute ride.

The streets in Moscow aren't that nice for driving around. First of all, there are no traffic laws. It's one giant mayhem on the streets, and driving is at best a hair-raising experience. At its worst, it's one traffic jam after another, congestion, smog, and dirty snow. Driving gets a lot better at night.

In the day, take the Metro and walk. At night, take a car.

The Money Plays
GAMBLING SETUP—THE QUICK FACTS

CASINOS There are about forty-five casinos in Moscow, but there's no reason to pay attention to most of them. Stick to the good ones in the good places. Stuff does go on. I would stick to the Casino Cosmos. Corona Casino, Cherry Casino, Crystal Palace, and Golden Palace are also good casinos. The Cherry Casino has an especially nice atmosphere, located in the Metelista Entertainment Complex.

HOURS Most casinos in Moscow are twenty-four hours. Gambling is a late-night activity, the casino ranks don't swell until after 8 P.M., at the earliest.

ADMITTANCE Admittance is for anyone who can get past the security and the metal detector. They'll probably ask for your passport the first time. They may ask for your passport every time. You are supposed to be eighteen, but some of the dealers are under that for sure, so I don't know. Scowling usually helps. There is no official dress code, but it helps to be presentable. A jacket and tie is not out of place.

AMBIANCE AND AMENITIES Free food, free drinks, free caviar, free cigarettes. What more could they do?

GAMES ON OFFER Blackjack, roulette, Caribbean stud, and poker. And maybe a wheel of "money in the ditch."

LIMITS From $5 minimum to about $500. Bigger limits are definitely available on request. The $10,000 buy-in pot limit five-card stud game at the Casino Cosmos, for instance.

MONEY Gambling in the casinos takes place in dollars. They have dollar chips, and that's what you buy in and cash out for.

LEGALITY They're legal. I mean, the good ones are secure and will pay you if you win. And it's not that they operate within the law. In most cases, they are the law.

TIPPING POLICIES IN THE CASINO Dealers seem to appreciate tips. They get paid about $300 a month, which most of them are thrilled with. But I always found the dealers appreciative and friendly when I tipped, most of them are quite professional in any respect. You have to be very professional to be a dealer in Moscow because Russian gamblers can be very emotional. I'll leave it at that.

AND . . . "There is a rule in Russian casinos," Mandy told me. "Never ask where the money's from."

In Moscow, you must yell to get things done. People don't do things unless they're scared or have no choice.

I'll Take the Odds
BREAKING APART THE GAME

SLOTS There are a few joints in the center of town that aren't open twenty-four hours, but they are mostly slot halls and not worth bothering with. What do you think, the slots are loose? Put your money in a drainage pipe if you have to.

POKER It was a big success for the Casino Cosmos's Inaugural Poker tournament. More than seventy adventurers representing twenty different countries showed up for the amenities and stayed for the poker. Players enjoyed the benefits of free food, free drinks, and free accommodation. All generously supplied by Australian poker boss Jeff Lissandro and his accomplished staff. Tournament coordinators Mel Judah and

Marsha Waggoner worked overtime to ensure that every player's wishes were catered to. The pioneer spirit and preferential treatment that players received was reminiscent of the old days at Binion's Horseshoe in Las Vegas. Where else but Moscow do you snap your fingers for vodka and black caviar on toast and then look down and find someone has raised the pot with you holding a set of aces?

Everybody who made the trip will return for the next tournament without hesitation, because Lissandro went overboard to ensure that players had no reason to be apprehensive.

Money transfers out of the country were aided by Lissandro himself. Hotel and casino security guards are the twenty-four-hour norm both at the casino entrance and hotel elevator entrance. Players were met and delivered from and to the airport by chauffeured cars and bodyguards. Even a sight-seeing trip was arranged by the Cosmos staff for players who could find time between the twenty-four-hour pot limit Omaha and Hold'em action to check out the Kremlin and eight hundred years of Russian history.

Between the twenty-four-hour buffet in the main casino, and the lavish spread set out in the poker room during each daily tournament, it was difficult to find anything to use money for—except of course for the games, which were fast and furious. The locals showed little hesitation in plunging into games that they "learned as they went."

In order to come to Moscow to play or participate in the Cosmos poker week, you must contact the poker room directly. Maria Kournikova is the very friendly poker room coordinator, fax her at +(7095) 215-7980, or fax the casino director Vadim Bereslavsky at +(7095) 234-1078. Tell her what dates you would like to come and passport information and she will fax you back an invitation.

They do play Hold'em and Omaha here, but the main game is five-card stud played with a stripped deck. Twos through sixes are removed from the deck, leaving only thirty-two cards. The game is then played pot limit. A straight beats a flush. It takes a bit of getting used to, and the Russians play this game pretty well.

Well, leave it to an Australian to bring good American casino know-how to Moscow. Although from what I hear, they been gambling in Australia just about as long as they have in the States. And its history is just as wild.

Enter Young Jeff Lissandro, who is barely old enough to be a floor-man, let alone hobnobbing with gnarly-toothed KGB mobsters squeezing millions from the local poker action. But Young Jeff can run a poker game. And he may be the only one in the world with the know-how to keep a $10,000 buy-in pot-limit five-card stripped deck stud game going virtually twenty-four hours a day in the murky regions of Moscow. He knows how to do it, Young Jeff has been running poker games around the world since he was sixteen years old. Now he's thirty-five and in Russia.

Jeff stays at the Marriott, which he says is the only hotel where the security can't be bought, and he rents the poker room out from the Casino Cosmos owners for a pretty steep fee, payment of which is dependent on the poker room's monthly proceeds. But he runs a fair game, and if you go to Moscow to play poker, if you go for the tournament, he will take care of you. Completely. And you can count on him if you get in a tough spot.

For the day-to-day tournament details, Lissandro brought over two more Australians, names well known on the international poker scene. Both Marsha Waggoner and Mel Judah have well deserved reputations for honesty and efficiency, two qualities you will most appreciate if you make the trip.

BLACKJACK The blackjack rules are in general very liberal in Moscow, featuring early surrender and the dealer sticking on soft seventeen. They are aware of the existence of card counters, knowledge occasioned in the last several years by one man in particular who reportedly won a figure totaling several million. Despite this, they are still a little stubborn about the possibility of someone beating the casino at blackjack in the long run. However, I would not want to be a person barred from a Moscow casino and also be expecting to get paid. In that case, I'd settle for getting back to my hotel safely. I played a great deal of blackjack in Moscow, was paid every time I won, and received nothing but friendly treatment. But if you're really good, you should be careful.

ROULETTE Roulette features only one zero throughout Moscow, and in some places they have twenty-five- and fifty-cent chips, so this is a very good place to play the game. The wheels look fair to me. Have fun.

CARIBBEAN STUD Don't bother. I'm told it's only a 5 percent edge, but that's still more than any other game in the house.

Casinos and Lodging
THE POINT

HOTEL AND CASINO COSMOS
Two great things about staying at the Hotel Cosmos. It's safe, and the casino is right downstairs. Just make sure you get a room with a working

refrigerator. Although that's generally the kind of thing you'll just have to hope for. I consider the Cosmos a good place to stay for a first time in Moscow. It's not overly touristy, and there's enough of the real Moscow here to satisfy, including overweight men with large gold teeth who smile unconvincingly while betting the size of the pot in an Omaha game.

Casino

HOURS Twenty-four hours.

LANGUAGE Russian, and enough people speak English so that you will be fine. A person who speaks only German will have some trouble in Moscow, as was evidenced by my good friend who couldn't even find a good German speaker at the Moscow branch of Bank Austria, where he was trying to transfer some money to Vienna. In the end, he just carried it out with him.

LAYOUT Nice casino, metal detector, good security. The casino is a nice space. Of course, there's the metal detector, and a complete search, if they feel it's necessary. Every once in a while you'll see three older guys in suits come in and walk through the metal detector and it goes *bleep, bleep, bleep,* and no one stops them. They're the owners of the casino. There's a coat check at the casino entrance, but the coat guy is sometimes a bit obstinate. If you have a bag to check as well, a dollar up front will usually placate him, a fiver is a lot of money in a tight spot. Moscow is a question of who you have to pay how much.

The table games are all in the center room, and then there is a dining area in the back of the casino with a buffet and a big-screen TV permanently tuned in to Eurosport. There's a separate room for poker with its own bar.

GAMES Blackjack, roulette, Caribbean stud, poker.

LIMITS $5 to $100, $10 to $200, $25 to $500 blackjack, roulette fifty-cent chips up to $25 on a number and a few hundred on the outside. Higher roulette limits can certainly be arranged.

RULES AND NOTES I don't think the raffle is on the square. It's one of those things where I'm not sure, but I'd be willing to lay 9–1 against. Raffle tickets are handed out very liberally every week and drawn for a small car on Sunday nights at midnight. You might win one of the smaller prizes, but I don't think you're gonna win the car. No matter how many raffle tickets you might have. And if you play blackjack, you're liable to get a lot of them because you get a ticket for every blackjack.

FOOD AND DRINK The best thing to get is caviar on toast. The food off the menu is fine and reasonably priced. The casino buffet is very Russian, but not very spectacular. The breakfast buffet in the hotel restaurant is a nice spread.

THE PEOPLE THERE The Casino Cosmos is a very local place. Mostly Russians gambling. And the main poker action in Moscow.

Hotel

The hotel room rate varies, but in my opinion, is always a fair price for Moscow. I mean, the rooms are nothing to shout about, believe me they are nothing to shout about, but they are clean and they are fairly well equipped. They are wooden Panaflex from the seventies, or late sixties, and the hot water, on the right, may be brown for three seconds when you turn it on. No matter—you're in Moscow. And when you get the view at night from the hotel windows, the tower lit up over Moscow, if it's your first time in Moscow, it's a beautiful city.

The casino rate is only about $50 per night. This is obviously exceptional value. 1,700 rooms, this place is big.

Another bright spot is your safety. Guests are meticulously checked for room keys and reservation cards on their way to the elevators. You are probably not in danger in this place. Twenty-six stories.

Bowling alley downstairs, seven days a week from 2 P.M. to 10:30.

Rooms usually come with a buffet breakfast, which is a pretty nice spread in a very Russian way. The buffet: What's that, what's that, what is that? But it's buffet, so a great time to try out some real farfels and strange rolled cheeses and meats plus blintzes with sour cream and everything else under the sun.

 PRACTICALITIES
Hotel Phone Number: 7095-234-1206, 7095-215-6791
Casino Phone Number: fax: 7095-215-7980, attention Maria Kournikova
Location: Prospectus Mira 150, Moscow. A little bit north of the downtown area, the Cosmos isn't really in walking distance to anywhere. But the Metro stop is just across the street from the hotel, and from there you can get anywhere very easily for 2 rubles. About forty minutes from the airport, and a good twenty-minute ride to downtown because of the traffic hassles. The Metro is the best way for getting around.

RADISSON SLAVJANSKAYA HOTEL

This is a nice and safe hotel to stay at, and an excellent place to come for first run American movies. Every seat in the lovely five-hundred-seat theater is equipped with an individual headset for simultaneous translation during the film. If you don't understand Arnold Schwarzenegger's brand of English. $8 ticket, $2 popcorn, look in the English-language paper under "American House of Cinema" for listings.

Casino

The Grand Prix Casino is located here, but reports have not been so encouraging. You're better off playing at the Casino Cosmos.

FOOD AND DRINK Excellent but pricey casual sushi bar in a Japanese garden, favorite of Russians in the know when they have the money. Also an American steak house here.

Hotel

407 guest rooms and 24 suites. King-size or double beds, individual air-conditioning and heating control, direct dial international telephones with personal voicemail and computer port, cable/satellite TV, in-room minirefrigerators, and work area. Superior rooms and suites feature hair dryers, bathrobes, coffee makers, and upgraded amenities. Health club with weights, pool, sauna, and massage services. Rack rates standard room, single or double, $155. Superior rooms start around $230. Ask for their Internet promotion rate. Access to the hotel's Internet server at a minimal charge—currently ten cents per minute.

PRACTICALITIES
Hotel Phone Number: 7-095-941-8020, 7-502-224-1225, fax: 7-502-224-1225, 7-095-240-3217. From the U.S., 1-800-333-3333
Internet: *www.radisson.com*
Location: 1 Berezhkovskaya Naberezhnaya, 121059 Moscow, very near to Metro and rail stations. Close to town, forty minutes to the airport.

MARRIOTT MOSCOW GRAND HOTEL

This is where President Clinton stayed. That's the first thing you need to know about the $300 per night Marriott, which is unquestionably the safest hotel in town. This is a nice hotel, but you don't need to stay here. Built in 1997.

Casino

No casino.

THE PEOPLE THERE Anybody who's anyone.

Hotel

ROOM	RACK RATES (USD)	
	SINGLE	DOUBLE
Deluxe	315	315
Concierge	345	345
Junior Suite	700	700
Ambassador Suite	1150	1150
Presidential Suite	1400	1400

All room rates do not include applicable taxes (currently 20 percent). Facilities: three restaurants, theme buffets, Russian tavern, lobby lounge, health club, wet and dry sauna, indoor pool, Jacuzzi, beauty salon, retail shops.

PRACTICALITIES
Hotel Phone Number: 7-502-935-8500, fax: 7-502-935-8501
Location: In the center of town. Not far from the Red Square, and where everything's happening. 26 Tverskaya Street, 103050 Moscow, Russia.

Entertainment and Nightlife

By the time I'd been in Moscow six days, I'd heard Night Flight mentioned eight times by seven different people. So I was glad to have the opportunity to visit it on my last night in the Ponderosa city.

It's downtown, it's open late, and there's no bones about it. Entrance at night is about $20 per person, but this gets you a free drink. I think it's free during the day, where you can just go to eat lunch upstairs and pick up a prostitute on your way back down, if you want. You don't have to get a prostitute if you don't want to. Don't worry. You can just eat, drink, dance, and check things out. Night Flight is open noon–5 A.M. Restaurant till 4 A.M. 550 rubles entrance. Prostitutes about $200, they all look like models. Apparently you should always negotiate. Then you take them back to your hotel.

Cheaper prostitutes, and not as good-looking ones either (although I thought most women in Moscow were beautiful), can be found at the American bar Chesterfields for $50–$100, or at the twenty-four-hour bar in the Casino Cosmos, about $100. Prostitution is very legal.

FOOD Some kind of meat, some kind of fish, something with cheese, something with sauce. Most of the food you eat will fall into these categories. Most of your meals will be something like this. You sort of know what you're eating, but you don't know exactly what you're eating. It tastes different than anything you've ever had before, but not especially good or bad. Unless you're having caviar on toast. And really, there's no time of the day you shouldn't be having this. For breakfast, caviar on buttered toast and *chai* (tea) with milk. For a snack, caviar on buttered toast and *chai* with milk. For a light dinner, two orders of caviar on buttered toast and *chai* with milk. Late night, vodka and caviar.

The Russian word for caviar is *Ikra*, pronounced *(ee KRA)*, and the way they eat it is best—spread on toast with butter. The black caviar is from sturgeon, the orange caviar is bigger and is from salmon. The salmon caviar is saltier as well, if you can believe that. Beluga is the top-grade caviar from sturgeon, and you can get it pretty cheap if you look around. I saw a one-kilogram box for $100, and I was told I could get it at half that. But that's a lot of caviar. You could have one awful big party with that. Most caviar comes in 50 or 100 gram containers. While you're in Russia, however, be sure to take advantage of the fact that you can eat star quality caviar at every meal for virtually nothing. It is truly the food of kings.

SIGHTSEEING The sightseeing trip was a question of extremes. Every poker player was thinking the same thing. "I'm bad, but I ain't that bad." Never have you seen a more motley and tired rag-tag bunch of don't give a fuck sight-seers who were too embarrassed to go back home and admit they'd been to Moscow and never left the damn hotel. We just wanted to see the Kremlin and get back to the tables—or bed, for that matter. But the Cosmos poker room set us up good. They set us up with an English-speaking guide on the steps of the Kremlin, the man was a Russian history professor, and for $6 each our group of two Swedes, three Finns, four Brits, and an American learned more about Russian culture than you can imagine. All in subzero weather.

The Kremlin is a must when in Moscow, give yourself about two hours and get a guide. The Diamond Fund, where they have all the state jewels, is not really worth the $10 extra to go in there. Much of Russia's jewels and gold has been systematically stolen.

SHOPPING I think Moscow is a shopper's paradise. I mean, aside from the fact that they don't make a wide variety of things well. But they make some nice caviar, *Matrushkas*, and everything having to do with fur. Hats, coats, and gloves.

I picked up my first hat at the Kremlin. It was actually my first time outside, we were all standing in the lobby waiting for the tour buses to get arranged and I had said, "What is it outside anyway, like zero or something?" And a Brit had turned and laughed at me and said, "Try thirty below." I said, "What? Thirty below? What the hell is that?" And I still don't know if he was talking Celsius or Fahrenheit.

The illegal CD market is alive and well in Moscow. Pick up pirated American CDs on the street and in Metro stations for 70–80 rubles, less if you buy volume and bargain, great value at less than $3. And even if the cases are defective, the quality of the discs is fine. I brought home about fifteen, for $30.

Matrushkas are those carved wooden dolls that are actually dolls inside dolls, in some cases, up to ten or I've even heard of thirty-five dolls snuggled together in one. They are distinctly Russian, the nice ones are hand-painted and -lacquered, and they make a great souvenir or even better gift. There's some shops downtown around the Red Square that specialize in *Matrushkas,* but I had trouble finding them. Give yourself some time.

Izmailovsky outdoor shopping park is only open on weekends and is huge. Hundreds of stalls selling everything. Take the Metro to Izmailovsky Park.

OTHER STUFF

CIGARS Good cigars are cheap and plentiful, read Cubans, and you can smoke them in the poker room and casino with reckless abandon. You can smoke all over Moscow with reckless abandon, and most people do.

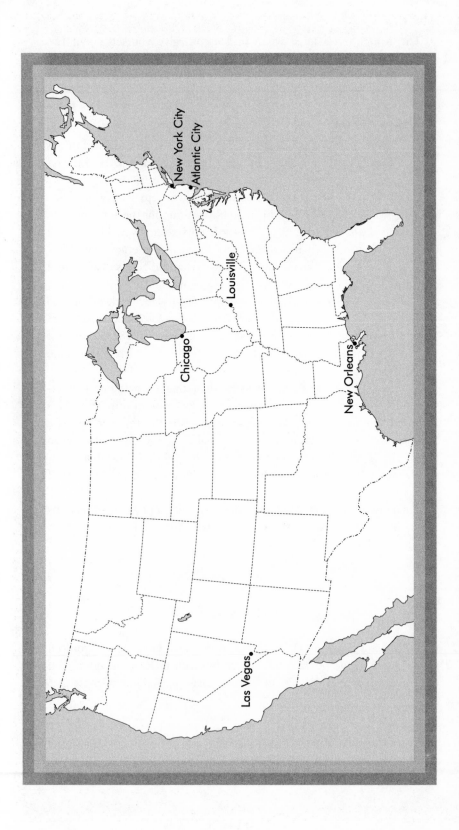

THE U.S. OF A.

PART

5

CHAPTER TWELVE

ATLANTIC CITY, NEW JERSEY

LAY OF THE LAND

Morty and I get down to Atlantic City on a Friday night, and I mean we're on the scam. We got a free room hooked up with this dude from *Swing* magazine, and the girls coming down in a separate car for a night of fun. The scene is the Taj Mahal, full of glittering lights and the cheesiest piano bar in hokeydum, a perfect place to begin an evening even though the drinks are overpriced and light on the alcohol. Order something straight.

◆

Later on, when the boys are finished playing poker, we head over to the AC Bar and Grill. The pitchers of beer start to pile up, as do plates of king crab legs and calamari and clams. Dealers just off shift from the Taj Mahal show up and the place begins to rock. We're lining up shots of tequila and some blue liquid called shooters. The dude from *Swing* magazine has been drinking straight Scotch all night long and he bails. Morty takes the girls over to the Tropicana, where the *Swing* dude has set me up with a free room. Morty orders breakfast for five and signs it to the room. The sun goddess and I continue on until we can't see and then stagger out into the bright sunlight of midmorning in Atlantic City. We head back to our room at the top of the Taj Mahal and crumple in a heap.

◆

Atlantic City has always been a place that catered to wise guys who like to play craps, and they still do. But now they've branched out into three other main areas. Seniors who like to play slots and crazy games, Asians who like to play hi-limit Asian games, and poker players who like to play everything. They don't particularly care for blackjack players. They are rather suspicious of blackjack players, Atlantic City being the former stomping ground of Ken Uston and all the big blackjack teams of note when they opened their doors in the late seventies, and the site of many famous court cases involving blackjack. That doesn't mean you can't play high. But if you play too well, they are going to notice.

◆◆◆

Atlantic City, New Jersey
GENERAL INFORMATION

YOU'RE NOT IN KANSAS ANYMORE Atlantic City, the home of the original Boardwalk and all the other streets from Monopoly, including Mediterranean Avenue, has finally cleaned up its act enough to compete with any top tier gambling destination in the world.

WHERE Atlantic City is in southern New Jersey, 100 miles south of New York City. Just take the Garden State Parkway south to Exit 40 and follow the signs. It's only about three hours from Atlantic City to Virginia and Washington, D.C., and an hour to Philadelphia.

WHEN Summers are hot in AC, what with the beach and the Boardwalk and lots of amusement options. December sees a month-long poker tournament at the Taj Mahal, which is fast becoming one of the most happening events of its kind.

INFO Visitor information and room reservations, 1-888-ACVISIT.

HISTORY Funny history, Atlantic City. It had a prime in the 1940s and '50s as a beach resort, and it was the site of the infamous meeting of the "Big Eight," the big Jewish and Italian bootleggers from New Jersey, when they carved up the illegal businesses for the whole state with one giant deal.

It spiraled downward, and by the 1970s Atlantic City had become one of the toughest and most depressed towns in the nation. The legalization of gambling was meant to change all that, to provide revenue and jobs for the whole area. But in the beginning, it didn't work like that. As late as 1986, the casinos were still bussing employees down from northern New Jersey rather than hire from the local population. The town was still depressed, and very dangerous. Very dangerous.

Things have really been changing in the last ten years, and even more so in the last five. Atlantic City is a thriving town, and virtually all of the people who work there now live in the community as well. It still pays to be careful. But there are some really nice places to go outside of the casinos, and the town need not be looked at with dread or fear.

TELEPHONES You'll have a lot of trouble getting your cell phone to work inside a casino floor. Most hotels charge for local calls.

ATMS ATMs are everywhere. Absolutely everywhere.

SAFETY Back in the day, you were always in fear. But no more. The Boardwalk has cleaned up its act, and I would be confident in all situations except late night when I'm carrying money. In that spot, drive or take a cab. Just because.

It is generally safe to park on the street while you are eating dinner or picking up a White House Sub. You always want to park in a casino parking lot when you can, however. Your car is really safe in those.

CLIMATE Summers are beautiful here. Winters are cold. It's New Jersey, a four-season state.

I'll Walk There Barefoot
TRANSPORTATION ISSUES

FLIGHTS A guy from Texas that I met in Moscow brought up an interesting point to me, over a buffet breakfast of Russian who-knows-what in the Casino Cosmos dining room. What is the quickest way to Atlantic City? Is it to fly into New York City and drive down there or take a cab? Or is it to change planes in New York and go to Philadelphia and drive from there?

The answer is that I guess it depends. JFK can be a very time-consuming place to drive out of, especially when it's busy. The drive from JFK to Atlantic City could conceivably take anywhere from three to five hours on the road. On the other hand, the drive from Newark Airport to Atlantic City should be about two hours on the button every time, and under exceptional conditions the Newark Airport to Trump Taj Mahal distance can be covered in one hour and thirty minutes. In fact, I believe that's the land speed record.

You can get a cab from Newark Airport to Atlantic City for about $125. It's been done. More than once.

The ride from Philadelphia Airport to Atlantic City is about an hour. From forty minutes in exceptional conditions, to an hour and twenty minutes most of the time, to two hours if things are really going badly on that road.

AIRPORT The Atlantic City airport should probably be used more than it is, and I'm sure it will be if Steve Wynn comes into town. Regular flights run to New York and Philadelphia and other places. The airport is about a fifteen- to twenty-minute ride from the casinos. Spirit Airlines 1-800-772-7117, or US Air Express 1-800-428-4322. AC Airport Taxi 1-609-383-1457.

BY LAND New Jersey Transit Rail 1-800-772-2222. Greyhound Bus 1-800-231-2222. Academy Bus Line 1-800-922-0451.

TRANSPORTATION AROUND TOWN Atlantic City is a place where you will appreciate having a car. It's no fun to be completely stuck in the casino in Atlantic City. Each casino charges a $2 parking charge and you get a transfer, which is good one more time, like a bus ticket.

There is a trolley that runs from casino to casino, but this isn't the greatest thing to travel on. Taxis are fine, and not expensive because you're not going far. It's only a fifteen- or twenty-minute walk from one end of the Boardwalk to the other.

The Money Plays
GAMBLING SETUP—THE QUICK FACTS

CASINOS have been legal in Atlantic City since 1978. Poker has been legal since summer 1993. Donald Trump is the main player in town. He owns the Trump Taj Mahal, Trump Marina, and Trump Plaza (the World's Fair). (Words fail.) Bally's Park Place Casino Management Company runs the casinos at Bally's, the Hilton, Caesars, and the Wild Wild West. Merv Griffin's Resorts is a fading player. And then there's Steve Wynn, if he opens his proposed blockbuster which is scheduled to open sometime in the years of the new millennium. The thing about Steve Wynn's casino is that you never know when it will be finished and opened, especially since the Bellagio has not been as big a success as was intended.

HOURS All the casinos are open twenty-four hours. Back in the day, the casinos shut at 4 A.M., no fun for all-night losers on the ride back home. Atlantic City became a far better place when the casinos went twenty-four hours.

ADMITTANCE You must be twenty-one and have ID to prove it. That said, I've seen quite a few underage people in Atlantic City casinos. But it's only a matter of time before you get kicked out and you will never be allowed to win any serious money without an ID. When I was sixteen, I had moderate success with a jacket and tie and counting an open wad of cash as I walked in the doors.

AMBIANCE AND AMENITIES Drinks are free while you're gambling. A $1 tip for every drink will ensure that they come regularly, more should ensure that you can get it whenever you want. Most casinos have comp cards, which accumulate points wherever you gamble.

GAMES ON OFFER Blackjack, roulette, craps, baccarat, slots, Pai-Gow, horse simulcasting, poker, Asian games, blackjack variations, keno, everything's here except for sports betting. But there's plenty of bookies who hang out in the Taj Mahal poker room.

LIMITS You don't have to worry about the high bet in Atlantic City. What you have to worry about is the low bet. (See Pushing Up the Limit on page 230.)

MONEY Dollars. The green ones.

LEGALITY Casinos are legal and licensed by the government. If you cash out for $10,000 or more, then you need to fill out a form and it's reported to the IRS.

TIPPING POLICIES IN THE CASINO Poker dealers have recently become allowed to keep their own tips. This has helped to improve the overall level of dealing drastically and is of great benefit to the players. It is proper to tip a poker dealer at least $1 every time you win a pot.

AND . . . Though it has cleaned up dramatically in the past five years, Atlantic City can be a tough town. One needs to be careful when traveling outside the casinos.

I'll Take the Odds
BREAKING APART THE GAME

PUSHING UP THE LIMIT Atlantic City invented the concept of pushing up the limit, in my mind. And a lot of the mind-set had to do with the fact that the casinos didn't used to be twenty-four hours.

It works like this. You get down to Atlantic City at one o'clock on a Friday afternoon and are pleased to see a $5 minimum blackjack game, which you sit down at without a whisper. Between one o'clock and ten o'clock at night, that table limit will be raised at least twice, first to $10 minimum bet, and then to $15 or $25. By ten o'clock at night, there's only a few tables in town with a minimum under $15. And most of them are $25 or $50. It's because Atlantic City always was a one-night town. It's a town where people drove down for an evening and drove back home when they were done gambling. And a lot of people still do that. So they push up the limits. They figure, if they force you to bet high, then not only will their table handle be bigger, but they'll get you through your money quicker. Either you'll get lucky and win and play on, or you'll go bust quick and make room for a player with some fresh dough. Look, you're gonna need a lot of money to play $25 minimum bet all night long. Or you might not need more than $200. But you certainly aren't gonna play that money for as long as you would at a $5 table.

That is just the way Atlantic City is. On a weekend evening, be prepared to gamble a little higher. During the day, the wee hours of the morning, and during the week, low limits can be found all over town. You can always bet high. You just can't always bet low.

I remember sometimes driving two and a half hours down to play in Atlantic City, and because of the high limits going bust in twenty minutes. And then having to drive the two and a half hours back home again. It happens.

CRAPS If anybody tells you that they've found something more exciting than craps, I'd assume it involves some very dangerous chemicals. Once you learn it, craps is simply, under the right circumstances, the most exciting gambling game known to man. That's a fact.

Before you learn craps, it is a mind-numbing and confusing conglomeration of bets and propositions. Once you learn it—and it's not hard—a good craps game is nothing more than a well-oiled machine. Clicking like clockwork.

The most complicated thing about craps is the board, and so the easiest way to learn craps is to forget the board. Learn craps the way they learned it when there was no table, when all there was was a blanket and a pair of dice. And that's the best way to think about the game. Just a blanket and a pair of dice.

There are only two bets you need to be concerned with when learning craps: Pass and Don't Pass. That's it. That's the game of craps.

Craps begins with the come out roll. It is at this point that you choose to bet either Pass or Don't Pass. Each bet pays even money. On the come out roll, the Pass line wins with a come out roll of seven or eleven and loses with a roll of two, three, or twelve (craps). Conversely, the Don't Pass loses with a come out roll of seven or eleven and wins with a two or three. A twelve is a push for the Don't Pass, so the house can get their edge. Each of these bets is approximately 1 percent in favor of the house, not a large edge.

If the come out roll is a two, three, seven, eleven, or twelve, the shooter rolls again. He rolls until he establishes a point, rolls a four, five, six, eight, nine, or ten. Now the game changes. Once the point has been established, nothing matters except that point and the number seven. The Pass line wins if the point is rerolled before a seven comes up. The Don't Pass wins if a seven comes up before the point number. If the point is six, the shooter keeps rolling until he hits a six or seven. No other number rolls affect the Pass and Don't Pass bets once the point has been established.

If the shooter "sevens out," hits a seven before his point, he passes the dice. If he hits his point, he keeps rolling. This is why a hot table is one where someone has held the dice for a long time. If someone hits six Passes in a row, you can make some money.

The only other bet worth explaining on the table is the one where you back up your bet. This is a gift given to you by the casino, a gift to gamblers, because this bet is always offered at true odds, that is, with no percentage against you. Once the point has been established, the house gives you the offer of increasing your Pass or Don't Pass bet, according to what the odds are. If the point is six, you can back up your bet at odds of 6–5, the true odds of a seven coming up before a six. If the point is four, the odds are 2–1.

For example, say you have a $5 Pass line bet and the come out roll is a pair of fours, eight. The point is now eight. To back up your bet, place $10 behind your $5 bet. Now you will have $15 on the line, $5 backed up $10. If an eight comes, you win $17, $5 at even money, and $10 at 6–5, which pays $12. If a casino claims to give five times odds, that means that you can back up a $5 bet for $25 more behind the line. This is pretty good. At that point, you're practically playing all your money on an even gamble, that is, with no percentages against you. It's an adrenaline thing.

FUNNY GAMES You can find some strange new games in Atlantic City. Funny games. The primary feature of most of these games is that the house has a big advantage. A bigger advantage than they do in the more traditional games. Or else they wouldn't have invented them.

THE BIG SIX WHEEL Take the big six wheel, for instance. This game is a simplified version of roulette. What they've done is they've taken a roulette wheel, made it bigger and turned it sideways, and changed the odds in their favor. If you bet on the even money option on the big six wheel, you have 23 out of 54 spaces to hit. That's 42 percent, compared with 47 percent if you make the exact same even money bet on the roulette wheel five feet away, where your chances are 18 out of 38. The game is the same, the odds are heavier against you. Big six wheel is the kind of thing people play when they're walking around and killing time. Just because you're killing time doesn't mean you have to kill your bankroll, too.

SLOTS Atlantic City is a major slots town. About a third of the retirement age people in North America keep it that way, and you can always expect to find good slots, lots of them, and fantastic deals and promotions for slot players, including cash back cards, very loose paying slots, and a variety of comps. I know a whole bunch of people who live in that town virtually for free because they play video poker every day where they reckon the game is almost even anyway if you play it correctly, and the comps they build up by virtue of all this play is a living unto itself. Every Atlantic City casino considers the slot player a valued customer. If I owned a casino, I'd give them the red carpet treatment as well.

ASIAN GAMES There are a lot of Asians who come to gamble in Atlantic City, drawing off the large ethnic Asian populations of New York City, as well as Virginia and Maryland. Atlantic City has not only seen a tremendous rise in the spread of Asian games in the last ten years, but also an explosion of Asian gambler–oriented services and facilities. The Taj Mahal and Claridge, among others, have very authentic noodle bars adjacent to their gaming areas. The Taj Mahal has an entire Asian hospitality department, with staff who speak a variety of languages. The Chinese or Vietnamese speaking gambler will find a host of opportunities in Atlantic City specifically catering to them, if they look.

POKER Poker was legalized in Atlantic City in the summer of 1993, and it took the town by storm. A pitched battle was waged between the poker rooms during the first two years of operations, and when the smoke cleared, only the Taj Mahal was left thriving. Their seventy gleaming tables in a beautiful room in a hot location single-handedly put poker rooms at Resorts, Bally's, and the Sands out of business. A few years ago, the Tropicana reinvested in a new poker room that complements rather than competes with the Taj Mahal, and it's well run and successful. They offer a niche for nonsmokers and for small to low-medium-limit games, and they have established a successful series of daily tournaments. The Taj Mahal, however, is the place for the best action, the best games, and the best atmosphere.

In all limits below $10–$20, rakes are taken from the pot, up to a few dollars per hand. In all limits $10–$20 and higher, a time rake is charged per half hour. This ranges from about $5 per half hour for $10–$20 to about $12 per half hour for $100–$200 limit. It's a fair rake, and although higher than Vegas I do not consider it too high.

While there were not many people in the area who knew how to play poker in 1993, that situation has changed by the turn of the new millennium. Wise guys have been quick to learn the game, and while you will find some excellent action in Atlantic City, particularly during the summer months, don't expect everybody to have a banana in their ear. Not anymore.

The Taj poker room is one of the best in the business. The space is first-class, the staff is first-class, the amenities of staying at the Taj Mahal are first-class. The poker room has made many changes over its six years of operations, all for the benefit of the player. Floor people are experienced, and the whole poker room is capably run by Tom Gitto, with longtime shift managers Gerry Jordan and David Marshall. Tony Marino is the poker room host, in charge of all things room, comp, and player related. They are all good people, and they're good at their jobs.

Donald Trump likes poker players, as well. He surfaces in the poker room from time to time, most notably during the Trump Taj Mahal poker tournament in December, but he has made many high-rolling VIPs feel welcome at the Taj poker room, including Roger King, and the prince of some oil-producing emirate.

You never have to worry about anything at the Taj because the dealers know the rules. The dealers all know the rules and they all know how to run the games, and if any problem should arise a floor person will come over, and you better believe that they know all the rules and will make a fair decision without any bias whatsoever. You know that, 100 percent for certain, and I've played enough hours there to make that claim without a shred of hesitation. If you have any larger problem, the shift managers are friendly, approachable, and knowledgeable about what goes on in that room. And if you play there, if you sincerely put in hours at the poker table, you will find that you are treated well and receive good comp value for your play, both in room and food discounts.

Atlantic City is primarily a stud town, seven-card stud is usually the big game in the Taj Mahal poker room, they regularly play up to $400–$800 on the weekends, but with seventy tables to choose from, you can always find a limit to suit you. Popular games at the Taj include seven-card stud $1–$5, $10–$20, $15–$30, $30–$60, $75–$150, and Texas Hold'em $3–$6, $10–$20, $20–$40, $50–$100, $75–$150. They also regularly spread rotation games, where you change the game every half hour and add games like Omaha Hi-Lo, Seven-Stud Hi-Lo, and Omaha Hi only. Rotation games are usually only played $50–$100 and higher, but they do have a $20–$40 half Hold'em and half Omaha Hi, which goes quite often.

Casinos and Lodging
THE POINT

Atlantic City is a weekend town, that's always been its mainstay. You will always find excellent hotel deals midweek throughout the year, but not surprisingly, Atlantic City is a lot more fun on the weekends. It is crucial to make a reservation in advance. The longer in advance you make the reservation the better the rate you will get, and the earlier in the day that you get there, the better the room you may get. It is not un-heard of for someone to arrive on a Monday without a reservation for the weekend, but expecting to stay in their room all week and then just extend it at the last minute, because there's always something available, and strike out. In Atlantic City, there's not always something available. They get sold out every weekend for real and, for sure, and as often as not, they'll turn you out on Friday morning, say, "We're all full, sorry," and send you down Route 30 to find some overpriced motel. In this case, tipping the front desk clerk $20 first thing Friday morning and saying, "If any-thing opens, please call me," is a good option. Of course it may not work.

In short, Atlantic City is not a good place to arrive on a weekend without a reservation. You won't be staying at a casino. Try Route 30. Without a reservation, try and arrive as early in the week as possible.

The comps policy at most casinos is now done with the cash cards. Every casino has its own cash card, which is used to keep track of every game you play in the casino. Points are awarded based on hours, limits played, and games played. These points can then be redeemed for a variety of things, including food, shop items, and hotel rooms. If you reach a certain level on the card, you are eligible for the casino rate, which is severely discounted. Some cards even have cash back options.

As far as lodging goes in Atlantic City, the Taj Mahal has always been the place to play and they do have the biggest poker room. But recently they have gotten more stingy about giving poker room rates on the weekend, which at $69 are excellent value simply because the rooms at the Taj Mahal are so nice. But a very good alternative is the Tropicana, which has expanded and now has a very big poker room, with a good selection of medium-limit games, $10–$20, $15–$30, $20–$40, as well as low-limit games. It's a nice place to play, you can order at the table, and they give good room rates and points to players as they play. October and November are very slow times in Atlantic City, the advantage being hotel rooms will be cheap and plentiful, the disadvantage being the games might not be fantastic. If you stay at the Tropicana, make sure to get a room in the West Tower, which is the new tower. I can't overemphasize the importance of this. If you stay at the Taj Mahal, get a room as high up as possible, certainly above the twenty-ninth floor.

TRUMP TAJ MAHAL

When you drive into the Taj Mahal, you know you're in for something special. It comes on you all of a sudden, you turn down the corridor called Virginia Avenue and there it is, like a glittering palace in the deserts of Rajastan. The Trump Taj Mahal. A fountain greets you along with the marble columns and gold gilt parapets of this architectural maelstrom. You can't see it from the front, but the Taj is huge. It's a whole city in there, and I know more than a few people who have gone for months at a time without ever leaving the confines of the hotel. You don't need to. It's all there. And if you're on a comp, you're in for a real treat.

There ain't much that tops eating for free at Scheherazade or the Dynasty Chinese Restaurant. There ain't much that beats pampering yourself in the spa, or padding the luxurious corridors to your fiftieth-floor room, from which you can sit on the giant window sill in the morning and watch the sunrise over the Atlantic Ocean. And all the way down the Boardwalk. There ain't much that beats the Maharajah Club, and there ain't much that beats a seventy-two-hour poker game at the Trump Taj Mahal.

Simply the best. The best place to stay in Atlantic City and one of the best places to gamble, anywhere. If you know how to do it right. The Taj is four star, but the rater must have been there on a bad day, or perhaps he didn't go to the Spa. Maybe he made the mistake of eating at the buffet.

If you're feeling romantic and want something special, get a midweek suite special. You may not leave your room.

Casino

HOURS Twenty-four hours.

LAYOUT The casino is very big, it's very easy to get in a spot from which you can't see any exit. All the games, with separate hi-limit pit. Slots galore. The poker room is completely separate from the casino, across the lobby, but it is actually in a more prime location than the casino itself, if you can believe it. When you descend the escalators under the biggest chandelier you've ever seen into the Taj lobby, all you can see on your right through the huge plate-glass windows is the poker room. And it's the same on a Saturday night, when the place is teeming with people coming out of the showroom. All they can see is a whole lot of poker games going on. The ceilings are huge, it's quiet, and smoke is not a problem. The air is clean. No smoking in the end seats, if you are sitting next to the dealer.

RULES AND NOTES At the Taj, as with other places, you're gonna need a casino player's card to get any comps and room deals. They're free, they're all free, and there are machines located throughout the hotel and casino where you can swipe your card and see how many points you have.

As they say, playing has its privileges. And if you can qualify for the Taj's Maharajah Club, do so at your first opportunity. The club is located on the forty-ninth floor, and you need a special key to get up there. Beautiful furnishings, views, televisions, a twenty-four-hour buffet, and a private bar. You can just hang out, if you want. Sometimes, if you have a room on the fiftieth floor, you can sneak in there anyway with your key and room number.

The craps games here rock. They absolutely hum with electricity. The Taj Mahal is a prime place to play any table game, as high as you want.

I may be wrong on this, but as far as I know, the Trump Taj Mahal was the first poker room anywhere to offer professional massage services while you play poker. Now there's a lot of rooms that do it, but the issue is that the people at the Taj are essentially the best. They are all professional masseuses and masseurs, and they know what they are doing. They know how to take twelve hours of cramps out of your neck while you are hunched over a poker game, and they charge a ridiculously reasonable fee. I think a twenty-minute massage is something like $25, but most people tip them also. It's one of the nicest perks about gambling. A professional massage while you're sitting there. You don't even have to leave the table. The Taj massage staff works the poker room evenings and weekends. They are easily recognizable, dressed in white and carrying cushions. They are friendly, approachable, and capable of magic. Strong hands. Alternatively, you can get a more comprehensive massage at the spa, but make a reservation.

The poker room hits its busiest periods during the summer, as does most of Atlantic City. Call for reservations.

UNITED STATES POKER CHAMPIONSHIPS The United States Poker Championships is a month-long event hosted by Donald Trump and the Taj Mahal, held every December. It culminates in a $7,500 buy-in no-limit Hold'em tournament held over the last three days, which attracts adventurers from far and wide. What it primarily features, however, is an opportunity to stay at the Taj Mahal for a reduced room rate during a period when there's a lot of action. And you are welcome in the casino as well. You don't have to play that much poker to come. It's just nice to gamble however you want, but in that atmosphere. During most of the tournament, small buy-in events with big prize payouts are held every day, most of them with a $200 to $500 buy-in.

FOOD AND DRINK The Starbucks coffee shop on the second floor serves the real thing and should be utilized. Lattés, espressos, damn good coffee, and don't forget to take a few biscotti with you for dipping or just crunching. This is good for pleasant gambling.

The poker room now offers hot dogs and pretzels free to poker players for about an hour at dinnertime. If you're stuck nine hours in a game, you'll appreciate it.

Avoid the **Stage Deli** at all costs. This is not a good New York deli. Not even if you're really hankering for it. Try the Taj room service menu instead, which is one of the better-quality room service menus out there. They now have this thing where there's a Stage Deli menu in the room. Don't use this. First of all you have to go down to the Stage Deli and pick it up. Second, the food's not as good as room service. It's from a different kitchen, not the Taj Mahal kitchen.

Don't bother with the buffet. You'll get a stomachache.

The Chinese restaurant **Dynasty** is the best spot to go on a comp. The **Sushi Bar** in the forecourt of the Chinese restaurant is not cheap, but it is damn good sushi.

The **All Star Sports Café** is there, in the back. Not as nice as the one in Manhattan, but it's the same drill.

The **Bombay Café** is just ever so slightly below average. The breakfast buffet at the Bombay Café, however, is a bright spot, especially when you're on a comp and you've been playing poker all night.

There's a piano bar in the back toward the Boardwalk that gets a classic cheesy piano act nightly. That's a nice place to have a drink for atmosphere and people watching, but the prices are rather outrageous. If you get something straight, at least you'll know how much alcohol you're getting.

The in-room dining is excellent as well. I particularly like breakfast, a carafe of fresh-squeezed orange juice and granola with strawberries and skim milk and then either a toasted bagel with cream cheese or an order of rye toast, or a plate of bacon and eggs and potatoes. It's a good way to start the day, all wheeled in for your disposal. Don't forget the pot of coffee.

Late night, my favorite has always been the portabello mushroom burger, which pops on and off the menu, or the reuben, which uses far better corned beef and pastrami than the Stage Deli, or a chicken salad sandwich. The salads are excellent as well, Mediterranean or seafood or Caesar. And the chicken with matzo ball soup is not to be underrated as an accompaniment to any meal. If you have a comp, go nuts. The entrees, while high priced, do not disappoint.

Scheherazade is a gourmet restaurant that overlooks the baccarat pit. Very fine dining, this is where most of the regular Taj high rollers eat. They say the food here is the best in the joint. Open for dinner from 6:00 P.M. to 11:00 P.M. Closed annually from December 7 to December 23.

THE PEOPLE THERE This is one of the classiest casinos in the world, and it's no wonder that a lot of high rollers come for the experience. The Taj is also a great place to people watch for men in the "cement business."

The Taj has a lot of things in Chinese, including a special office for Asian clients to deal with comps and room services, plus all the menus and room literature in Chinese. They have a lot of programs designed to facilitate and attract Asian clients.

Hotel

Poker rate, $65 plus $7.80 tax and $2 tourism promotion fee, but it's very hard to get the rate on the weekends. You should always have a reservation when coming to the Taj. And you should always try and get there as early as possible to get the best room. The best rooms at the Taj are the ones high up. It's a fact. Everything over twenty-nine is better. If you can get yourself on fifty or fifty-one, you're living a dream. The sun goddess and I once spent a few blissful weeks up on fifty, but it takes effort to get up there. Your best bet is to arrive midweek, any time between Monday and Wednesday, or Thursday. Besides that, there's an all suites floor I think on fourteen, but I'll take a standard room high up with a king-size bed anytime. Or of course a corner suite with the Jacuzzi. They are absolutely lovely.

Local calls eighty cents. Pay TV movies $9.50, lots of pay per view movies on the television. Health club $12.50 per day. They are very helpful at the front desk if any problem charges have been made to your room, for instance movies that you didn't watch. I have spent a lot of time dealing with people at the Taj's front desk and I have found them to be among the most friendly and professional in the business. You are truly in for a different level of service when you are a guest of the Trump Taj Mahal. It means something.

All the rooms have free safes that should be utilized. They are an excellent place to keep things safe while you're in Atlantic City. They are large and can fit more than just money. You can also get a box in the casino, if you're not staying at the Taj and you win a lot of money there, just ask. They'll let you leave it on deposit at the cage or give you your own box. No problem.

You see, the nice thing about playing poker at the Taj Mahal while you're a guest there is that you can go up to your room. You can leave your chips on the table for about an hour and a half without them getting picked up, that is, you keep your seat in a busy game. This is plenty of time to go up to the room, take a shower, change, relax, lie in bed and have a cigarette and think about the game. Or have a bite to eat.

And if you like to play poker and you will be playing all day, it's so nice to be able to come up to your room whenever you want, even if it's just for thirty minutes, and have your chips sitting down there on the table in the poker room below, and know that there is no problem, none whatsoever. When you're ready you just go down and your money and seat will still be there waiting for you. Don't worry. The cameras are on. And if you stay away too long, if you hit a hot craps roll while walking through the casino and can't leave the table, they'll pick up your chips after you get three no player buttons and then you can get them when you go back to the poker room and go to the top of the list. No problem. The Taj Mahal is ultimately professional. On the top-notch.

As far as getting poker rates goes, you'll have an easy time of getting that $65 rate from Monday to Thursday nights, but on the weekends, it's very tough. They only give out a few rooms at the poker rate on the weekends, and you really have to be playing there regularly to get one of those rooms. Or have some pull. During the tournament month, however, poker rooms are cheap and plentiful. It's a fine time to be in Atlantic City.

The suites at the Taj are among the nicest anywhere. Ask about their Sunday night suite deals and midweek specials, because if you're not on a comp the suites are still a luxurious and worthwhile expense. The corner ones on high floors is what you want. With two rooms and whirlpool Jacuzzi and a circular bed with a TV at the foot of it and a bigger TV in the living room. It's a nice place to party. One nice thing about the suites is that they can really sleep five or six absolutely comfortably, so it can be a nice splurge. The bedroom door can be closed to the living room, for privacy. The Jacuzzi tub is very comfortable for two, in any position. The suite, however, is also just perfect for two.

Housekeeping is excellent. This is a place where you should make an effort to tip your maid. You will be rewarded. Laundry is expensive but excellent, same day service before 9 A.M.

You really don't do better for this room rate in Atlantic City, even if you're not at a casino rate. So book early. Room rates at the Trump Taj Mahal vary, based on the season. Rack rates are as follows:

	MIDWEEK	WEEKEND
Jan.	$125	$150
Feb.	$125	$150
Mar.	$125	$150
Apr.	$150	$175
May	$150	$175
June	$150	$175
July	$175	$225
Aug.—Sept. 4	$175	$225
Sept. 5—30	$150	$175
Oct.	$150	$175
Nov.	$150	$175
Dec.	$125	$150

All rates are per night, single or double occupancy, and do not include 12 percent tax and $2 per night occupancy fee.

Midweek, the Taj offers a Sultan Suite Package, Mon.–Thurs. only, $250 total per night, for which you get to stay in a premium suite, plus turndown service, chocolate and fruit basket, $50 gourmet dining credit, complimentary welcome cocktails in either the Oasis or Princess

Lounge, free admission to the spa, and 20 percent off services in the Salon at the Taj. This is one of the romantic deals of a lifetime. Based on availability. Or you can book a regular room, show up on a Monday and try to finagle a suite upgrade from the check-in clerk. It's been known to happen.

SUNDRIES Cigarettes are some outrageous price in the casinos, like more than double, so bring your own if you smoke. A lot of them. But you can get *The New York Times* and a good selection of local papers at the Taj gift shop. Don't get there too late for the Sunday *New York Times*. It goes quick.

There's a fairly decent arcade on ground level next to the Boardwalk. Some better video games can be had in summer if you walk down the Boardwalk, but the Taj arcade is a fine place to go on tilt for $20 and kill a whole bunch of aliens.

The Salon at the Taj is also a hidden gem. My wife always has a facial and a haircut there and she raves about it. The Taj is a surprisingly luxurious place to bring a wife or girlfriend for the weekend. Chances are, they'll love it even if they never gamble.

The indoor pool on the fourteenth floor is nice, but the gem is the spa: $12 per day for use of the spa for hotel guests and just accept that you should go to the spa every day. It's a genius place, an East Coast answer to Caesars Palace Las Vegas. Sauna, steam room, whirlpools, and a truly excellent staff of massage people. And a lot of fitness equipment. Plus your own robe and slippers and juice. It's a nice place to be between gambling. Separate spas for men and women, share the fitness equipment.

Taj valet is free, you only have to tip the parking attendant. And it's so nice to drive right into the front driveway of the Trump Taj Mahal.

 PRACTICALITIES
Hotel Phone Number: 1-609-449-1000, 1-800-825-8888
Casino Phone Number: Poker room, 1-800-72-POKER
Internet: *www.trumptaj.com*
Location: 1000 Boardwalk at Virginia Avenue. The northern end of the Boardwalk. When driving to the Taj, take Route 30 all the way to Virginia Avenue and drive all the way down. That way you get the full effect of the Taj and Atlantic City.

SHOWBOAT CASINO

Completely decked out in a Mardi Gras theme, the Showboat makes no pretenses about the clientele it is trying to attract and service: the Mississippi steamer generation, that is, all persons born before 1880. It is a nice enough place, very bright all around. This hotel is always busy with day buses and senior vacation packages, a Dixieland three-piece playing in the lobby, '50s beach fashion, slot machines to beat the band, and a whole bunch of crazy game tables to keep people interested all day. And a lot of low- and medium-limit options. I think it's a fun place to hang out, mostly because I like that multiple action blackjack game. It is definitely a good game.

Casino

LAYOUT One big room, with one level raised up a few steps above the other. The noise level is high, owing to the fact that you are never more than an arm's reach from a slot machine lever. The race book is small, crowded, and ill equipped for the hordes of old men who crowd it each day.

GAMES Slots, blackjack, multiple action blackjack, craps, roulette, baccarat, let it ride poker, Caribbean stud poker, sic bo, Pai-Gow poker, Pai-Gow tiles, race book, they've got a lot of gambling games here.

LIMITS One of the casinos that you can expect to find minimum bets among the lowest in town.

RULES AND NOTES The Showboat has been famous for not charging its patrons the $2 citywide parking fee since that tax was established about five or six years ago. But now you do have to have a Showboat cash card to get the free parking. However, the cards are free. So just go get one. Some people walk an awful long way just to park there.

Craps here offers 5x odds.

Multiple action blackjack is a game where you can play your blackjack hand up to three times against the dealer. It's quite an exciting game if you like blackjack. They also offer double exposure twenty-one here, where you exchange the right to see both of the dealers' cards in exchange for losing on all ties, and some other things.

All models of slot machines return at least 83 percent of the coins played to the customer.

FOOD AND DRINK Ho-hum. The saving grace, however, is the **Basin Street Café,** the ground-floor ice cream and pastry shop, which will satisfy completely.

THE PEOPLE THERE Guys wearing shorts with brown socks pulled up to the knee. Here you will find the epitome of kitsch, casino fashion. In short, no care about dressing whatsoever. You can dress like you're going to the living room or the grocery store.

This hotel specializes in senior charter trips that bus down from Jersey and north. There are very few Asians here whatsoever.

Hotel

Rack rates. Standard rooms, $120 midweek, $170 weekend, $200 holiday. Suite rates, Carousel Suites $200. Garden Court Suites $250. One-bedroom Mardi Gras $300. Two-bedroom Mardi Gras $420. One-bedroom Grand Balcony $350. Two-bedroom Grand Balcony $472. 1-800-621-0200.

One perk here is a sixty-lane bowling center open twenty-four hours a day. 800 rooms.

 PRACTICALITIES
Hotel Phone Number: 1-609-343-4000, 1-800-257-8580
Location: All the way on the north end of the Boardwalk, next to the Taj Mahal.

BALLY'S PARK PLACE AND WILD WILD WEST

Bally's Park Place and the Wild Wild West Casino. It's two adjacent casinos with the same owner and the same everything else. What I can tell you is that I'd prefer to play slots in Bally's Park Place and any table games in the Wild Wild West. The Park Place Casino is large, loud, and ungainly, in my opinion. There's no atmosphere to hold it all together, except for some tenuous carnival theme, which gets a little stretched when they bring out the industrial-size vacuums and start whooshing the floor at 4 A.M. Then again, the race and sports book at the Park Place is one of the best in town. And quiet. Wow. Quiet.

The Wild Wild West has got some atmosphere. The space is kind of quirky, and being able to play $5 minimum bet craps with 10x odds is like a privilege, worth taking a cab ride all over town for, which you don't have to do. Just go to the casino.

Casino

BALLY'S PARK PLACE LAYOUT The race book and poker room and keno lounge are upstairs, you really gotta walk. One of the nicest race books in town, private, quiet, scads of TVs. You can bet on any race anywhere. The poker room is empty but for a single $1 to $5 stud table. Lots of poker rooms opened in 1993, and now the smoke has cleared. Bally's is not a player. The regular casino is Mardi Gras decor in one big room with a glittering rug.

WILD WILD WEST LAYOUT The theme is there. At least it's not jarring to the senses. The slot chairs don't look especially comfortable, hard-backed in some saddle motif. Craps dealers know exactly what the fuck is going on. I like the Wild Wild West. It's the only place in town that offers $5 craps with 10x odds. What does 10x odds mean? It means if you get lucky, you're gonna crush them. It means that if you play it right, you are practically gambling for free. Practically gambling for nothing at all.

FOOD AND DRINK Bally's Park Place has the standards. A twenty-four-hour coffee shop, a northern Italian restaurant, a Chinese restaurant, a steak house, and a buffet. Yawn. The only interesting thing is the Sunday buffet, which offers rack of lamb.

The Wild Wild West only has a few informal options, but you can always eat at the ninety-foot-long bar, which is nice.

Hotel
Single or double occupancy at same rate.

January 1–April 1: $75–$195
April 2–June 17: $85–$215
June 18–September 5: $95–$245
September 6–November 27: $85–$215
November 28–December 30: $75–$195

Check-in time is 4 P.M.; checkout is noon. Spa.

 PRACTICALITIES
Hotel Phone Number: 1-609-340-2000, 1-800-BALLYS7, reservations call 1-800-225-5977.
Location: On the Boardwalk. These casinos are two casinos, or one casino, depending on how you want to look at it. They are adjacent to each other.

TROPICANA HOTEL
About four years after poker had been established in Atlantic City, just when it looked like the Taj Mahal was going to be the only poker room left in town, the Tropicana hired away a goodly amount of poker dealers and floor people from the Taj, offered them better pay and benefits, and opened up what has become a very successful low-limit poker room. The Tropicana now offers a good option for poker players looking to play lower limits and $20 buy-in daily poker tournaments, as well as good

comp value for your poker play. The Tropicana can be a nice enough place to stay, as long as you're in the West Tower.

Casino

LAYOUT As far as the casino itself goes, the rug has been in place since the original Atlantic City opening in 1978, I think. And the decor has aged into a little bad taste. The casino space is okay, it's not one big squared room like the Hilton. The slot areas have very low ceilings, but it's much nicer in the table game section.

GAMES Everything but keno. Usually when a big casino doesn't have keno it means that someone hit the jackpot and they discontinued the game. In Mario Puzo's classic novel *Fools Die*, the casino owner fired all his keno personnel when the jackpot got hit, because he figured the odds were far greater that someone was cheating than someone just getting lucky. This should give you some indication that keno is not the best game in terms of odds for the player.

LIMITS Craps $15 to $5,000, $10 to $2,500, 5x odds. Blackjack $25 minimum, roulette $15 minimum on a Saturday night.

RULES AND NOTES Caribbean stud progressive jackpot, $110,000 and rising. Self-park is $2 up to eight hours, after that it's $8 or $20 or more. Why the penalty? The Luma Kid once left a Ford Taurus for two and a half months in the self-park of the Taj Mahal, and nobody touched it. And it started right up.

POKER ROOM AT THE TROPICANA The poker room is a nice space, separate from the main casino, but in a place where passersby can find it. There's also a glass enclosed nonsmoking poker room which gets a steady flow of games in a completely smoke-free atmosphere. Sealed and ventilated no smoking room with glass doors, $1–$5 and $2–$10 limits. The rest of the sixty tables are mostly low to mid stakes. One $30–$60 stud, one or two $20–$40 stud, and two $10–$20 Hold'em tables. Then a lot of $1–$5, $3–$6, and $5–$10 games. Poker dealers keep their own tips here. The staff is very friendly and eager to please poker players. They definitely value their poker players here.

Sunday–Thursday, $59 poker room rate slightly undercuts the Taj. Four hours minimum play. $89 Friday and $99 Saturday poker rate is a good option when the Taj fills up on the weekends. Make sure you get in the West Tower.

50 table poker/simulcast facility. Yes the horse races are right there. Table side food service and complimentary drinks. Lots and lots of TVs

for sweating a variety of things twenty-four hours. Up to $2 per hour in comps back from the poker. Call 1-888-Poker-AC for poker reservations.

THE TROP POKER CLUB—EVENT CALENDAR Sunday through Friday, there is a poker tournament every day at the Tropicana. Now that's nice. Current schedule is as follows. Maximum number of participants: Hold'em events, 117. Stud events, 112.

Sundays	1:15 P.M.	$40 buy-in, $10 entry	Stud Hi-Lo
Mondays	12:15 P.M.	$30 buy-in, $10 entry	7-Card Stud
Tuesdays	7:15 P.M.	$10 buy-in, $10 entry, $500 guaranteed prize pool	7-Card Stud
Wednesdays	4:15 P.M.	$50 buy-in, $10 entry	Hold'em
Thursdays	7:15 P.M.	$10 buy-in, $10 entry, $500 guaranteed prize pool	Hold'em
Fridays	4:15 P.M.	$100 buy-in, $15 entry	Hold'em

FOOD AND DRINK The Tropicana poker room has the advantage of table side food service. The menu is neither complicated nor expensive, but the prices are fair to cheap and you can find something filling. Wait and see what the regulars are ordering.

Standard restaurants plus Hooters, which is what it is.

Hotel

The West Tower is the new tower, and that's where the nice rooms are. The rates are the same, West Tower or East Tower, but the rooms are no comparison, and you can't reserve a tower in advance. You just have to get there as early as possible and consider whether or not a tip will help you at check-in. Because it's worth it. Rack rates, summer weekend $250, $125 to $200, poker rate $59.

 PRACTICALITIES
Hotel Phone Number: 1-800-TheTrop, 1-609-340-1000, 1-800-228-2828
Poker Room Phone Number: 1-888-Poker-AC
Location: All the way down the Boardwalk, but north of the Atlantic City Hilton.

SANDS

Sands is old-time. When a casino shrinks, the top management stays. It's an interesting phenomenon, old shitty casinos with unbelievable personnel, like the Stardust in Las Vegas, and the Sands here in Atlantic City. The place needs some cash, and it shows no signs of getting it soon.

Casino

LAYOUT Low ceilings with sparkled mirrors are an instant headache. Clear '70s design. The sports book is nice. Personal TVs set down in the desk so you can look down on them. The poker room has 19 tables, but I can't imagine they get more than one going except on the weekends, and the games are virtually all $1 to $5 stud day games, where you get only seventy cents per hour on the comps.

FOOD AND DRINK Keep on walking.

Hotel

Rooms at the Sands are looking very old. Like eastern European Panaflex from the outside of the building. Hotel guests can use the Sands golf course in Somers Point, about thirty minutes away.

 PRACTICALITIES
Hotel Phone Number: 1-609-441-4000, 1-800-257-8580
Internet: *www.acsands.com*
Location: Center of the Boardwalk, accessible via a moving walkway.

CLARIDGE

The Claridge, recently renovated, is one of the premier Asian games spots in Atlantic City. A very nice section with Pai-Gow, baccarat, and minibaccarat and an authentic Chinese noodle bar. They love the Asian games here. Besides that room, the casino is not very large.

Casino

LAYOUT Casino is small but on three or four levels. The table games pit is small, with craps and blackjack. The Asian games pit is on a different level down some stairs, nice and private.

FOOD AND DRINK The best food is undoubtedly found at the noodle bar inside of the Asian games section of the casino. The coffee shop might be worth a try.

THE PEOPLE THERE Large Asian clientele on account of the very good Asian games section.

Hotel

Good winter midweek package deals. All phone calls, seventy-five cents, pool and spa, 10 A.M.–6 P.M.

PRACTICALITIES
Hotel Phone Number: 1-609-340-3434, 1-800-257-8585
Location: Center of the Boardwalk, but set back. Accessible via a moving walkway from the Boardwalk that also goes to Sands.

CAESARS

All Caesars are not the Palace in Las Vegas. This hotel is nice enough, but it's missing that extra edge that makes things memorable. A cash injection is planned, and hopefully this will get things past the point where everyone is just going through the motions. Don't expect to find a game in the poker room, but you won't get bothered there either.

Casino

LAYOUT The casino is spacious, the noise level is okay. The second-floor level sedately holds a poker room race and keno book. There is a nice spot upstairs to play table games in peace and quiet, just next to shopping and boutique alleyways.

GAMES Caribbean stud, let it ride, roulette, blackjack.

LIMITS Craps 2x odds on $5 table, you can do better than that. 5x odds on $10 minimum table. Blackjack, $5 to $1,000.

RULES AND NOTES Blackjack twist called 21 madness. It's blackjack, but you put up a side bet of $1, and if you get dealt blackjack, hit the bonus button and you get paid from $5 to $1,000 extra, average is about $10. The odds on this proposition are way against you. Way against you, but it does look like fun.

This is a nice Pai-Gow casino. $20 min bet tables with comfy chairs, nice pace, you can play forever, best slow game in Atlantic City.

FOOD AND DRINK Caesars has got a lot of dining options, including a branch of Nero's grill, which if it's anything like it is in Las Vegas you should head there at all costs. My fear, however, is that it's not Caesars Las Vegas, but at the same price. A Japanese restaurant and a Chinese restaurant plus sushi in the lobby give you the idea that they know something about Asian food. Also a Planet Hollywood.

Hotel

Not very many rooms for an Atlantic City hotel. Only about 500.

 PRACTICALITIES
Hotel Phone Number: 1-609-348-4411, 1-800-582-7600
Location: Directly across from Ocean One Mall. On the
Boardwalk, between Trump Plaza and Bally's.

ATLANTIC CITY HILTON

This hotel used to be the Bally's Grand. Now it's the Atlantic City Hilton. The management is the same, the hotel is a different name. The same casino management company runs Bally's Park Place, the Hilton (BG), Caesars, and the Wild Wild West.

This is the south end of the Boardwalk, all the way on the end, and walking to anywhere from here is a pain. You are on the fringe of the action here, rather than inside it. This place is your classic push up the limit joint, getting a cheap bet down here on a weekend is not very likely.

Nice enough lobby, if obvious lack of couch space or any place to sit, for that matter. Some people bring entire families down to Atlantic City and leave the small children to sit outside in the lobby and wait while the men gamble, and this hotel is obviously taking steps to discourage that.

Casino

LAYOUT The casino is new, no bones about it, and clean, and slots are the major attraction. The table games are surrounded, loud! Noise level here is an absolute maximum. This place is cold. Don't forget to layer in the middle of summer, as the Hilton checks in at about forty-five degrees. The simulcast area is big and new, every seat has a personal TV. But it's not really separate from the casino. I guess it means you can find time to get some blackjack hands in between races.

LIMITS $50 tables, no mid-shoe entry. Craps, 5x odds $10 to $3,000, roulette $15 to $200 number, $5,000 on the outside.

FOOD AND DRINK The Sterling Brunch, 10 A.M.–3 P.M. on Sunday, $50 prix fixe, looks more than worth it. Everybody's talking about this thing. Australian rack of lamb, Washington State oysters, Maine lobster tails, and Tattinger champagne. I talk to a guy who says it's worth it, and he's not a spender.

Casino drinks are pleasantly strong. Dizzy Dolphin Beachfront Bar adjacent to Boardwalk is a nice enough spot, with live music at night.

Hotel

804 rooms, salon, spa. Rather expensive. $120 in the off season midweek up to $500 in peak times.

 PRACTICALITIES
Hotel Phone Number: 1-609-347-7111, 1-800-257-8677, group rates 1-800-231-8687
Location: South end of the Boardwalk. All the way on the end.

TRUMP PLAZA AND WORLD'S FAIR CASINO

I don't rightly know what all the slot club deals are, important for a slot player, but as far as comfort and selection go, I'd go no farther than the Trump Plaza and World's Fair. Words fail. It's just so big and so clean and so airy and new—all over.

The lobby is all marble, grand, if a bit cold and austere. Trump believes the place sets the mood, not the people. Donald Trump is the father of this town. He had faith in this town when no one else did, he poured money in when it was still a pit and stuck with it. I mean, it's done well for him, but still, the first time I came down to Atlantic City, what a pit. And no Donald Trump.

Casino

LAYOUT Lots of walls break up the noise here, pretty nice for a slaughterhouse. The main casino floor is a touch noisy, but that's owing only to the tremendous action.

World's Fair: All slots on two floors, but don't get lost in the section that houses all the old ones. The casino is spread over several levels and lots and lots of different-size rooms. It's kind of fun in that get yourself lost kind of wandering and gambling way.

FOOD AND DRINK The New Yorker restaurant looks inviting twenty-four hours, well above average twenty-four-hour coffee shop, offering attractive seating options with comfort and privacy, or not. Counter seating, pleasantly lit, nice menu, standard, and QUICK and attentive service. Homemade mozzarella wedges are far better than the deep-frozen standards known the world over. The food's just a few notches better.

Besides that, all the standard restaurants I wouldn't normally bother with.

Hotel

Rack rates. January–March and November–December, $115 weekday, $140 weekend. April–June and September–October, $140 weekday, $165 weekend. July–August, $165 weekday, $265 weekend. Rooms befitting a Trump hotel.

PRACTICALITIES
Hotel Phone Number: 1-609-441-6000, 1-800-677-7378
Location: On the south part of the Boardwalk, between Caesars and the Tropicana.

RESORTS

Resorts had two choices. Renovate the entire casino. Or spend a lot less money on a huge and flashy new ad campaign. They went for the marketing. It's just a new ad campaign, not a new casino.

Absolutely nothing has changed about this place in over ten years. The casino is one big room with one old rug. They made a stab at a nice poker room, but lost early in a battle with the Taj Mahal next door. Now they've taken out the poker room and replaced it with an entire roomful of nickel slots. How's that for an insult? That shows you just where they rate the value of poker players these days.

Casino

What can I say? The entire casino is in one big room, with the exception of the race book, which has a nice and private location, although it's a hell of a long walk. This is a place to find $5 limits at 5 A.M. on a Monday morning.

FOOD AND DRINK The deli at the Resorts is nice because tables have views directly of the Boardwalk and beach and the morning sun through the plate glass in your air-conditioned street level booth. Other than that, I would strongly recommend against eating anywhere else in the joint.

THE PEOPLE THERE People who haven't been to Atlantic City in a while, and who still think Merv's name means something.

Hotel

The rooms are aged. This place needs a heavy cash injection.

PRACTICALITIES
Hotel Phone Number: 1-609-344-6000, 1-800-GETRICH
Location: Near the top of the Boardwalk, next door to Resorts. You can travel between Resorts and the Taj Mahal without having to go outside, via an indoor second level bridge.

TRUMP MARINA AND HARRAHS

These two casinos exist. They are both located away from the other casinos, on the water. I've been going to Atlantic City all my life and I don't know that I've ever been in Harrahs. The only time I was in Trump Marina is when I was with someone who parked his yacht there, and that's probably when you should go.

Entertainment and Nightlife

One of the main things about Atlantic City that you have to realize is that nobody really drinks at the casino bars. Not for fun, anyway. All the fun bars to drink at in Atlantic City are outside of the casinos. But they're not too far.

The two best bars in town are the Atlantic City Bar and Grill on Pacific Avenue and Los Amigos on Atlantic Avenue. They pick up steam when the swing shift gets off at 2 A.M. You can get some fine food at both those places as well, excellent fresh king crab legs at the AC Bar and Grill.

Atlantic City Bar and Grill—this place is open twenty-four hours, at least I think it is. I mean, it's never been closed when I've been there. Maybe it closes for a few hours in the daytime or something. This bar is right on Pacific Avenue, just a few blocks south of the Taj Mahal and Resorts. It is a top drinking spot, because it's open late, it's cheap, it's friendly, and they serve some unbelievable seafood to wash down your pitchers of beer. King crab legs and fried calamari will get you started. 1219 Pacific Avenue, at South Carolina Avenue, 348-8080. Kitchen open until 6 A.M. Very reasonable prices, they also offer lobster and filet mignon specials.

Los Amigos—they're always talking about tearing this building down, but they never do, probably because it's such a great bar. The building that Los Amigos is in has had adjacent buildings torn down to the right and left of it, and the entire building that Los Amigos now resides in is no more than ten feet wide. Three stories high and ten feet wide. An architectural classic. Although there are tables to sit and eat at in the very back, you generally don't sit down at Los Amigos. The bar runs down fifty feet, and it's primarily a favorite of the swing shift crowd in Atlantic City, who get off between 2 and 3 A.M. and drink until past sunrise. Coronas flow freely, as do large nacho plates and chips. One of the most happening spots in Atlantic City between 2 and 5 A.M. Weekends are good.

Los Amigos is located on Atlantic Avenue, it's hard to find sometimes, and they do close, and if you leave your car in the parking lot, it will get towed by 10 A.M. and you will have to produce about $60 to $100 and deal with one of the nastiest men you shall ever care to meet over at one of the private towing concerns in Atlantic City. I've tried that, with the Luma Kid.

You can see some good shows at the casinos. Some unbelievable people make the rounds of these casinos. Most of these places have things for a night or two and that's it. Not many regular shows. I've seen Bob Dylan, the Neville Brothers, and the Radiators in Atlantic City. But that's just who I like. And the Moody Blues. Everybody plays there. Go to *casinocapsule.com* for information about what's going on in different showrooms. Or check *www.attheshore.net.* If you'd rather call, try any or all of these phone numbers:

Bally's Park Place 1-609-340-2709, 1-800-772-7777
Caesars 1-800-677-SHOW
Claridge 1-609-340-3700, 1-800-752-7469
Harrahs 1-609-441-5165, 1-800-2HARRAH
Hilton 1-609-340-7200, 340-7160
Resorts 1-888-771-1sun, 1-800-322-SHOW
Sands 1-609-441-4137, 1-800-AC-SANDS
Showboat 1-609-343-4000, 1-800-621-0200
Tropicana 1-609-340-4020, 1-800-526-2935
Trump Marina 1-609-441-8300, 1-800-284-8786
Trump Plaza 1-800-759-8786
Trump Taj Mahal 1-609-449-5150

AMUSEMENT PARK The Steel Pier amusement area is located on the Boardwalk just across from the Taj Mahal in the summer. Roller coaster, rides, games, and food. 100-foot Ferris wheel. Virginia and the Board-walk. Open daily June through Labor Day, 1 P.M. until midnight. Week-ends Palm Sunday through October, noon until midnight. 1-609-345-4893, *www.steelpier.com.*

FOOD Atlantic City is one of the culinary gems of the East Coast. All the good eats are to be had outside the casinos. Unlike Las Vegas. In general, any good restaurants in At-lantic City casinos are very overpriced and any cheap restaurants are hor-ribly lacking in quality. It makes sense to eat in the casinos when you're on a comp. But when you're not on a comp, experience the culinary de-lights Atlantic City has to offer. This area of the country is long famous for fresh seafood and good southern Italian home cooking, along with some regional specialties of the indigenous population of big-haired mall people of the South Jersey shore. Local food here is good eating.

This section of the world, from a culinary standpoint, is responsible for inventing two things and presenting them to the world: the cheese steak sandwich. And funnel cake. Now don't grimace. You may have had a cheese steak before. You may have even eaten funnel cake. But if you haven't had a cheese steak from South Jersey or Philly, then the chances are 10–1 that you have no idea what I'm talking about. Welcome to the source, baby. Both of these specialties can be sampled on the Boardwalk, along with some absolutely killer fresh-squeezed lemonade.

My personal favorite spot is **Joe Italiano's Maplewood II,** which I will put up against any Italian restaurant anywhere. This is not complicated food. This is homemade spaghetti with red sauce, salad that will knock your socks off, fresh bread, and an entree of veal parmigiana or calamari or seafood fra diavolo. The most expensive thing on the menu is $15. Make sure you order the homemade spaghetti rather than the imported one. Joe Italiano's Maplewood II is a thirty- to forty-minute drive from downtown Atlantic City. It's located on the Black Horse Pike in Mays Landing, N.J., and it's not really that hard to find except that you always think you've gone too far, but you haven't. You just get on the Black Horse Pike in Atlantic City and stay on it, and eventually Joe's Maplewood will be on your right side. Keep going past the mall. Phone number is 1-609-625-1181. Cash only, I believe.

White House Subs begs to be mentioned, because if you spend any time in Atlantic City you have to go there. You just have to go there. First of all, just for the pictures, to see the gallery of people and culture who have eaten at the White House Subs during its seventy-five years of existence. This is where Burt Lancaster hung out while filming the movie *Atlantic City*. This is the kind of place where people tip the guy who makes their sandwich.

It is, quite simply, the quintessential submarine sandwich. This is the arete, this is what all submarine sandwiches strive to be. Perfect in every aspect. Get whatever you want, a half a sub can feed a person, a whole sub can feed a starving maniac. If you want to eat there, you may have to wait, but it's worth it to look at the pictures on the walls. Most people get subs to go, and you still have to wait. The White House Special Sub with everything is a personal favorite. Located on the corner of Arctic and Mississippi avenues, across from Trump Plaza. 10 A.M.–11 P.M. Phone 1-609-345-1564. Cash.

If you have any sort of affinity for Asian food whatsoever, then you must go to **Little Saigon** Vietnamese restaurant, which is located right inside Atlantic City. At the risk of sounding repetitive, this may be the best Vietnamese restaurant in the country. And if you've never had Vietnamese food, order the cold spring rolls, not the fried ones, and if you like coffee order a *café sua da (café sooey dah)*, it's an iced coffee sweetened with condensed milk, so refreshing. Then you can have either *pho*, Vietnamese soup which is actually a delicious meal, or anything else on the menu. Try the broken rice.

Vietnamese food is light and not at all greasy. There's a beaming family who runs the joint, and their popularity is such that now you need reservations in the evening. The very bright interior has about twelve tables, seating for thirty or forty. Clean wood, overhead fans, music, and pink mats.

Little Saigon is located at 2801 Arctic Avenue, on the corner of Iowa Avenue, three blocks from the Trop World. Phone 1-609-347-9119, open lunch and dinner every day but Wednesday, 11 A.M.–11 P.M. Lunch specials available Monday–Friday, 11 A.M.–3 P.M.

If you need a good steak, **The Library Restaurant** is known as the top steak joint in the area for the price. You pick out your own steak and they cook it right there for you. It's also on the Black Horse Pike, but closer to Atlantic City than Joe Italiano's Maplewood II.

Late night Italian can be had at **Angeloni's II.** It's a nice space and a fair meal, good basic red Italian. It's not the level of Joe's Maplewood, but it is only two blocks from the casinos, and there is a late night menu from midnight–3 A.M. You can have dinner there as well. 2400 Arctic Avenue, at Georgia Avenue, 1-609-344-7875. Credit cards accepted, and they always show the Yankee games on TV.

LUCY THE ELEPHANT If you have a car in the summer, drive all the way down Pacific Avenue and keep going, into and through Margate. It's a great long drive next to the beach, and beside the great old and new beach houses, if you go far enough, you'll see Lucy the elephant, who I think is the biggest free-standing elephant, anywhere. 65 feet tall, built in the late 1800s. Decatur and Atlantic avenues, Margate. You can also climb inside of Lucy, call 1-609-823-6473 for opening hours.

GOLF You'll need a car to play golf in Atlantic City, and you'll need a tee time. During the week, it's a little easier. Don't expect to make a reservation for Saturday on a Friday. Not during the summer.

Green fees are on the high side, up to $75 or $100 at the nicer public courses. Brigantine has an all right public course at the lower end of the scale, and it's only about ten minutes from the casinos. There's some fun holes, but don't go if it's muddy. Around $40 for eighteen holes.

SHOPPING The Ocean One Mall on the Boardwalk across from Caesars Palace is a good mall. It juts out on a pier over the water and is three stories high. Good cheap shopping, particularly useful for wives or girlfriends who don't gamble. A few hundred bucks and they'll be in there all day. Cheap shoes, clothes, a shopper's delight. Also a food court and video arcade. Open daytime hours every day. On the south end of the Boardwalk.

THE BEACH The beach. Well, I wouldn't go swimming. But people do. The beach runs right along the Boardwalk. If you're serious about lying out, drive along Atlantic Avenue until you hit Margate and check out the beach there. It's pretty nice, but I still wouldn't go swimming.

THE BOARDWALK This is the Boardwalk. The one from the song and the one from the Monopoly game, and there is a spot to sit under the Boardwalk and kiss, so that's nice. And a sunrise stroll along the Boardwalk is the perfect slot noise antidote, exchanging ringing bells for cawing gulls and oxygen suffused smoke rings for salty tangy sea air. Morning walkers and joggers. The Boardwalk runs southwest, from the Showboat down to the Atlantic City Hilton.

The Boardwalk is in a constant state of repair. There are two people whose only job is to replace one wooden board, one after the other. It takes them like three years and then they start at the beginning again. Wow. And they keep it in good shape—in a very literal sense, it is a "board walk."

BIKE RENTALS 1-609-344-8008, summer 6:30 A.M.–10 A.M., between Sands and Claridge at the bottom of the ramp leading to the Boardwalk. Morning rides are where it's at. The Boardwalk boards are the perfect surface for bike riding.

CHAPTER FOURTEEN

LAS VEGAS, NEVADA

LAY OF THE LAND

The Super Bowl has always taken place in Las Vegas. I mean, there's always someone who will say, when you tell them that you're going to Vegas for the Super Bowl, some guy will always say, "But I thought it was in California this year." Or New Orleans or something like that. But for those in the know it has always taken place in Las Vegas. The most wagered on sporting event in the history of our country. Like the year the Bengals played the 49ers and everybody remembers it as the Bengals winning, because even though they lost the game by two points, they covered the spread, and that was the year Bob Stupak won a million dollars by betting on them. That's when the Super Bowl took place in Vegas.

◆

In Vegas, where you are is everything, and you can be anywhere. Don't get stuck! Don't get stuck at a crappy casino at a crappy hotel playing at some two-bit blackjack table, when Vegas can be done in full-blown style. Yes, Vegas is a gambling town. But it's a town for excitement, for hype, and for drinking all hours, so don't mix it all up.

In 1989, I stayed in a $20 a night motel downtown where there were holes in the curtains and everything was dirty because we didn't want to spend the money and get a regular room. This is after having been up for over twenty-four hours because we didn't want to get a room the first night. That's almost the last time I did that.

Don't go to Vegas unless you can spend a little money to have some fun. It's too grim. The sweet side of Vegas, the party and entertainment town, is where to focus your energies, because this is where Vegas shines.

Las Vegas, Nevada
GENERAL INFORMATION

YOU'RE NOT IN KANSAS ANYMORE I don't consider Vegas a place for kids. Of course, having said that, it should be noted that I first went there at sixteen and was there a dozen times before I turned twenty-one.

WHERE Vegas is in the middle of the desert. Don't ever forget that. It's a wild paradise, but it's in the middle of the desert.

WHEN Room rates are two to three times or more on Friday and Saturday nights than they are during the week. Some hotels will give you cheap rooms for all nights if you check in like on a Wednesday or Thursday. Cheap rooms go to those who book early. Most reservations are easily held and then canceled by credit card on short notice with no penalty. So I usually make a reservation as soon as I have even an inkling that I might be there.

TELEPHONES Most hotels charge you $1 every time you make a call, even if it's to a 1-800 number or your calling card. House phones inside most casinos in Vegas are the deal, however. From a Bally's house phone it should be possible to get the operator, ask for the Las Vegas Hilton, and make dinner reservations at the Barronshire prime rib room. Or page someone in the Bellagio poker room.

There's a classic bank of pay phones just outside the Stardust sports book. Before everyone had cell phones, that's where runners would phone wise guys to find out how much to bet. And on what game.

MONEY Any hotel room worth its salt will have an in room safety deposit box. If you're not sure, ask when making a reservation. You are advised to make use of this safe. Carrying a lot of money around is a bad idea if you're going out, that is to bars, nightclubs, and anything sordid. It's better to just bring what you need and leave the rest behind. That way you can't get snared by a sharp sniping craps table either.

One of the first times I was in Vegas, a guy we were staying with named Pooky showed up and claimed he had been robbed in the Frontier parking lot on the way back to the Stardust from the Mirage. We think he may have gotten mugged by the craps table at the Frontier. Either way, he would have been better off leaving his money in the safe.

CURRENCY Dollars. If you cash out for more than $10,000 at a time, you might have to fill in a form, so don't if you can help it. Chips are almost currency in Vegas. They're not, and they're not usually exchangeable between casinos, but you can carry chips around in Vegas without a problem. And you know you'll get your money back.

ATMS There's a million ways to get money in Vegas. Everything is at your disposal. Be careful.

CLIMATE You could probably fry an egg in downtown Las Vegas in the middle of summer. It's that hot. Oven-blasted temperatures of 110 degrees without a speck of humidity. Then it gets down to 55 degrees at night. The winter is more mild in the 60s with some rain.

SAFETY You're all too safe in the casinos. In Vegas, the problems happen when you get outside the casinos and off the Strip. You're also safe on the Strip between the Stardust and the Bellagio at any time day or night. It's a much longer walk and there's not as many people farther up the Strip toward the Excalibur, but it's generally safe. Once you get off the Strip, more care must be had. Dangerous situations at massage parlors and nightclubs are not unheard of, getting rolled and robbed in some back room of a place your cab driver took you. It's better to know where you're going rather than asking your cabby for a suggestion.

The guys I know who've gotten robbed or rolled at a strip or massage parlor, it always started out that they went someplace that their cab driver suggested.

WHAT THEY WEAR Being dressed properly in Las Vegas comes down to one thing—always layer. As for fashion, it doesn't matter how you look. Vegas is kind of beyond that.

The first thing that comes to mind when I consider Vegas fashion is about a section from the book *Letters from a Nut*, when a guy writes a formal letter to Bally's in Las Vegas telling them he likes to dress up as a giant shrimp when he gambles and making sure it's okay in their casino. I can't exactly remember Bally's response, but they took him seriously. And that's the whole thing about Vegas. Everything goes. It's not anything goes. It's everything goes. Think about it.

TIPPING IN TOWN Basically, you should always be thinking about tipping in Las Vegas and what it can get you. Everybody takes tips, and everybody is on the lookout for them. They are the pipeline of Vegas.

A Little Green Can Grease the Wheels

You need to know that a little green can grease the wheels. Vegas is a town where everything's on a sliding scale. No matter where you are, no matter what you're doing in Vegas, the difference between the best and the worst is always huge. That's just the way Vegas is set up. And money is how you climb the ranks there.

An example. You have a reservation for dinner at a nice restaurant. So does everybody else. The best tables go to the people with the comps, guests of the casino, the high rollers. Who else gets the best tables? The tippers. No tip and you are automatically shuffled to the back.

Success in Vegas is about understanding that people can do things for you. In Vegas, employees have a lot of freedom about exactly how they execute their jobs, and they can go above and beyond their call of duty at any time. They really can. There are a lot of people in Vegas that can do things for you. Here are a few of them.

Maids: Ever see what's on those little carts? Everything. I always tip my housekeeper the first time I see her, especially if I'm going to be in town for more than one or two nights. First of all, I like to have personal contact with anyone who's going to be in the intimate vicinity of my stuff. Also, I like to have someone who's not going to complain if things should get a little messy, you never know. My standard line is: "I would really appreciate if I could have a few extra towels in my room." Well, I love to take lots of showers, anyway.

And then I give them from $2 to $5. It does wonders. One time I tipped $10 and when I got back to the room I could have opened up a store. I had about thirteen fresh towels and ten of every bottle they had, plus stuff I had never seen before like, toothbrush, shaving kit, deodorant, conditioner, mouthwash, cologne, hairbrush. And for the whole week. Housekeeping is good to have on your side.

Maitre D's: Maitre d's are the big guns in Vegas. They're in charge of those seating plans, deadly in charge. It ain't like a New Jersey diner, where your table's too cold and you move to another booth. The big move to make with a maitre d' is early in the day, before you actually come for dinner. At a nice place, showing up with a $20 bill when you make your reservation in the afternoon should get you a good table, $50 is not out of line if there are several in your party. In Vegas, there is truly nothing like a good table at a good restaurant.

Check-in Clerks: It's important to understand that when you have a room reservation at a big hotel, you are not assigned a specific room. When you go to check in, the clerk looks down on her big computer screen and she basically has the option of assigning you any room that is available in the hotel. With some limitations, I'm sure. This is a person who can do something for you, because all rooms are not the same. In fact, my experience suggests that different rooms in the same hotel can vary widely in quality. There are new towers, floors with new furniture, different decor, and different room layouts in corners or on different floors, adjoining rooms, rooms with an obnoxiously long walk to the elevator, rooms with a great view. It helps to know what you want. It really helps.

Here are some tendencies I have noticed. Treat them with bias.

1. The higher the room, the better the view. I love a room high up.

2. Rooms with one king bed are better than those with two doubles. Just nicer, but you obviously have to treat need first.

3. Ask for a room in the "new section" or a newer room. Big hotels are in a constant state of renovation. There's always something new and something old.

How to Do It: I maintain that the reason most people don't tip in some circumstances is because of their fear that it could be interpreted as a bribe or something worse, that it could be bad. At least that's the way it is with me.

It's important to be smooth. Here's an example. You're checking in at a hotel and check-in time is not until 2 P.M. It's 9:30 in the morning and you've been gambling all night. You'd really like to get to sleep and don't like your chances of surviving until 2 P.M. It's a very busy holiday weekend. They're turning people away at the front desk. You approach the front desk with a tired smile. You don't begin to speak until you reach the front desk. Put the money next to your credit card, not on top of it.

I'll Walk There Barefoot
TRANSPORTATION ISSUES

FLIGHTS If you need help in getting to Vegas, then you've never left home before. Everywhere goes to Vegas. There are so many flights flying into Vegas all the time that absolutely abnormal prices exist if you have plenty of advance planning or you live in a gateway city. Good fares can also be gotten at the last minute if it's not an insane holiday or convention weekend.

Red-eye flights are the Vegas special. Never has a group of passengers looked so weary and forlorn.

Don't go for the deals that promise you a special hotel rate based on a number of hours of play at a minimum bet table. That's a clear bankroll killer.

Air/hotel packages can be a good deal if made through travel agencies. *Travelscape.com* has some pretty darn cheap combinations at all times.

STREETS The Strip. You always hear about it, but what is it? The Strip is Las Vegas Boulevard. Las Vegas Boulevard is a broad street that runs all the way from downtown Las Vegas southward until it crosses the highway, or becomes one itself. Any casino with property fronting on that road can call itself "on the Strip." But in my mind, the Strip really refers to that section of road that runs between about the Sahara Hotel up until Bally's on the left and Caesars on the right. That's because, if you drive on that stretch of road in a nice car, at the right time, then you are cruising on the Strip. And that is what everyone wants to do.

The Strip can get so packed on the weekends that it'll take you an hour to get anywhere. It's better to use back roads or the highway if you actually need to get somewhere. Vegas is very easy, it's mostly a grid. Get a map.

TRANSPORTATION AROUND TOWN Unless you plan on always being drunk, a serious possibility, renting a car is the way to go in Vegas. This affords you the possibility of prowling, and there is nothing quite like being on the prowl, driving through Vegas at night. Besides that, taxis are reasonable and affordable. In Las Vegas, you can only get a taxi at a hotel, and sometimes you have to wait in a long line, and sometimes you have to tip the hotel doorman $1. The lines move fast, but that's the way it works. It's usually about $15 to get from the Mirage to Binion's if they take the highway.

I always make an effort to rent a really nice car when I'm in Vegas. There's something about the combination of driving down the Strip in a really nice car that seems to obscure money considerations.

The Strip trolley is an easy and inexpensive way to travel in Las Vegas. The trolley just runs up and down the Strip, from downtown all the way to the south end, and that's a pretty long way. I think it costs about $1. The trolleys seem to run rather frequently, but if you're gonna wait you're gonna wait. Those decisions you can make when it comes down to it.

The Money Plays
GAMBLING SETUP—THE QUICK FACTS

CASINOS Vegas is casinos. A trend in the last fifteen years has seen large casinos move toward corporate ownership and away from the mob-infested shady ownership deals of the past. Binion's Horseshoe is still under independent ownership, although control has recently shifted from Vegas old-time establishment Jack Binion, to his sister Becky.

New developments may transform the town further still. Mirage Resorts and holdings have been sold to Kirk Krekorian and MGM. It is unclear if Steve Wynn will now have a role in the future of Las Vegas. But as one of Krekorian's first moves was to sell the Bellagio's billion-dollar art collection, it appears that another part of Vegas may surrender to cost sheets and the bottom line, rather than over-the-top lavishness.

HOURS Some of the restaurants in Las Vegas close sometimes. So do some of the stores. Not a damn thing else ever does.

ADMITTANCE Minimum gaming age is twenty-one. ID required. As someone has actually found out, most casinos do not permit you to wear a large shrimp costume while gambling because it may upset other people. To my knowledge, this is the only dress restriction in Las Vegas.

AMBIANCE AND AMENITIES You won't believe your eyes. That said, at some point you'll wish you could just turn it all off. Vegas has the biggest, the newest, the wildest, it's in a constant state of growth. Atmosphere ranges from the sedate and refined elegance of the Dunes to the wild and skimpily clad waitresses of the Rio to the over the top lavishness of the Bellagio, and every theme in between. Most casinos are themed, some more charmingly than others.

GAMES ON OFFER Wow. Sport books, poker, craps, slots, blackjack, roulette, baccarat, keno, Caribbean stud, Big Red, Chuck a Luck and the big wheel and all those crazy new games they have, Pai-Gow, and everything else. Everything in Las Vegas is a game on offer. What tickles your fancy.

LIMITS This is where it all hangs out. This is where the whales come to play, and this is where busted-out old men in threadbare clothes looking for a bowl of beans at the lunch counter come to gamble. You can find a limit to suit your bankroll, and most likely, you'll find one a little higher.

TOP-TIER PLACES TO GAMBLE As far as gambling goes, the top-tier places are the ones who've been in the business the longest, and things associated with Steve Wynn. In no particular order. Caesars Palace, Bellagio, Mirage, Stardust, Golden Nugget, Desert Inn.

MONEY Everything takes place in dollars. Vegas is a place that gives substantial credit to players, if you set yourself up properly. I have very little experience in that area.

LEGALITY Everything is legal, and everything is regulated. Vegas is not a place where you have to worry about being cheated anymore. What you have to worry about is being careful.

Basically, you need to be twenty-one. If you're not twenty-one, you can probably still dive into some places and gamble until you get carded. Then you say you don't have your ID or wallet with you, but you are over twenty-one. You will be allowed to cash out your chips and leave. Unless you have a lot of chips. Then they may hold them until you can produce an ID.

TIPPING POLICIES IN THE CASINO Most everybody who works in Vegas makes most of their money from tips. You don't have to be a big tipper, but you should be a fair tipper.

THE RULES OF VEGAS Rule number one: No plans are fixed. And rule number two: Every man has the right to gamble alone.

AND . . . ON THE SQUARE The games in Vegas are on the square. They're on the square in the sense that there are no marked cards, there are no cheating dealers, no phony dice passed into the game, and no magnets under the roulette table to move the ball. In that sense, Vegas games are on the square and you don't have to worry about getting a fair gamble. But you should be careful. For instance, let's say you're at a busy craps table with multiple bets on every number and the layout is packed shoulder to shoulder with every sort of come bet and hard way proposition known to two dice and you happen to be playing the Don't. You're playing the Don't and hoping it won't, the only one at the table hoping so and you have quite a few numbers up in the Don't come and then shooter rolls a seven and the croupier just sweeps all the chips. Because that's what they do when shooter sevens out, and your bets are gone and you have to tell the croupier and the floorman that you're owed a bunch of money, but you don't want to make too big a stink because everyone else at the table just got crushed. You see, in that case, and things like that aren't so rare, there's certain casinos I'd rather not be in. Because I want a competent box man who has already taken care of the problem, because even in a very busy game he's seen every bet. And that's why every casino is not really the same.

I'll Take the Odds
BREAKING APART THE GAME

CRAPS As any craps player will tell you, a good craps game depends on how many times odds they'll let you back up your line bet. In my mind, the other thing is how busy the table is, because I think there's nothing more appealing than a humming craps game when I have a few moist bills in my pocket. Craps odds in Vegas are competitive and vary—the Stratosphere was offering 100x odds behind the line, but that's probably a little excessive. Vegas is a very decent place to play craps and competition keeps the odds at different casinos on a general par. Usually 5x your bet behind the line, sometimes more.

POKER There was a time when Vegas was just about the only place in the world that you could find a legal poker game, and if you wanted to be a poker player, that was where you went to make your bones. From time back until the present, Las Vegas has been the undisputed poker capital of the world. In my mind, however, this is changing, perhaps even as soon as the new millennium. Las Vegas is still a great place to play poker. The plethora of games at every limit and the low rakes make Las Vegas a great poker atmosphere. However, a little care should be taken. Because in Vegas there are always sharks treading the waters. And in a poker room, there's always sharks in the woodwork.

Some poker rooms offer hotel room rates based on you playing a certain number of hours in their poker room during your stay. Be wary of this deal. The poker room may be fairly empty, the game might be bad. When playing poker, I think a large part of your potential profit comes from game selection, and if you must commit four hours of every day to a certain poker room, where you have no knowledge of the games, you could be a tad frustrated. Not every poker room has sixty tables.

Imagine having to leave a rocking game at the Mirage where they're capping every flop because you have to put in four hours at a drip drip game at the MGM in order to get your reduced room rate. It's like having a job.

Binion's poker room always maintained a strong presence, at least as long as Johnny Moss, the Grand Old Man of Poker, was still alive and living there and playing every day in Binion's $20–$40 Hold'em game. But now Binion's has changed ownership. Mr. Moss has passed away and there's little hope that the Horseshoe Poker Room will continue to function as an everyday force. As long as the World Series of Poker continues to be held there, however, the Horseshoe will be the center of the poker and entire gambling world for those two weeks in May. The World Series of Poker is continuing to grow every year.

The Stardust continues to have a good low-limit room, perhaps as a testament to the dealers, who are basically the best poker dealers in the business. The least experienced dealer has been at the Stardust about fifteen years. $1 to $5 seven-card stud and $3 to $6 Texas Hold'em.

The Mirage Poker Room opened in 1988 and changed the face of poker in Vegas. It immediately put the Las Vegas Hilton's rather successful poker room out of business. 70 tables gleaming green in an enclosed area that manages to be simultaneously in the dead center of the casino and shielded from all unwanted noise. An architectural miracle. All the hi-limit action in Vegas took place at the Mirage until the opening of the Bellagio next door.

Bellagio is now the most happening poker room in Vegas, and the place to go if you want to play higher than $10–$20 stakes. If you are playing $10–$20 or lower, some other poker room might be recommended. The Mirage continues to be a nice place to play. The Mirage plays $5–$10, $10–$20, and $20–$40 limits, the Bellagio plays $15–$30, $30–$60, $75–$150, and much higher.

Some tips about playing poker in Vegas: The most important poker decision you will make in Las Vegas is game selection, I believe. There are good games and there are bad games. In limit poker, which is the primary type of poker played in Vegas these days, good games are those where a lot of players are playing a lot of hands. Bad games are those where players don't play very many hands at all. Part of good limit poker play involves folding a lot of hands at your earliest convenience.

Good games can be found in busy casinos at night and all the way up until about 6 A.M. Bad games can be found during the day. That is a general tendency in Las Vegas.

If you really want to make money at poker in Las Vegas, take a nap and set your alarm for 3 A.M. Then when you go down into the casino to play, you'll have everything working for you. It still doesn't mean you'll win.

BLACKJACK Competition keeps the blackjack rules fairly attractive in Vegas. They vary slightly from casino to casino, and there's always some single and double deck games downtown. But they are very wary of counters in Las Vegas, and very experienced in being able to tell if you know what you are doing at the blackjack table. That said, if you like to gamble high at blackjack and the casinos like your action, then you will find a whole host of comps at your fingertips.

PAI-GOW POKER Pai-Gow poker with cards is played in many places around town. The Mirage and Bellagio, among others, also have Chinese Pai-Gow, played with dominos.

SLOTS America is the place to play slots, and Vegas has the newest and the loosest slots in the world. Paybacks vary wildly, however. There's some huge jackpots to go for. Bellagio has lots of the new Odyssey machines. Make sure you have a cash card, for comps are there for the asking for slot players. If you have the wherewithal to play $25 video poker, a full-suite comp is yours for the action. $5 players can expect a regular comped room or at the very least, a casino rate.

HORSE RACING It's all simulcasting, which is the nice thing about betting horses in Vegas. You can't be at the track, but you've got any of eight tracks, or twenty-eight, to choose from to bet all at the same time, so you can pick out one good horse in one race and plunk something down. It doesn't have to cost much, and it's a nice way to while away an hour or two.

SPORTS BOOKS The Mirage sports book is a classic, but it tends to become so overcrowded on the weekends that you can't even stand in there. Forget about getting a seat. The Caesars sports book is a much better alternative. It's big and it's not too bright, so you can see all the TV screens and betting boards. You just might get a seat. Bally's sports book is out of the way, way in the back out of the casino and down an escalator, and it's a bit strange in there, being so far away from everything else. Not a great place to sweat, although the beers run freely here. The nicest obscure sports book by far is the one in the Las Vegas Hilton. Big, plush, and quiet, if you happen to be hanging at the Las Vegas Hilton, it's a pleasure to place any bet and be able to sweat it here, sipping a drink in the cool confines of the big-screen TVs all around the sports book. I sweated some great Australian Open tennis matches in that place, I'll tell you.

Now the Bellagio is the toast of the town. If you can get there early enough, commander's chairs are yours for the taking, where you can sit and have an armchair view of every game, all at once, and all the lines.

The Imperial Palace is for betting only, but you will find some crazy proposition bets at that place that don't exist anywhere else in town.

Binion's Horseshoe race book is old and run-down, but very classic. Nice if you can get a good seat. Hang out with real toothless broken-down horse players, and then sidle over to the lunch counter for a bowl of ham and beans that will cost you seventy-five cents.

The Gambler's Book Club

Perhaps ironically befitting the most invaluably profitable locale for the gambler in Las Vegas, the Gambler's Book Club is tucked away on a side street where the uninformed gambler will never trip over it.

This ain't no tourist trap. Books on gambling, all the books on gambling, and the people who run the shop know those books inside and out. It's a family atmosphere, feel free to spend a while and browse and schmooze and find what suits your fancy. I guess a lot of people have the attitude, "Well, I'm gambling anyway, I have to get lucky to win, and I know all I need to know if I'm going to get lucky."

There's a lot to know about gambling. And anybody looking to put their money into action can only help themselves by going there. I know a fellow who likes to play blackjack, been playing a long time, wanders into the store one day picks up a blackjack book, takes it back to the hotel, and reads it by the pool in the afternoon, takes a nap, wakes up that evening, and gets crushed worse than ever before at the blackjack table. So you never know.

But the GBC has it all. Whether you like to bet football or baseball, basketball or horse racing, or if you're into poker or blackjack or video poker, then the GBC has got all the serious books, treatises, and software available. The first time I ever walked into that place I must have been about nineteen or so and taken a cab from the Strip and gotten one of those Malmouth–Sklansky books on advanced Hold'em. Or maybe the Luma Kid bought it. But that was in like 1989 and the Gambler's Book Club was in the same place, in the same location, and even then the store was crowded with tomes, although I don't think they'd built their addition on back then. I also bought a bunch of books on sleight of hand. There again, if you're willing to practice and want to learn how, the secrets of Ricky Jay are there for the grasping, although don't ever expect to be able to deal from the middle of the deck.

The Gambler's Book Club is the premier place not only in Las Vegas, but also the country for gaming educational resources. And someone there has read every book. Serious gamblers are always slipping into the GBC. Slipping in and not talking to anyone, just buried off in a corner leafing through a book. One guy who I started a conversation with was a horse player, but very secretive about his system and obviously not very much comfortable with anyone but rather effusive, I guess he was doing well lately. I see a guy who I think maybe I played Hold'em with at the Stardust eight years before named Willie M. Herb recommends to me a biography of Steve Wynn, which I pick up along with a reprint of an 1880s treatise of a Mississippi riverboat card sharp. And an old paperback which was only $3.95 and a book about Bear Bryant for my father.

Later, when I wanted to get into the serious instructional stuff, I consulted with Peter, the resident blackjack guru. (See Adventures in Card Counting, page 149.) I told him what my time parameters were and how much time I was willing to devote to serious study. He recommended an ambitious arsenal of materials, but at a reasonable price. I got the Ne Plus Ultra Blackjack Master and Practicum computer simulator, which is actually both a tutor and a computer simulator that tells you when you make mistakes and lets you set any playing conditions for only $39.95, and I got Lawrence Revere's classic *Blackjack as a Business* and Stanford Wong's *Professional Blackjack.* The first book proved so accessible and yet time-consuming in conjunction with practicing on the computer, that I didn't even open the second book until forever. But I was excited, because Peter set me up really well. If I followed that book to the T and put the time in to memorize the charts, all the charts, then I might be of some significance in a casino. At the midpoint, situations weren't too encouraging. I was stuck $12,000 to the computer and had a tendency to go on tilt and lose the count. But I kept at it.

The Gambler's Book Club is a humble abode, they've even had the name of the Gambler's Book Store copyrighted out from under them by a two-bit outfit in Reno, so they labor ignominiously under the moniker of the Gambler's Book Club. The walls of the store boast a picture gallery of Vegas gambling icons, past and present. The original owner, Edna, still works at the store at nights. Howard Schwartz has been at the GBC since the beginning and has a filing cabinet that would be the envy of any newspaper chief in the world. He has read and reviewed every book in the store. Peter Ruchman has been playing blackjack for twenty years. Asking him about the count is like asking Einstein about the atom. Or any of the other laid-back GBC family members who dwell in the pleasantly air-conditioned refuge where they take gamblers seriously. As long as you take yourself seriously. Located on 630 South 11th Street, Las Vegas. Store hours Monday–Saturday, 9 A.M.–5 P.M. Closed Sunday. Toll-free order lines 1-800-522-1777 and 1-800-634-6243. Phone 1-702-382-7555 / fax 1-702-382-7594. Call for the free catalog. On the Internet at *www.gamblersbook.com.*

Casinos and Lodging
THE POINT

CHOOSING A HOTEL Choosing where to stay is the single most important decision you'll make for your trip to Vegas, aside from the decision about how much money you're prepared to blow. The three factors to consider are how much you're willing to spend per night, what amenity atmosphere package you want, and what location in Vegas you want to be in.

Vegas is always changing. Some of the new resorts have nice facility offerings, but they're so far out, like the MGM, where you have to walk a minimum of a mile to get anywhere. The center of the Strip now is that place where Caesars and the Bellagio and the Mirage and Bally's are all together, the giants of Vegas now. Then you have down the Strip, you have Treasure Island, which is an all right joint but doesn't have the action for the money and the Desert Inn farther down, which is like an old-time classic Vegas casino, probably the most elegantly fashioned casino in Vegas. But don't stay there to party.

The reason your hotel is so important is that you'll end up spending so much of your time there. Even if you never sleep, which in Vegas is always the possibility looming on the horizon, where you will find yourself most likely is in your own hotel, in the casino or at the bar.

It's like this. You're lying in bed winding down about to fall asleep or just waking up and ordering room service and you realize there's a basketball game about to come on TV in twenty minutes. Now if you're staying in hotel with a great sports book, you can throw something on and run down and bet on the game and be back up in bed just as the room service gets there and the game starts. See, why miss out on that?

Vegas is not so much a question of best and worst as what you want. As for location, center Strip is where it's at. I don't care what newfangled conglomerations (contraptions) they're putting up God knows where in Vegas. The central part of Las Vegas Boulevard that houses Caesars Palace, the Mirage, and the Bellagio is where the action is at. That's where the hottest sports book, casino, and poker action is in Las Vegas and looks to be for at least the foreseeable future. Bally's is a great less expensive option directly across from the Bellagio and Caesars. Everywhere else you stay on the Strip is basically a long walk to anywhere.

These casinos can all be traversed together on foot. Although in Vegas these days, you should always have a good pair of walking shoes. If you don't, check out the massive Foot Locker in the Caesars Palace shopping forum, which has very good prices.

Stretching south from the Bellagio on the Strip, you have all the new themed hotels, the Excalibur, MGM, NYNY, the Venetian, Mandalay Bay, and whatever else they're putting up. These are worth checking out. But they will restrict you mostly to the hotel that you choose, so don't stay there unless you feel comfortable spending most of your time there.

New places arise, but because of their slightly remote locations, the test of time is on to see if they can remain at the forefront of casinos after a year or two of operation. Casinos like MGM and NYNY, and Luxor, in my mind, have not sufficiently shown that they possess any depth beneath their gimmicky themes, which wear off after a while. Although Luxor does have some exceptional rooms for the price. Not as nice rooms as the Golden Nugget, however.

North of Center Strip you find some long-standing fixtures on the Strip. The string of low-budget sausage house places like the Holiday Inn and the Barbary Coast, the low-volume five-star elegance of the Desert Inn, where you can still catch Don Rickles if you're lucky, and the Stardust, with a history stretching far back into Vegas lore and still a decent and fairly recently renovated casino hotel that may be lacking from a clear identity. Then the Strip kind of turns a little seedier and it's a mile or so of motels and pawnshops and chapels until you get to downtown. And there, that's old-time Vegas.

Downtown does have its charms. Most of them have to do with price. I love to start off a Vegas weekend downtown. Tradition has it that the players meet at the Binion's Horseshoe at midnight or 2 A.M. for some steak and eggs. The Horseshoe coffee shop has the longest running midnight steak special in Vegas. And it hasn't changed. A decent steak in the middle of the night for like $2.95. Upstairs is new management. I don't think they still boast the highest betting limits in the world. But the sports book, while small, has some surprisingly good lines and is always worth checking out if you are price shopping. But you have to come back downtown to collect your ticket.

Not much else for downtown except for the Fremont Experience, which is a midnight light and laser show that takes place under the iron canopy now covering the whole of Fremont Street. It's worth watching one time.

And then there's the Golden Nugget, which may be the best value in town, considering it's a virtual palace, the food is good, and the rooms are large and gorgeous. But it is downtown, so rent a car and park it valet.

Vegas is changing faster than the speed of my typewriter. That's the nature of the town. Go bigger or go home. Go newer and better all the time. Here, however, is a quick ranking of atmosphere and amenity packages in some major Vegas hotels.

CRÈME DE LA CRÈME. These places have a service level that is truly exceptional. They are also sedate: **Desert Inn, Caesar's Palace**

OVER-THE-TOP EXTRAVAGANCE-ON-A-BIGGER-SCALE-AND-A-BIT-CROWDED: Bellagio, Mirage

GOOD SERVICE / GAMBLING PACKAGE: Golden Nugget, Rio, Bally's, Treasure Island, Stardust

A STEP BELOW, BUT NOT WITHOUT SOME ATTRACTION: Binion's Horseshoe, Circus Circus, Luxor, Gold Coast, Imperial Palace, Hard Rock

NOT RECOMMENDED: MGM, NYNY, Excalibur, Frontier, Holiday Inn, Flamingo Hilton, Barbary Coast, Las Vegas Hilton, any other downtown hotel

UNCLEAR: Mandalay Bay, Venetian.

CAESARS PALACE

"Hail, noble guest, we hope you enjoy your stay in Caesars wonderful kingdom."

We had caught up with Morty in Vegas, along with the Luma Kid again and it was kind of like a minireunion, for the opening of the Bellagio. Morty had the usual suite at Caesars because he's a mad Russian gambler, but we really went over the top in experiencing Caesars charms.

The place is just so damn classy. I mean, especially in Vegas, where cut corners are all over the place and what is promised is a technicality. Surely Caesars is an anomaly, keeping to a five-star service policy throughout their resort. And when Morty wanted to bet a $2,600 teaser, they didn't even blink. The guy just shouted over his shoulder, teaser for $2.50, to the woman manager who came behind him and looked at his screen, and Morty gave them his card to be rated. Why would anyone want to tease the Niners to −8½?

Every casino goes through its heyday, and hey, that's why it's Vegas. At one time the Las Vegas Hilton was the newest and classiest joint in town. But then the Mirage opened up and blew everything out of the water and there have been so many new openings since then: the MGM, the Luxor, New York New York, Treasure Island, to name a few, and each one bigger and better than the last. And all along, Caesars Palace has remained at the top of the pack. The last ten years have seen continual rebuilding and expansion for Caesars and the package is now pretty impressive, what with the forum shops and the restaurants and the swimming pool and the spa facilities and the casino with the high ceilings, Caesars has got what we'd call luxurious. And hip. Hanging out down in that sports book is a pleasure. All the televisions, dark room for the better picture and the odds sheets and lines on the big betting screens behind the teller windows. Or the long tables where you can sit and bet the horses, relaxing to handicap any of the tracks available through simulcast.

Wow, is Caesars Palace a nice place or what. I mean, when you walk into that spa, you know that you're ready to be pampered in style. First you go to your locker, don your towel and robe and slippers, and head for the showers for a hot rinse or directly into the wet spa in order to get warm. From here into the dry sauna to really get warm and sweat out that hangover. Now into the shower to cool down and rinse off. Grab a new towel or two and retire out to the cushioned chairs and couches to have some water or juice and watch the game or pregame or "Sports-Center" until you're ready to go back into the wet sauna. This time Morty signals the attendant and he brings us new razors and paper cups of lather. There's a sink and mirror in the wet sauna, so we indulge in a shave, after which we go back into the dry sauna for a final blast of real sweating.

After another cold shower and a brief respite watching the Bears fumble against the Cowboys, we were in no hurry, Morty and I were ready to tackle the whirlpool, the Olympic-size Roman tub spouting with steam. Very nice. Then a hot shower with soap and shampoo and deodorant and the new toothbrush with the toothpaste and a little after shave and a few more towels and some more juice while sitting on the couch watching TV with my feet up and waiting for Morty. We were sparing no expense. We arrived back into the room very refreshed to find the Luma Kid sitting up in the room at two tables surrounded by six plates of food. He looked like he could handle all of them. We had just made a reservation at Nero's and were quite content to just have a few chicken tenders and let the Luma Kid finish his filet while we thought about what soon awaited. There was only the question of rousing the sun goddess from her crash, where she'd spent the whole day asleep after heroically succeeding in getting nine of us very drunk the previous night. And the room service menu is good. I mean really good. So good that the Luma Kid would pass up a trip to the steak house in order to sit in the room and order everything off the room service menu and watch games that he was betting on.

But then again, maybe the Luma Kid really didn't understand Nero's steak house. Because with a menu like it has and service to go with it, well, you just can't go wrong. Morty of course went for the caviar, it being just to the left of the market price sign. I got pate foie gras and almost had another order as my main course, rare pieces thinly grilled with walnuts and the whole bit on pears. The sun goddess had crab cakes, excellent crab cakes that had her swooning, and she's very picky. They had delightful onion soup while I went with a gorgonzola salad. Presentation is genius here. Morty asked what the best thing on the menu was and the waiter told him to have a steak and when I ordered a veal chop he steered me to the steak and boy was I glad that he did.

Caesars Palace general information goes like this. It's a $1 charge for local calls and 1-800 # calls. The spa opens at six. Nobody says you have to sleep before you go there. They have about twenty different spa packages, treatments, facials, the works, including the famous Ultimate Synchro Massage, where you get massaged by two people at the same time. The rooms in the new tower, the Roman Tower, are like six times better than the other rooms. Go for the Roman Tower rooms. They are stupendous.

PRACTICALITIES
Hotel Phone: 1-702-731-7110, 1-800-634-6001
Location: 3570 Las Vegas Boulevard South, Center Strip.

DESERT INN

The Desert Inn is a very special place. First of all, Lord knows how many people are buried there. It's Vegas the way Vegas began, but that's not to say it's old or lacking. It's old, it's austere, it's really magnificent. The casino is a centerpiece, understated. No loud and unsightly slot machines all over the damn place. It's really a one of a kind place. If you know who Lorna Luft is, then you'll know what it means when I say she's a regular in a packed showroom with Don Rickles. And if you don't know what I mean, you should catch the show. Rooms are in the $300 per night range, but they're worth it. The morning brunch at the sunlit coffee shop will make your jaw drop. The Desert Inn also has an on site golf course—arguably the top course in Vegas. If you're serious about playing on it, you should be staying there to have a chance at all. (A little green can grease the wheels.)

PRACTICALITIES
Hotel Phone: 1-702-733-4444, 1-800-634-6906
Location: 2535 Las Vegas Boulevard South, a smidgen north of Center Strip.

MIRAGE

The Mirage opened in 1988 and changed the face of Vegas. A million dollars a day in operating expenses. A tropical walkway forest of flowers. A 200-foot-long 10-foot-high aquarium, with live monsters of the deep and tropical beauties, an erupting volcano out front, and acres of beautiful gambling inside, set off by a huge hushed poker room with seventy tables and a Gauguin-like mural on one whole wall of the room with a few bare breasts. And Siegfried and Roy and white tigers out back. Steve Wynn owns the Mirage, and the Golden Nugget and Treasure Island and the Bellagio, and he believes in quality and service.

The Mirage is convenient, has among the nicest rooms in town, and has a convenient place to stop for a cheap but filling meal in the California pizza kitchen, where the spaghetti bolognese is a sleeper choice at $8.95. Soup is also good there.

 PRACTICALITIES
Hotel Phone: 1-702-791-7111, 1-800-627-6667
Location: 3400 Las Vegas Boulevard South, Center Strip.

BELLAGIO

It's not that the Bellagio is a bad place. It's just that, from Steve Wynn, you've come to expect the moon. I mean, the opening of this place was trumpeted to beat the band. There was actually a rumor circulating that this would be the first Vegas locale with a dress code, jacket and tie, and the smallest limit table here would be $100 minimum. No dice, on both counts.

It's a nice place, don't get me wrong. The likes of the glass sculpture on the ceiling of the lobby have never been seen before, anywhere. I don't know who came up with it, but it should be preserved forever. The casino is so big that it needs public transportation. Everything at every limit, and the absolute newest slots that you've seen anywhere. Tons of them. The poker room is the only place to play, and the sports book is the place in the world that you would choose to sweat a game if you had a good seat. The rooms are luxurious and the list of restaurants reads like a who's who in *Gourmet Today*. The buffet serves duck.

A word about the art collection. Steve Wynn decided he wanted an art collection for the Bellagio, and he figured he had a billion dollars to spend. And he knew that he wanted at least one Van Gogh, some Picassos, a Kandinsky, a Pollock, a Rodin, a Rembrandt, a Monet, a Manet, a Matisse, and some Gauguin. And he had about a year to do it. And he got them.

Then Kirk Krekorian bought the Bellagio and sold the whole collection.

A shame, really, because as my friend Dave liked to say, a lot of people were getting to see those works who ordinarily would never be caught inside a museum. They were on display daily just off the lobby, and they were a testament to just how lavish Vegas had gotten.

The Bellagio is still lavish. And time will show if the new owners can keep it that way. Even if you're not staying there, and since room rates are reasonable there is no reason not to stay there, the Bellagio is a place you want to go and check out. Because you gotta check out everything big in Vegas.

PRACTICALITIES
Hotel Phone: 1-702-693-7291
Location: Las Vegas Boulevard South, Center Strip, next door to Caesars Palace and across the street from Bally's.

TREASURE ISLAND

Treasure Island has a hell of an arcade. And pirate ships out front with a buccaneer fight every half hour. It's a Steve Wynn project, built on top of what was formerly the Mirage's parking lot. I guess it's Wynn's concession to families and kids. There's nothing very special about the inside, or the food, that I have found, but the rooms are spacious and comfortable, like you'd expect from Wynn. On the whole, this hotel is a niche rather than a cornerstone to the Wynn empire, and the minitram that runs between the Mirage and Treasure Island is the primary reason most people stay there. The Mirage fills up fast. The rooms facing the Strip have great views.

PRACTICALITIES
Hotel Phone: 1-702-894-7111, 1-800-944-7444
Location: 3300 Las Vegas Boulevard South, Center Strip, next door to the Mirage.

GOLDEN NUGGET

A lot of real gamblers who have been coming to Vegas for about twenty years always stay at the Golden Nugget. See, twenty years ago, the Golden Nugget was the nicest place in town, in the center of downtown, and the only thing that's slipped about the Golden Nugget in twenty years is the neighborhood. But the neighborhood has plunged. It's not the center of Vegas anymore, Center Strip is. And downtown Las Vegas has come to be known politely as a "budget gambling" area. Downtown now houses a lot of the down-and-out.

The Golden Nugget, however, is a different world. An oasis in the middle of a sandstorm, with beautiful rooms, excellent food and service and amenities, and a nice casino. The Italian restaurant here is a real find. Because the Golden Nugget is downtown, prices reflect it. But the service and quality don't. You can usually be staying at the Nugget for like $59 a night. This is an unbelievable deal. And you are safe inside the Golden Nugget and can leave your car with the valet, and watch the Fremont Experience light show.

 PRACTICALITIES
Hotel Phone: 1-702-385-7111, 1-800-634-3454
Location: 129 E. Fremont Street, downtown Las Vegas.

RIO

The Rio is commonly considered as the place with the nicest-looking dealers and cocktail waitresses in town. It's pretty good. The rooftop bar is one of the most happening casino bars in Las Vegas, as is the disco. Besides that, it's an okay if loud place to gamble, when you can find a seat. The casino is mammoth, so big and so labyrinthine that you are always lost, all the time. If you lose someone in there, good luck finding him again.

One attraction of the Rio is that it is all suites. All the rooms are big, and very nice. And you can get a pretty attractive room rate. The Rio is located opposite from the Gold Coast. You can't walk from these two casinos to anywhere else. They are quite close to Center Strip, and there's always the twenty-four-hour free shuttle that will take you back and forth.

The Rio specializes in buffets. Both the World Buffet and the Seafood Buffet offer exactly what they promise, and lots of it.

Club Rio is happening at night. No sneakers, collar, $10 cover. Women are decked. Gorgeous from Southern California. Yes yes.

 PRACTICALITIES
Hotel Phone: 1-702-252-7777, 1-800-888-1808
Location: 3700 West Flamingo Road, west of the Strip.

BALLY'S

My only real complaint with Bally's is the walk to get to the sports book. And oh yeah, the showroom is nonsmoking. We were in line to get tickets for Penn and Teller when we decided the money could be put to far better use at the blackjack table.

The biggest advantages to Bally's are that the location is perfect and the room rates are low. Lower than any other decent hotel on Center Strip. The rooms aren't beautiful, but they are fair at $89, or $119, or something like that, which is 50 to 100 percent lower than you will probably find across the street at Caesars or the Mirage. It's completely convenient to travel from Bally's, action is right outside the door.

 PRACTICALITIES
Hotel Phone: 1-702-739-4111, 1-800-634-434
Location: 3645 Las Vegas Boulevard South, Center Strip.

STARDUST

Back in the day, the place to stay was the Stardust, out back in their motor lodge. You could get a room at the poker rate of $18.95 and split it three ways. Then you could get $5 food comps from the poker room and live virtually for nothing. Except your gambling. But people aren't going to Vegas for three months as much anymore. It's a town for a weekend or a convention and you might as well have some fun.

I remember my first time at the Stardust. It was just after its heyday, but it was still basking in the glow, fifteen tables going regularly in the $3 to $6 Hold'em backbone of Las Vegas. At the Motor Inn, the rooms out back that stretch down from the hotel and you have to walk a little bit to get to them, we got a room at the poker rate for $18 plus tax, which we split three ways. And we used the $5 food comps from the poker room, which could be applied either to the snack bar or the seven-page menu of Toucan Harry's twenty-four-hour coffee shop. We spent all our time in the poker room. If we weren't playing, we were soaking up the chatter, the atmosphere, for all the Vegas old-timers were here. The poker dealers had a minimum of ten years of service and most of them far more. Chuck, who has been in Vegas at the Stardust since it was a one-horse town, was there, with stories about every gambler and casino that's been through Vegas.

In the early '90s the Stardust had a major renovation and they built a new tower with nice rooms for the price. The Stardust is, in my mind, a pleasant low-pressure place where you can get nice rooms for a good price, get good service amenities including a pool, and still have some very economical quality options to make daily life in Vegas a little lighter on your wallet. The Rock 'n' Roll diner has an excellent burger, meat loaf, or blue plate special with mashed potatoes or fries and a great milk shake, which will never set you back more than $5. Small-package liquor store for that all-important cold beer in your room. You know, things you need.

 PRACTICALITIES
Hotel Phone: 1-702-732-6111, 1-800-634-6757
Location: 3000 Las Vegas Boulevard South, just north of Center Strip, but walkable.

GOLD COAST

The Gold Coast has always had some quirky attractions. They set themselves on the map that Washington–Buffalo Super Bowl when the line was 7 and they offered +7½ Buffalo and −6½ Washington, middling themselves. The whole of the sports world took the 20–1 odds on that proposition and the Gold Coast held all the Super Bowl action and actually risked going under if the Super Bowl number fell on 7.

What the Gold Coast now features is quality service at budget prices. In my mind, it's the best you can get for these prices and still be somewhere. First of all, Gold Coast has a twenty-four-hour bowling alley that's got a lot of lanes. And they have a two-screen movie theater, and a very good ice cream parlor. The sports book is fair, but crowded, as is the casino. The bonus is that the Rio is right next door, and if you like to party, that's where all the action is at. The Gold Coast had a great low-limit poker room. It's probably still worth checking out.

 PRACTICALITIES
Hotel Phone: 1-702-367-7111, 1-800-331-5334
Location: 4000 West Flamingo Road, next door to the Rio.

HARD ROCK CASINO

Right now the Hard Rock Casino lays serious claim to being the wildest spot in Vegas. Hit the place about 3:30 A.M. on a Friday night and you'll see what I mean. It is, however, a little out of the way in the sense that you can't walk there or walk from there. But it's an easy cab ride. Personally, I would never stay at the hotel. I just like to go when I'm loaded. It's a really good place to be drunk. I like to go to the bar in the middle of the night. It's just that I think the rooms and service level are sort of geared toward young people having wild parties. Now, I am all for wild parties. It's just that I'd prefer to have them in a really nice room where the TV's not bolted down. I'd prefer to have the option of throwing the TV. If it should get to that.

 PRACTICALITIES
Hotel Phone: 1-702-693-5000, 1-800-HRD-ROCK
Location: 4455 Paradise Road, east of the Strip.

Party On

There hadn't been much reason to leave Caesars Palace. But what with the Coronas and the Heinekens and the rum and champagne, we were raring to go. Lenny had his zoot suit on and at three-thirty we figured it was a good time to check out the Hard Rock Casino. When they say Vegas never sleeps, they mean you can party—truly party—at any hour.

The Hard Rock was in full-blown force. The sun goddess was trying to pick up a woman for the Luma Kid. Women were trying to pick her up instead. Morty was passing out his phone number to some chick at a blackjack table, I was smoking Morty's Montecristo and drinking white wine very fast. Loud music was playing and a Jimi Hendrix guitar hung behind glass. The bar is in the center of the room from which you can see everything, the whole casino. All the casino chips have rock stars on them. The sun goddess got a hold of a $25 chip with Jimi Hendrix on it and decided to keep it for a souvenir. It wasn't even hers.

Morty spotted a porn star from Playboy's "Up All Night." She walked through the room with a hunk. People were dancing at the bar and drinking up a storm. Drinks were fairly reasonable, or so said Lenny, who is used to L.A. prices and was surprised to get back a chunk of change from his $20 bill after buying a round.

IMPERIAL PALACE

The Imperial Palace needs to be mentioned, because everybody figures to end up passing through there at some point on a trip to Vegas. Usually by accident. It's just so damn central, and stairs lead right from the street straight up to the sports book and fast-food restaurant. What a combination. The theme of the IP is Oriental, much in the same manner as chop suey. During Super Bowl time, the IP sports book is a must. They always lead the pack in wildly original Super Bowl propositions and are credited with originating the famous Michael Jordan points scored on Super

Bowl Sunday vs. the points scored by both Super Bowl teams that day. Michael Jordan usually won. I wouldn't recommend staying there.

 **PRACTICALITIES**
Hotel Phone: 1-702-731-3311, 1-800-634-6441
Location: 3535 Las Vegas Boulevard South, Center Strip.

BINION'S HORSESHOE

Johnny Moss passed away two years ago, without hardly so much as a ripple. Johnny Moss. The Grand Old Man of Poker. Stu Ungar died last year and he got an obituary in *The New York Times* and radio shows and articles about his life, but Johnny Moss passed away without hardly so much as a ripple. And I figure it was because, by then, no one really liked him. Up until his death, Johnny Moss spent eight or more hours a day in the 20–40 Hold'em game at the Binion's Horseshoe, and I didn't spend that much time there, but I spent enough time there over the course of the years to play with Mr. Moss quite a number of times, and listen to him and talk to him and watch him, and I mean I never saw any of the establishment old-timers say hi to him. I never saw Doyle Brunson or Chip Reese, Bobby Baldwin or Puggy Pearson, no one ever said hi to Johnny Moss, came up to shoot the bull with him or talk about the weather. And I don't know, but I figure he just never went in with any of them. He just beat them all flat on his own. Now I don't know. But there are a couple things I do know about the life of Johnny Moss.

I know that there was a time when Nick The Greek Dandalos came into Las Vegas and put up the challenge that he would play any man in poker for any amount of money until one of them was busted. The year was 1949. And Benny Binion, a young fellow from Texas who had just bought a sawdust joint downtown that he renamed Binion's Horseshoe, Benny Binion said he'd run a poker game like that for free, on one condition—that it be held in full view of the public. Dandalos agreed, and then Benny Binion made a phone call—to his childhood friend Johnny Moss.

Johnny Moss was in Odessa, Texas, where he had been up for four days straight playing poker, and he put down the phone and got in his car and drove straight to Las Vegas without any sleep and he walked right into Benny Binion's casino and put his money down on the table and they started up the game. And Nick the Greek drew a jack on the last card—his board read jack, three, four, seven—playing five-card stud no-limit with one card in the hole. Johnny Moss's board read two, three, nine, six, and he had a nine in the hole, so when Nick the Greek bet $50,000 into a pot that was already over $100,000, Johnny Moss moved in with all his chips. And Nick the Greek Dandalos, in full view of the public, said in a soft voice, "I believe I got a jack in the hole, Mr. Moss." And Johnny Moss said, "Greek, if you got a jack, you're liable to win one hell of a pot." And Nick the Greek pushed in his chips and flipped over the jack of diamonds. And Nick the Greek Dandalos raked a pot that, at best estimates, was almost $1 million. This really happened.

And then Johnny Moss went to sleep and got some more money and came back and busted Nick the Greek Dandalos. He busted him. After losing a $1 million pot, Johnny Moss went to sleep and then came back and busted Nick the Greek Dandalos for many millions more. Did you hear me? The game lasted five months. Other players drifted in and out, but it was only Johnny Moss and Nick the Greek. And at the end, Nick the Greek Dandalos said in a soft voice, "Mr. Moss, I'm gonna have to let you go." One of the greatest gamblers in the history of the world, after five months, he said to Johnny Moss in a small voice, "Mr. Moss, I'm gonna have to let you go." And in his later years he was playing $5 and $10 limit in Gardena, California. This is true.

Johnny Moss once bet everything he had on a golf match. He had to shoot an eighty using only his seven-iron and his putter and he'd put up $275,000, which was all the money he had, and it got down to the eighteenth green and Johnny Moss had to sink a seventeen-foot putt in order to make eighty strokes, and everyone was standing there on the eighteenth green, and Johnny Moss just lined up that putt and put it right down into the middle of the hole. And the men with the money grumbled and said something to the effect of lucky fuckin' putt, and do you know what Johnny Moss did? He said, "Let's go double or nothing," and then he went over to the first tee and stood and waited for them. They didn't follow.

So that's the history that Binion's Horseshoe has behind it, and up until a few years ago they also held a claim that they had no maximum betting limit. And that's where some of the really big sports bets got made, and where some fellow named Archie almost busted the whole casino when he got ahold of $30 million and then lost it all again.

In 1998, the casino was sold from Jack Binion to his sister Becky Binion. Both are children of Benny Binion. Becky Binion seems determined to put her own stamp on the casino, and this will be evidenced primarily by the direction that the World Series of Poker takes in the future. Bigger media coverage could mean big things for this world championship in the future, which features a four-day $10,000 buy-in no-limit Hold'em tournament with a first prize of about $2 million.

The rooms and facilities at Binion's are sadly in need of an upgrade. The deli across from the sports book will always be a gem, as will the 3 A.M. steak at the coffee shop, and the atmosphere of the horse racing book. The rooftop steak house offers a fine view of the city.

PRACTICALITIES
Hotel Phone: 1-702-382-1600, 1-800-237-6537
Location: 128 Fremont Street, downtown.

CIRCUS CIRCUS

I never thought I'd say this, but it's official. The Circus Circus has been around long enough to be considered a classic. This place was a horror show back when it first opened. All the dealers wearing bright pink, tons of low-budget gambling, families all over, and an actual circus performing nonstop on wires and nets hung above the casino floor. A true madhouse. No gambler would be caught dead inside, except perhaps to play in the $1 to $5 no smoking stud game as some sort of Sisyphean punishment. Now, the Circus Circus harkens back to those days of the late eighties, when style was a Fila jogging suit and a clown juggling three milk bottles.

For some mind-boggling reason, the Circus Circus steak house is among the best in town.

PRACTICALITIES
Hotel Phone: 1-702-734-0410, 1-800-634-3450
Location: 2880 Las Vegas Boulevard South, north of Center Strip.

LUXOR

The first thing you notice about the Luxor is that all the elevators go sideways. The Luxor is shaped as a giant pyramid, and the rooms, while big, all have that pyramid slant to them. No matter. It's a pleasant place to stay for the price, the knock, as usual, being location. It's a ways down to Center Strip. You can get a good "pyramid burger" in the coffee shop, and take a boat ride along the banks of the Nile.

PRACTICALITIES
Hotel Phone: 1-702-262-4000, 1-800-288-1000
Location: 3900 Las Vegas Boulevard South, south of Center Strip, and it's a little bit of a hike.

LAS VEGAS HILTON

The Las Vegas Hilton has always been a class joint, but I think it's severely in need of a makeover if it wants to compete with top-tier hotels in Vegas. I mean, they almost charge top hotel prices. The Hilton has always faced the drawback of being slightly off the Strip. It was a little more plausible a few years ago, when that corridor between the Stardust and the Hilton was populated with the Landmark, the Paddlewheel, the Silver Slipper, all since closed down. Now it's a hefty walk or much more, probably a cab ride to anywhere else.

Actually, it's not *that* far out of the way. But a walk will only get you to the Riviera, Stardust, or Circus Circus, and where's that?

On the plus side, Las Vegas Hilton does have exceptional convention facilities, so you might end up there if you're attending something big. One of the best sports books in town.

The sad truth is the Las Vegas Hilton has come way down in class. Way down.

PRACTICALITIES
Hotel Phone: 1-702-732-5111, 1-800-732-7117
Location: 3000 Paradise Road, east of the Strip.

NYNY

I haven't spent that much time in NYNY. It was kind of empty when I was there and Kid Sam had been drinking all night and we were looking to get some Bloody Marys and breakfast, in that order. Well, the Bloody Marys had no alcohol in them and cost $5.75 each, the breakfast was weak, and the casino, when we walked through it, was empty. And the only place you're within football field walking distance of is the MGM. I'd rather be in Las Vegas.

PRACTICALITIES
Hotel Phone: 1-702-740-NYNY
Location: 3790 Las Vegas Boulevard South, way south of Center Strip.

FLAMINGO HILTON

My complaint with the Flamingo Hilton is that it's utterly devoid of charm. In fact, it has no character whatsoever other than that damned pink flamingo. The rooms are equally as bland. The location is excellent.

PRACTICALITIES
Hotel Phone: 1-702-733-3111, 1-800-732-2111
Location: 3555 Las Vegas Boulevard South, Center Strip.

FRONTIER

Ever since anyone can remember, the Frontier suffered under the ignominy of the longest-running labor strike in the history of the modern world. I don't know exactly how long the strike lasted, but it shattered the ten-year mark, that's for sure. A twenty-four-hour picket line staked out the sidewalk in front of the Frontier, and there was no reason to go inside. Why cross a picket line when you can cross the street and go to a different casino? There was nothing so special about the Frontier. And the management refused to give in to the strikers. They hired scabs for years and years and finally the casino got sold to people who had already negotiated a deal with the union and the strike was over. That was 1998. The Frontier is freely open now, but it has been neglected for so long that it will take a major renovation to even compete with the second-tier hotels in Vegas. I'm sure the owners are planning a major cash injection into this property, unless they're thinking of tearing the whole thing down and building another.

PRACTICALITIES
Hotel Phone: 1-702-734-0110, 1-800-634-6966
Location: 3120 Las Vegas Boulevard South, north of Center Strip.

HOLIDAY CASINO

The Holiday is best described by their centerpiece, the Holiday buffet, where you can eat all you want for $4.95 and there's no way you can eat $4.95 worth of food. The total value of your meal is equivalent to its value in weight after you put it in the trash compactor and take it down to the junkyard. You may find some scrap metal in there, and plenty of reusable oil.

I once ate there with a guy who choked on a chicken bone, turned blue, and almost expired right there in the Holiday buffet. Ain't nobody who wants to die while eating at a red-and-white-checked table in the Holiday casino.

PRACTICALITIES
Hotel Phone: 1-702-737-3500
Location: Las Vegas Boulevard South, Center Strip, across from the Mirage.

MGM

I once stayed at the MGM, and I always had a hard time getting to Las Vegas from there. Because I never felt like I was in Las Vegas while I was in the hotel. The rooms are tiny, among the smallest in town. I actually don't know why you would want to stay there.

PRACTICALITIES
Hotel Phone: 1-702-891-7777, 1-800-929-1111
Location: 3799 Las Vegas Boulevard South, several football fields from Center Strip. A long walk.

EXCALIBUR

This may be the worst hotel in Vegas. Everything smells like urine. My friend Battin describes the place as "officiated by the Gestapo." The rooms are so bare minimum it's not funny. Everything not bolted down is completely worthless. The towels look like postage stamps, thin as handkerchief lining. The bathroom mat is paper, the soap chip falls right down the drain the first time you use it. I don't know how strongly I can not recommend this hotel. Personally, I would rather sleep in the bus station.

PRACTICALITIES
Hotel Phone: 1-702-597-7700, 1-800-937-7777
Location: 3850 Las Vegas Boulevard South, south of Center Strip.

BARBARY COAST

This is a place you're likely to end up at one point with a plastic cup full of beer in your hand while cruising the Strip on foot. There's either a Burger King or a McDonald's in the back. Out front in the casino, which is open to the street, is good cheap gambling. This is a good place to gamble and drink, gamble and pound beers on your wild way. I imagine they have rooms there, but I would shudder to see them.

PRACTICALITIES
Hotel Phone: 1-702-737-7111, 1-800-634-6755
Location: 3595 Las Vegas Boulevard South, Center Strip.

Entertainment and Nightlife

Vegas is about as wild as it gets. If you have a habit of finding yourself in places as wild as Las Vegas, or wilder, then you really know where to look. There are also some clearly dead spots. Some of it has to do with timing. Las Vegas fluctuates between like 10 percent capacity during the week to like 100 percent on weekends. On weekends the town is crammed to the gills. And during the week, you might be the only one at the bar. As far as casinos go, the Rio and the Hard Rock Café are very happening, and Binion's features very cheap drinks. And Utopia is a nightclub just across the street from NYNY.

If you have your own party already, swing downtown to the Horseshoe to drink cheap before or after dinner. Drinks at the bar there are like one or two bucks each, so it's a great place to pound and check out the Binion's sports book.

FOOD Both Sahara and Charleston are fantastic streets to drive on east and west of the Strip in search of good ethnic food. There's stuff all over the place. Las Vegas is becoming a multinational American city, with strong populations of Filipinos and Chinese and Cubans and Koreans and Mexican and Vietnamese and Thai and there's some darn good authentic restaurants that aren't your fancy expensive joints.

Besides that, the newest and the best. Vegas is about eating in hotels, because there's so many things to choose from. All the new hotels are opening up new everything, and an orgy of choices await you. Will you go to Wolfgang Puck's new joint? Or is Bam-Bam Emeril Lagasse more to your liking?

One sleeper choice in Vegas that is a bit unexpected is the steak house at the **Circus Circus.** Don't ask me why. Just accept that it's damn good. And classic. Some Vegas buffets are a little too greasy. However, the buffet at the **Mirage** is an industry standard, the buffet at the **Palace Station** is always rated as best value in town, and the seafood buffet at the **Rio** has exceptional marks. The new buffet at the **Bellagio** has duck.

If you want an $800 bottle of wine, go to the **Palace Court** at Caesars Palace. I don't know if it's worth it, but it sure tastes good.

Just opposite the **Binion's** sports book is their deli, which has the most serious corned beef and pastrami sandwiches in Las Vegas. Bar none. For like $5, you'd swear you were at Second Avenue in New York. But it's only open daytime hours.

Morty the Hammer's Top 5 Spots in the Land of the Damned

One thing you can be sure of. Morty the Hammer knows where to party in Las Vegas. Here are his favorite spots.

On Wednesday night, go to **Ra** at the Luxor.
Friday night, **Babies** at the Hard Rock Casino.
Saturday night, **Utopia.**
Sunday night, go to the **House of Blues** at Mandalay Bay.

And every night is perfect for OG. **Olympic Gardens** nightclub, the best strip club in town. Two blocks off Las Vegas Boulevard, north of the Strip. Take a cab to OG.

A special addition, but it's hard to find and you should never go there before 7 A.M. **The Spearmint Rhino.** It is where the locals go to party after working all night. Truly the wildest spot in Vegas. Take a taxi, and don't get out unless the sign says THE SPEARMINT RHINO. In large letters.

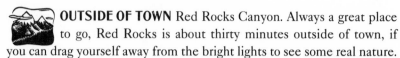

GOLF Vegas can be a tough place to find a golf reservation on a weekend. The best course in town is at the Desert Inn. Good luck, stay there if you're serious. For a reasonable chance of getting on the course, Las Vegas Golf Club, 4300 W. Washington, Las Vegas. Phone 1-702-646-3003. They take reservations and walk-ons, but it's nothing special. Also *http//www.intermind.net/im/golf.html* is a good listing of clubs in the area, most clubs take reservations two weeks in advance and you should do just that if you absolutely want to play.

OUTSIDE OF TOWN Red Rocks Canyon. Always a great place to go, Red Rocks is about thirty minutes outside of town, if you can drag yourself away from the bright lights to see some real nature.

For about three years running, there was always a bet in the group that I went to Vegas with about whether or not someone would go to see the Hoover Dam. Every time, a person ended up paying serious money not to have to go to the dam. You can make whatever plans you want, but it's hard to find time to get out of town when you're in Vegas. It's hard to find time for anything but gambling, actually.

THINGS TO SEE The Fremont Experience light show every midnight. The volcano at the Mirage, a pirate battle at Treasure Island, and a water show at the Bellagio, every hour. Steve Wynn's $1 billion art collection.

SHOPPING The mall in Caesars, the forum shops, is right now the best high-class shopping in Vegas. All the top designers are there. My mom bought her dress for my sister's wedding there, and she's a discerning shopper.

OTHER STUFF

CIGARS You cannot smoke cigars in Las Vegas casinos. Not most of them, no matter how nice your cigar is. It's all right in a lot of the bars, however. The Hard Rock Casino bar is a particularly nice place to smoke a cigar, while the melee rages around you.

BATHROOMS Cleanest bathrooms downtown? The Golden Nugget. Cleanest bathrooms on the Strip? The Mirage, next to the poker room.

INDEX

A

Addleman, Shelby, 43
Admiral am Kurpark, 184, 187
All Sports Bets, 31
All Star Sports Cafe, 237
Allegro Hotel and Royal Palm
Casino, 132–33
Alpino Hotel, 75–76
American Hotel, 192
Amsterdam, 176, 177, 189–94
accommodations in, 191–92
American Hotel, 192
Amsterdam Marriott, 192
Arrive Hotel, 192
bookstores in, 194
Bulldog Coffeeshop, 194
Filosoof Hotel de, 192
food and drink in, 191, 192–93
games in, 190
Golden Tulip Hotel, 192
Holland Casino, 189–91, 194
Kantjil and Tiger, 192–93
Khorat Top Thai, 192

marijuana in, 193–94
Master Classics of Poker in,
189–90
Omaha poker in, 190
Parkhotel, 192
poker in, 190–91
Pulitzer Hotel, 192
restaurants in, 192–93
Waterfront Hotel, 192
Angeloni's II, 255
Arc Élysées Hotel, 197
Arcade, 276
Argentina, 3, 8, 9. *See also* Buenos
Aires; Mar del Plata
blackjack in, 140
Casino Central, 3–4, 7
casinos in, 66
food in, 77
Art collection, 181, 275, 276
Aruba, 121–35
Allegro Hotel, 132, 33
baccarat in, 125
bingo in, 124, 131

Aruba (*con't*)
　blackjack in, 121, 127, 129, 130,
　　132, 133, 134
　Caribbean stud poker in, 124–25,
　　129, 132
　Casablanca Casino, 130
　casinos in, 123–24, 127–34
　craps in, 124
　Crystal Casino, 124, 125, 133–34
　currency in, 122
　diving in, 135
　entertainment and nightlife in,
　　134–35
　Excelsior Casino, 128–29
　food and drink in, 128, 129, 130,
　　132, 133, 134, 135
　games in, 124, 129, 130, 131, 133,
　　134
　Havana Night Club, 134
　Holiday Inn Hotel and Casino,
　　124, 125, 128–30
　horseracing in, 129, 134, 135–36
　lodging in, 127–34
　Marriott Resort and Casino, 124,
　　127–28
　money plays in, 123–24
　poker in, 124, 125–27, 129
　restaurants in, 129, 132, 133, 134
　roulette in, 125, 128, 130, 132, 133
　Royal Cabana Casino, 124, 131–32
　Royal Palm Casino, 132–33
　safety in, 122
　shopping in, 135
　slots in, 130
　Sonesta Hotel, 133–34
　sports betting in, 129
　Stellaris Casino, 127–28
　transportation in, 123
　Wyndham Hotel and Casino, 125,
　　130–31
Asian games, 232–33, 247
Atlantic City, 225–56
　All Star Sports Café, 237
　Angeloni's II, 255
　Asian games in, 232–33, 247
　Atlantic City Bar and Grill, 252
　baccarat in, 247

Bally's Park Place, 229, 243–44
Basin Street Cafe, 242
beach in, 256
Big Six Wheel in, 232
blackjack in, 242, 245, 249
Boardwalk in, 256
Bombay Cafe, 238
Caesars Hotel and Casino, 229,
　248–49
Caribbean stud in, 245
casinos in, 229, 234–52
Claridge Hotel and Casino, 233,
　247–48
craps in, 231–32, 236, 242, 245,
　248, 249
Dizzy Dolphin Beachfront Bar,
　250
Dynasty Chinese Restaurant, 235,
　237
entertainment and nightlife in,
　252–56
food and drink in, 242, 244, 246,
　247, 248, 249, 250, 251–55
games in, 229, 232, 242, 245, 248
golf in, 255
Harrahs, 252
Hilton Hotel and Casino, 229,
　249–50
history of, 226–27
Hold'em in, 234
Joe Italiano's Maplewood II, 254
Library Restaurant, 255
Little Saigon, 254–55
lodging in, 234–55
Los Amigos, 252–53
Lucy the Elephant in, 255
minibaccarat in, 247
money plays in, 229–30
new games in, 232
Omaha Hi-Lo in, 234
Pai-Gow poker in, 247, 248
poker in, 233–34, 245–46
and pushing up the limit, 230
Resorts (Merv Griffin's), 229, 251
roulette in, 245, 249
safety in, 227
Sands Hotel and Casino, 247

Scheherazade, 235, 238
Seven-Stud Hi-Lo in, 234
shopping in, 255–56
Showboat Casino, 242–43
slots in, 232, 242
Stage Deli, 237, 238
Starbuck's coffeeshop, 237
Sushi Bar, 237
transportation in, 227–28
Tropicana Hotel and Casino, 233,
    235, 244–46
Trump Marina, 229, 252
Trump Plaza, 229, 250–51
Trump Taj Mahal, 10, 225, 229,
    233, 235–41
Trump Taj Mahal poker
    tournament in, 226, 233–34
United States Poker
    Championships in, 237
White House Subs, 254
Wild Wild West Casino, 9, 229,
    243–44
World's Fair Casino, 229, 250–51
Atlantic City Bar and Grill, 252
Aurola Hotel. *See* Holiday Inn
    Aurola
Austria, 178. *See also* Baden; Vienna
Casinos Austria in, 178, 186, 188
entertainment and nightlife in,
    186–87
golf in, 186
skiing in, 186
tennis in, 186
Austrian Classics, 188
Aviation Club, 178, 195–97

B
Babies, 288
Babylon, Club
    in Europe, 186–87
    in San Juan, 86, 87, 96
Baccarat. *See also* Punto y banco
    in Aruba, 125
    in Atlantic City, 247
    defined, 12
    in Mar del Plata, 66, 69–70, 72
    in San Juan, 83

Back Street Hong Kong, 86
Baden, 181–86
    Admiral am Kurpark, 184, 187
    Baden Casino, 179, 182
    Brunn Golf and Country Club, 187
    casinos in, 184–87
    Do and Co., 185
    entertainment and nightlife in,
        186–87
    Enzesfeld Golf Club, 187
    Fontana Golf and Sportclub, 187
    food and drink in, 185
    golf in, 187
    Grandhotel Sauerhof, 184, 186,
        187
    Gutenbrunn Hotel, 184, 186
    Heurigenkalender wine schedule,
        187
    lodging in, 184–87
    Parkhotel Baden, 184, 186
    Poker European Masters Final in,
        181–82, 184, 188
    poker in, 181–82, 183
    transportation in, 183–84
Baden Casino, 179, 182
Baldwin, Bobby, 281
Bally's
    in Atlantic City, 229, 243–44
    in Las Vegas, 243–44, 270, 272,
        278
Balmoral Hotel, 25, 53
Balzac Hotel, 197
Banana Tree, 142
Banca gana, 70–71
Bankroll, defined, 11, 12
Barbary Coast, 272, 287
Barcela Amon, 28
Basin Street Cafe, 242
Beach
    Atlantic City and, 256
    Mar del Plata and, 76
    Puerto Rico and, 97
    San Juan and, 97
Beach Grill, 156
Bellagio, 229, 275–76
    Bally's and, 270
    gambling high at, 10, 266

Bellagio (*con't*)
Pai-Gow poker at, 267
poker at, 266, 267
service at, 272
water show at, 289
Bereslavsky, Vadim, 214
Big six wheel, 232
Big Wheel, defined, 12
Bikini Bar, 55
Billy Boys, 58
Bingo
in Aruba, 124, 131
in Curaçao, 156
in Mar del Plata, 67
Binion, Becky, 263, 282
Binion, Benny, 281–82
Binion, Jack, 263, 266, 282
Binion's Deli, 288
Binion's Horseshoe, 266, 268, 272,
281–82
coffee shop at, 271
drinks at, 287
Blackjack, 3. *See also* Rommy
in Argentina, 7, 140
in Aruba, 121, 127, 129, 130, 132,
133, 134
in Atlantic City, 242, 245, 248
best casino for, 9
in Bonaire, 140, 142
Canal 21 as variation on, 104–5
in Central America, 7
in Costa Rica, 140
in Curaçao, 140, 149–54, 156,
159, 160
defined, 12
in Europe, 179
in Las Vegas, 7, 26, 266–67
in Mar del Plata, 68–69, 72
in Moscow, 215, 216
in Panama City, 104, 105, 107,
109, 113
rommy instead of, 25, 26–27, 45
(*See also* Rommy)
in San José, 25, 26–27, 36, 40
in San Juan, 83, 91, 92, 93
in South America, 7
standard Vegas, 152

Blind, defined, 12
Blue Marlin Bar, 52
Bombay Cafe, 238
Bonaire, 137–43
Banana Tree, 142
blackjack in, 140, 142
Caribbean Point, 142
Caribbean stud poker in, 139, 141
casinos in, 140–42
currency in, 138
diving in, 143
entertainment and nightlife in, 143
food and drink in, 142
games in, 139
lodging in, 140–43
money plays in, 139
odds in, 139
Plaza Bonaire Casino, 139
Plaza Resort, 141–42
poker in, 139
restaurants in, 142
roulette in, 142
second-chance poker in, 139, 142
slots in, 142
Tipsy Seagull, 142
transportation in, 138
Boulevard Hotel, 75
Brandinelli, 78
Brennes, Humberto, 33
Brennes brothers, 32, 33
Brunn Golf and Country Club, 187
Brunson, Doyle, 281
Buenos Aires, 3–4
Alpino Hotel, 75–76
best hotel in, 75–76
horseracing in, 71
tourist office in, 74 (*See also*
Argentina)
Bulldog Coffeeshop, 194
Bust, defined, 12
Busted, defined, 12

C
Caesar Park Hotel and Casino
(Panama City), 103, 105, 112–14
Caesars Hotel and Casino (Atlantic
City), 229, 248–49

Caesars Palace (Las Vegas), 10,
270–71, 272–74, 288
Café Bahía, 112, 113
Cage, defined, 12
Calypso Terrace, 157
Camino Real, 22, 46–47
Canadian Thunderbird Corporation,
103
Canal 21, 104–5
Canasta
at Herradura Hotel, 45
roulette *vs.*, 25–26
in San José, 25, 39, 45, 52
Card counting (in Curaçao), 149–54
Caribbean Point, 142
Caribbean stud poker
in Aruba, 124–25, 129, 131
in Atlantic City, 245
in Bonaire, 139
defined, 12
in Moscow, 215
in San José, 26
in San Juan, 91, 93
second-chance poker *vs.*, 139
Casablanca Casino, 130
Cascante, Jose, 24
Casinos. *See also* Amsterdam; Aruba;
Atlantic City; Baden; Bonaire;
Curaçao; Dublin; Helsinki; Las
Vegas; Mar del Plata; Moscow;
Panama City; Paris; San José;
San Juan; Slovenia; Vienna
best, 9–10
with best cocktail, 9
best for blackjack, 9
best for craps ambiance, 10
best for craps odds, 9
best for gambling high, 10
best for sauna, 10
with best room service, 10
with best service and luxury, 10
with best strip club, 10
Ceasarito, 113
Central America, 3, 20
Central Casino, 3–4, 7, 68
Cerromar Casino, 95
Chateaubriand Hotel, 197

Cherry Casino, 212
Chop Game, defined, 12
Cigars, 58, 87, 221, 289
Circus Circus, 272, 283, 284, 288
Claridge Hotel and Casino, 233,
247–48
Clubs. *See also under specific name or
location*
Aviation Club, 178, 196–97
Brennes' poker club in, 32
Brunn Golf and Country Club, 187
casino with best strip club, 10
Club Babylon (Europe), 186–87
Club Babylon (San Juan), 86, 87,
97
Coco Club, 115
Coconut Bay Beach Club and
Restaurant, 157
Enzesfeld Golf Club, 187
Fontana Golf and Sportclub, 187
Gallistico Club, 83, 84
Gamblers Book Club, 150
268–69
Happyland, 115
Havana Night Club, 135
Josephine's, 115
Maharajah Club, 235, 236
Marriott's Aruba Ocean Club,
130
Merrion Club, 178, 200
Tropicana Poker Club, 246
Coach Sports Bar, 166
Cockfighting, 83–84, 90
Coco Club, 115
Coconut Bay Beach Club and
Restaurant, 157
Colonial Casino, 10, 24, 25, 27,
38–40, 105
Balmoral and, 53
craps in, 26, 43
hours for, 24
liquor in, 24
rommy in, 27
sports betting at, 27
Come, defined, 12
Concord Card Casino, 178, 187–88
Concord Casino, 39, 177, 178

Condado Plaza Hotel and Casino, 81, 82, 89–90
Continental Hotel (Panama City), 108–10
  Canal 21 at, 105
  clubs near, 115
  Crown Casinos and, 103
  horseracing at, 106
Corobici Hotel, 47–48
  Balmoral and, 53
  Japanese restaurant in, 58
  poker at, 32, 33, 34
Corona Casino, 212
Coronado resort, 115
Cosmos Hotel and Casino, 10, 206, 208, 212, 213–14, 215–17
Costa Rica, 9, 19–60. *See also* San José
  blackjack in, 140
  Gran Hotel Costa Rica in, 21, 22, 23, 24, 27
  poker in, 32–34
  safety in, 21
  slots in, 9
  Ticos and gringos in, 36–38, 46
Costa Rican Rummy, 104
Costa Rica International Sports (CRIS), 28, 35
Count defined, 12, 13
Craps. *See also* San José
  in Argentina, 9
  in Aruba, 124
  in Atlantic City, 231–32, 236, 242, 245, 248, 249
  best casino for ambiance, 10
  best casino for odds, 9, 10
  defined, 12, 13
  in El San Juan, 83
  in Europe, 180
  explanation of, 231–32
  horseracing compared with, 31
  in Las Vegas, 265
  in Mar del Plata, 66, 67, 72
  in Panama City, 104, 109, 113
  in San José, 25, 26, 39, 43
  in San Juan, 83
Crème de la Crème, 272

CRIS. *See* Costa Rica International Sports (CRIS)
Crown Casinos, 103, 105
Crystal Casino, 124, 125, 133–34
Crystal Palace, 212
Curaçao, 9, 145–68
  Beach Grill, 156
  blackjack in, 140, 149–54, 156, 159, 160
  Calypso Terrace, 157
  card counting in, 149–54
  Casino Curaçao Resort, 9, 148, 154–58
  casinos in, 154–66
  Coach Sports Bar, 166
  Coconut Bay Beach Club and Restaurant, 157
  currency in, 146, 148
  Denny's, 164
  diving in, 158, 168
  entertainment and nightlife in, 166–68
  food and drink in, 156–57, 159, 161, 165, 168
  games in, 148
  Garuda, 157
  golf in, 168
  high limits in, 156
  Holiday Beach Hotel and Casino, 159, 164–65
  Le Tournesol, 165
  lodging in, 154–66
  money plays in, 148
  odds in, 149–50
  Otrabanda Hotel and Casino, 158–59
  Pirates, 157
  Plaza Hotel Curaçao and Casino, 165–66
  poker in, 164
  Porto Paseo Hotel and Casino, 159, 162
  Ristorante Giorgio, 164
  roulette in, 159, 166
  San Marcos Hotel and Casino, 163
  shopping in, 168

slots in, 160, 163, 165
Sonesto Hotel and Casino, 155
transportation in, 147–48
Willemstad, 146–47
Curaçao Resort Casino, 9, 145,
    154–58

D
Dandalos, Nick the Greek, 175,
    281–82
Darsena, 94
Del Rey Hotel and Casino, 51–52
Denny's, 164
Desert Inn, 270, 272, 274
Diamond Palace, 93
Dime, defined, 12, 13, 28
Diving
    in Aruba, 135
    in Bonaire, 143
    in Curaçao, 158, 168
Dizzy Dolphin Beachfront Bar, 250
Do and Co., 185
Don't Come, defined, 13
Don't Pass defined, 13
Dos Reyes Hotel, 75
Double Down, defined, 12, 13
Draw, defined, 12, 13
Dublin, 200
    Hold'em in, 200
    hotels in, 200
    Irish Open in, 175, 177, 200
    Merrion Club, 178, 200
Dynasty Chinese Restaurant, 235,
    237

E
El Chico Mambo Dance Lounge,
    86–87
El Conquistador Hotel, 81, 97
El Imperial Marisqueria, 77
El Panama Hotel and Casino, 99,
    103, 106–8, 115
El Presidente Casino, 25
El Pueblo, 10, 22, 54–55
El San Juan, 9, 10, 82, 84–89, 96
El San Juan Towers, 89
Embassy Suites Hotel and Casino, 96

Empanda Nik Grik, 106
Entertainment/nightlife
    in Aruba, 134–35
    in Atlantic City, 252–56
    in Austria, 186–87
    in Baden, 186–87
    in Bonaire, 143
    in Curaçao, 166, 168
    in Las Vegas, 287–88
    in Mar del Plata, 76–78
    in Moscow, 212, 219–21
    in Panama City, 115–16
    in San José, 54–58
    in San Juan, 86–87, 96–97
Enzesfeld Golf Club, 187
EPPA. *See* European Poker Player's
    Association (EPPA)
Europe, 171–200
    blackjack in, 179
    casinos in, 178
    Club Babylon in, 186–87
    craps in, 180
    currency in, 179
    gambling differences in, 176–77
    gambling evolution in, 174
    games in, 179
    money plays in, 178–79
    odds in, 179
    Poker European Masters Final in,
        181–82, 184, 188
    poker in, 174, 176
    roulette in, 179
    shuffling machines in, 179
European Poker Players Association
    (EPPA), 10, 174, 175–78, 182
European Seven Eleven, 180
European Tour, 10, 174, 175–78, 182
    ranking events, 177
Eurosport, 216
Excalibur, 271, 272, 286
Excelsior Casino, 128–29

F
Fazio, George, 116
Fazio, Tom, 116
Field, defined, 13
Filosoof Hotel de, 192

Fishing, in San José, 58
Fitoussi, Bruno, 195
Flamingo Hilton, 272, 285
Flamingo Hotel, 75
Flood, Liam, 175, 200
Flynt, Larry, 130
Fontana Golf and Sportclub, 187
Food and drink. *See also* Restaurants
  in Amsterdam, 191, 192–93
  in Argentina, 77
  in Aruba, 128, 129, 130, 132, 133,
    134, 135
  in Atlantic City, 242, 244, 246,
    247, 248, 249, 250, 251–55
  in Baden, 185
  in Bonaire, 142
  in Curaçao, 156–57, 159, 161, 165,
    166
  in Las Vegas, 287–88 (*See also*
    specific casinos and hotels)
  in Mar del Plata, 10, 73, 77
  in Moscow, 217, 218, 220
  in Panama City, 107–8, 109, 112,
    113, 114, 116
  in Paris, 196
  in San José, 24, 36, 39, 42–43, 46,
    48, 49, 50, 51, 53, 55–58
  in San Juan, 85–86, 89, 90, 91, 92,
    94, 96–97
Foot Locker, 271
Frontier, 272, 285

G
Galeon Hotel, 75
Gallistico Club, 83, 84
Gamblers
  common mistakes of, 6
  on European Tour, 10
  makeup of, 3
Gamblers Book Club, 150, 268–69
Gambling
  addiction to, 5–6, 30
  dangers of, 6, 11
  defined, 1
  fate and, 4
  free will and, 5
  the government and, 30

  high, 10, 82, 94, 156
  legality of, 30–31
  for profit, 1
  rules for, 10
  superstition and, 5
  terms in, 12–15
Gambling tournaments
  Austrian Classics, 188
  Casino Cosmos's Inaugural Poker
    Tournament, 213–14
  Four Seasons Tournaments,
    196
  Irish Open, 175, 177, 200
  Poker European Masters, 181–82,
    184, 188, 189–190
  Trump Taj Mahal poker
    tournament, 233–34
  United States Poker
    Championships, 237
  World Series of Poker, 177, 188,
    266, 282
Garuda, 157
Gauchos, 132
Gitto, Tom, 233
Gold Coast, 272, 279
Golden Nugget, 271, 272, 276–77
Golden Palace, 212
Golden Tulip Hotel, 192
Golf
  in Aruba, 135
  in Atlantic City, 255
  in Austria, 186
  in Baden, 187
  in Curaçao, 168
  in Las Vegas, 274, 289
  in Mar del Plata, 78
  in San Juan, 97
Gran Hotel Costa Rica, 21, 22, 23,
    24, 49–51
  Balmoral and, 53
  Rommy in, 27
  sports betting at, 28
Granada Hotel, 103, 105
Grand Prix Casino, 218
Grand Soloy, 103
Griffin, Merv, 229
Gutenbrunn Hotel, 184, 186

H
Hampton Inn, 90–91
Happyland, 115
Hard Rock Café, 287
Hard Rock Casino, 272, 279–80, 288, 289
Harrahs, 229, 252
Havana Night Club, 134
Heads Up, defined, 12, 13
Helsinki, 197–98
    Casino Ray, 178, 197–98
    Hotel Ramada Presidentti, 198
Herb, Willie M., 268
Hermitage Hotel, 75
Herradura Hotel, 44–45
Hilton (Atlantic City), 229, 249–50
Hilton (Las Vegas), 266, 272, 284, 285
Hippodromo, 104
Hit, defined, 13
Hit Casino, 178
Hit Hotel Casino Park, 199
Hold'em, 32, 36, 200
    in Aruba, 129
    in Atlantic City, 234
    defined, 13
    in Dublin, 200
    in San José, 32, 36
Hole Cards, defined, 13
Holiday Beach Hotel and Casino (Curaçao), 164–65
Holiday Casino (Las Vegas), 285–86
Holiday Inn (Aruba), 124, 125, 128–30
Holiday Inn Aurola (San José), 24, 27
    Balmoral and, 53
    craps in, 26
Holiday Inn (Las Vegas), 272
Holland Casinos, 176, 178, 189–91, 194. *See also* Amsterdam
Horseracing, 30–31
    in Aruba, 129, 134
    as bad bet, 30
    in Buenos Aires, 71
    in Las Vegas, 267
    in Panama City, 104, 106
Hotel Arrive, 192

Hotels. *See* Amsterdam; Aruba; Atlantic City; Baden; Bonaire; Curaçao; Dublin; Helsinki; Las Vegas; Mar del Plata; Moscow; Panama City; Paris; San José; San Juan; Slovenia; Vienna
House, defined, 13
House of Blues, 288
Hyatt Cerromar, 97
Hyatt Dorado Hotel, 95, 97

I
Iguana Lounge, 132, 135
Iguazú Grand Hotel Resort and Casino, 76
Imperial Palace, 267–68, 272, 280–81
Internet
    EPPA Web site on, 178
    in Mar del Plata, 63
    in Moscow, 209, 218
    in Panama City, 101
    in San José, 22, 30
    in San Juan, 80
Irazú Hotel, 24, 32, 34, 53
Ireland. *See* Dublin
Irish Open, 175, 177, 200

J
Jay, Ricky, 268
Jesse's Besties, 9–10
Jimmy's, 116
Joe Italiano's Maplewood II, 254
Jordan, Gerry, 233
Jordan, Michael, 280–81
Josephine's, 115
Judah, Mel, 213–14, 215

K
Kantjil and Tiger, 192–93
Keno, 107, 245
Khorat Top Thai, 192
King, Roger, 233
Kournikova, Maria, 214
Krekorian, Kirk, 263, 275
Kremser, Thomas, 188
Kyl, Jon, 30
Kyl, Bill, 29, 30

L
La Hacienda Steak House, 57
La Piccola Fontana, 86
Landauer, Lothar, 181
Landmark, 284
Las Palmas BBQ, 108
Las Vegas, 3, 9, 257–89
    Babies, 288
    Bally's, 270, 272, 278
    Barbary Coast, 272, 287
    Bellagio (See Bellagio)
    Binion's Deli, 288
    Binion's Horseshoe, 272, 281–82
    blackjack in, 7, 26, 266–67
    Caesars Palace, 10, 270–71, 288
    casinos in, 263, 270–87
    cigars in, 289
    Circus Circus, 272, 283, 284, 288
    cleanest bathrooms in, 289
    craps in, 265
    Crème de la Crème, 272
    currency in, 259
    Desert Inn, 270, 272, 274
    entertainment and nightlife in,
        287–88
    Excalibur, 271, 272, 286
    Flamingo Hilton, 272, 285
    food and drink in, 287–88 (See also
        specific casinos and hotels)
    Foot Locker in, 271
    Fremont Experience light show
        in, 289
    Frontier, 272, 285
    Gamblers Book Club in, 268–69
    games in, 263
    Gold Coast, 272, 279
    Golden Nugget, 271, 272, 276–77
    golf in, 274, 289
    Hard Rock Café, 287
    Hard Rock Casino, 272, 279–80,
        288, 289
    Hilton, 272, 284
    Holiday Casino, 285–86
    Holiday Inn, 272
    Hoover Dam, 289
    horseracing in, 267, 269
    House of Blues, 288
    Imperial Palace, 267–68, 272,
        280–81
    Landmark, 284
    lodging in, 270–87
    Luxor, 271, 272, 283, 288
    Mandalay Bay, 271, 272
    MGM, 271, 272, 286
    Mirage, 266, 267, 270, 272, 275,
        288, 289
    money plays in, 263–65
    Nero's, 273
    NYNY, 271, 272, 284
    odds in, 265–69
    Olympic Gardens, 10, 288
    Paddlewheel, 284
    Pai-Gow poker in, 267
    Palace Station, 288
    poker in, 177, 265–66
    Ra, 288
    Red Rocks Canyon, 289
    Rio, 272, 277, 287
    Riviera, 284
    Rock 'n' Roll diner, 279
    safety in, 259
    shopping in, 271, 289
    sight-seeing in, 289
    Silver Slipper, 284
    slots in, 267
    Spearmint Rhino, 288
    sports betting in, 267–68
    Stardust, 272, 278–79, 284
    Strip in, 270–71
    Super Bowl betting in, 257, 280
    transportation in, 261–62
    Treasure Island, 270, 272, 276, 289
    Utopia, 287, 288
    Venetian, 271, 272
    World Series of Poker in, 177, 188,
        266, 282
Las Vegas hotel suites (in Panama
    City), 116
Le Tournesol, 165
Le Trianon Grill, 112, 113
Library Restaurant, 255
Limits, high, 10, 82, 94, 156, 229,
    230–31
Line Bet, defined, 13

Lissandro, Jeff, 213–14, 215
Little Saigon, 254–55
Lollapalooza story, 45–46
Lord Byron Hotel, 197
Los Amigos, 252–53
Losing, profit in, 5
Lottery, 30, 31
Luft, Lorna, 274
Lukas, 57
Luma Kid, 8, 245, 273
Lupis Restaurant, 90, 97
Luxor, 271, 272, 283, 288

M
Mafia, 31
Maharajah Club, 235, 236
Mandalay Bay (Las Vegas), 271, 272
Mandalay (San Juan), 89
Mar del Plata, 3, 10, 61–78. *See also*
    Argentina
    baccarat in, 69–70, 72
    banca gana in, 70–71
    beach in, 76
    bingo in, 67
    blackjack in, 68–69, 72
    Brandinelli, 78
    casinos in, 66, 71–76
    Central Casino, 71–74
    craps in, 66, 67, 72
    currency in, 63, 73
    El Imperial Marisqueria, 77
    entertainment and nightlife in,
        76–78
    food and drink in, 10, 73, 77
    games in, 66, 72
    golf in, 78
    Iguazú Grand Hotel Resort and
        Casino, 76
    lodging in, 71–76
    money plays in, 66
    odds in, 67–70
    Paella Liberto, 77
    restaurants in, 77
    Riviera Hotel, 74–75
    roulette in, 67–68, 72
    safety in, 64
    shopping in, 78

transportation in, 64–65
    waterfalls near, 76
    Yo Tu El Pizzas, 77
Marino, Tony, 233
Marriott (Amsterdam), 192
Marriott (Aruba), 124, 127–28
Marriott (Costa Rica), 54
Marriott Moscow Grand Hotel,
    218–19
Marriott (Panama), 114–15, 115
Marriott (Paris), 197
Marriott (San Juan), 91–92
Marriott's Aruba Ocean Club,
    130
Marshall, David, 233
Max's Deli, 89
Merrion Club, 178, 200
Metropol Restaurant, 90, 96
MGM, 271, 272, 286
Mirage, 270, 272, 275, 288, 289
Mirage Poker Room, 266, 267
Money in the Ditch, defined, 13
Money plays
    in Aruba, 123–24
    in Atlantic City, 229–233
    in Bonaire, 139
    in Curaçao, 148
    in Europe, 178–79
    in Las Vegas, 263–65
    in Mar del Plata, 66
    in Moscow, 212–13
    in Panama City, 103
    in San José, 24–25
    in San Juan, 82
Monte, Lucio, 156
Monte Carlo, 173–74
Morty the Hammer, 9, 272, 274, 280,
    288
Moscow, 2, 209–21
    blackjack in, 215, 216
    Caribbean stud, 215
    casinos in, 212, 215–19
    Cherry Casino, 212
    cigars in, 221
    Corona Casino, 212
    Cosmos Hotel and Casino, 10,
        206, 208, 212, 213–14, 215–17

Moscow (*con't*)
  Cosmos Inaugural Poker
    Tournament in, 213–14
  Crystal Palace, 212
  currency in, 206–7
  Diamond Fund in, 221
  entertainment and nightlife in,
    219–21
  food and drink in, 217, 218,
    220
  games in, 213
  Golden Palace, 212
  Grand Prix Casino, 218
  lodging in, 215–19
  Marriott Moscow Grand Hotel,
    215–19
  Metelista Entertainment
    Complex in, 212
  money plays in, 212–13
  and money transfers, 207, 214
  Night Flight, 10, 220
  odds in, 213–14
  poker in, 213–14
  prostitution in, 220
  Radisson Slavjanskaya Hotel, 209,
    218–19
  raffle in, 212
  roulette in, 215, 216
  safety in, 208
  shopping in, 221
  sight-seeing in, 220–21
  slots in, 213
  sports betting in, 216
  transportation in, 209–12
Moss, Johnny, 266, 281–82
Mustang Café, 76

N
Natural, defined, 13
Nero's, 273
New Jersey. *See* Atlantic City
Nick the Greek. *See* Dandalos, Nick
  the Greek
Night Flight, 10, 220
Niko's, 116
Nova Gorica, 199
  Hit Hotel Casino Park, 199

location of, 172, 200
  Park Hotel Complex, 199
NYNY, 271, 272, 284

O
Ocean Terrace, 91
Odds, 6
  best casino for craps, 9
  in Bonaire, 139–40
  in Curaçao, 149–50
  in Europe, 179
  in Las Vegas, 265–68
  in Mar del Plata, 66
  in Moscow, 213–14
  in Panama City, 104–6
  in San José, 25–27
  in San Juan, 83–84
Old San Juan Hotel, 94–95
Olympic Gardens, 10, 288
Omaha poker, 33, 182, 190, 234
Otrabanda Hotel and Casino,
  158–59
Outback Steakhouse, 96

P
Paddlewheel, 284
Paella Liberto, 77
Pai-Gow poker
  in Atlantic City, 247, 248
  in Las Vegas, 267
  in San José, 25, 26, 35, 47
Palace Station, 288
Palacio, 24, 26, 27, 34–36
  Balmoral and, 53
  games at, 35
  Pai-Gow poker at, 26, 35
  poker at, 32, 33, 34, 35
  sports betting at, 28
Palm Restaurant, 86
Panama City, 10, 99–116
  blackjack in, 104, 105, 107, 109, 113
  Caesar Park Hotel and Casino,
    103, 105, 112–14
  Cafe Bahia, 112, 113
  Canadian Thunderbird
    Corporation, 103
  Canal 21 in, 104–5

casinos in, 103, 106–15
Ceasarito, 113
Coco Club, 115
Continental, 103, 105, 106, 108–10, 115
Coronado resort, 115
craps in, 104, 109, 113
Crown Casinos, 103, 105
currency in, 100
El Panama Hotel and Casino, 99, 103, 106–8, 115
entertainment and nightlife in, 115–16
food and drink in, 107–8, 109, 112, 113, 114, 116
games in, 103, 106, 107, 109, 111, 113
Granada Hotel, 103, 105
Grand Soloy, 103
Happyland, 115
Hippodromo, 104
horseracing in, 104, 106
Hotel Granada, 110–12
Jimmy's, 116
Josephine's, 115
Las Vegas Hotel Suites, 114, 116
Le Trianon Grill, 112, 113
lodging in, 106–15
Marriott Hotel, 114–15
Marriott (Panama), 115
money plays in, 103
Niko's, 116
odds in, 104–6
Panama Canal in, 115
poker in, 111, 112
restaurants in, 107, 109, 111, 112, 113, 114
Riande Continental, 103, 105, 106, 108–10, 115
roulette in, 104, 107, 113
safety in, 101
Salty's, 112, 113
slots in, 104, 107, 113
transportation in, 102–3
Papapez, 56–57
Paris, 195–97
    Arc Élysées Hotel, 197

Aviation Club, 178, 197
Balzac Hotel, 197
Chateaubriand Hotel, 197
food and drink in, 196
Four Seasons Tournaments, 196
games in, 196, 198
Lord Byron Hotel, 197
Marriott, 197
Parkhotel Baden, 184, 186, 187, 192
Pass, defined, 13
Pearson, Puggy, 281
Penn and Teller, 278
Philharmonic Pops, 87
Pirates, 157
Pit, defined, 13, 14
Planet Poker, 31
Players Lounge, 85
Plaza Hotel Curaçao, 165–66
Plaza Resort, 141–42
Point, defined, 13, 14
Poker
    in Amsterdam, 190–91
    in Aruba, 124, 125–27, 129
    in Atlantic City, 233–34, 245–46
    in Baden, 181–82, 183
    at Binion's Horseshoe, 266, 268, 271
    in Bonaire, 139
    Caribbean stud (*See* Caribbean stud poker)
    Casino Cosmos's Inaugural Poker Tournament, 213–14
    in Curaçao, 164
    defined, 13, 14
    in Europe, 174, 176
    in Las Vegas, 177, 265–66
    in Moscow, 213–14
    Omaha, 33, 182, 190, 234
    Pai-Gow (*See* Pai-Gow poker)
    in Panama City, 111, 112
    Poker European Masters, 181–82, 184, 188, 189–90
    in San José, 32–34, 35
    second-chance, 139
    Seven-Stud Hi-Lo, 234
    tournaments in (*See* Gambling tournaments)
    Tropicana Poker Club, 246

INDEX · 303

Poker (*con't*)
  Trump Taj Mahal poker
    tournament, 233–34
  tute, 25, 26, 39, 52
  United States Poker
    Championships, 237
  video, 107, 111, 160
  World Series of, 177, 188, 266, 282
Porto Paseo Hotel and Casino, 159,
  162
Price, Nick, 135
Puerto Rico. *See also* San Juan
  beaches in, 97
  high limits in, 82, 94
Pulitzer Hotel, 192
Punto y banco, 67
Push, defined, 13, 14

R
Ra, 284
Radisson Ambassador Plaza Hotel
  and Casino San Juan, 92
Radisson Slavjanskaya Hotel, 209,
  218–19
Rake, defined, 13, 14
Ramada Presidentti, 198
Ranch, 86
Ray Casino, 178, 197–98
Reese, Chip, 281
Resort, Casino Curaçao, 9, 148,
  154–58
Resorts (Merv Griffin's), 229, 251
Restaurants. *See also* Food and drink
  in Amsterdam, 192–94
  in Aruba, 129, 132, 133, 134
  in Atlantic City, 235, 237–38, 255
  in Bonaire, 142
  in Curaçao, 157
  in Mar del Plata, 77
  in Panama City, 107, 109, 111, 112,
    113, 114
  in San José, 56–58
  in San Juan, 85–86, 89–91, 90,
    94, 96–97
Revere, Lawrence, 151, 268
Riande Continental, 106, 108–10,
  115

Canal 21 at, 105
  clubs near, 115
  Crown Casinos and, 103
  horseracing at, 106
Rias Bajas, 57
Rickles, Don, 274
Rio, 272, 277, 287
Ristorante Giorgio, 164
Ritz Carlton (San Juan), 90, 93–94
Riviera (Las Vegas), 284
Riviera (San José), 74–75
Rock 'n' Roll diner, 279
Rogers, Terry, 200
Roland Hotel, 75
Rommy
  at Colonial Casino, 39, 40
  defined, 13, 14
  at Del Ray Hotel and Casino, 52
  at Gran Hotel Costa Rica, 50–51
  at Herradura Hotel, 45
  at Palacio, 35
  in San José, 25, 26–27, 35, 39–42,
    45, 50–52
Roulette
  in Aruba, 125, 128, 130, 132, 133
  in Atlantic City, 245, 249
  in Bonaire, 142
  canasta instead of, 25–26 (*See also*
    Canasta)
  in Curaçao, 156, 159
  defined, 13, 14
  in Europe, 179
  in Mar del Plata, 67–68, 72
  in Moscow, 215, 216
  in Panama City, 104, 107, 113
  in San José, 25–26, 45, 52
  in San Juan, 85, 92, 93
Royal Cabana Casino, 124, 131–32
Royal Dutch Casino, 25
Royal Palm Casino, 132–33
Ruchman, Peter, 150, 268
Russia. *See* Moscow

S
Safety
  in Aruba, 122
  in Atlantic City, 227

in Costa Rica, 21
in Las Vegas, 259
in Mar del Plata, 64
in Moscow, 208
in Panama City, 101
in San Juan, 80
Salty's, 112, 113
San José, 19–60. *See also* Costa Rica
Balmoral Hotel, 25, 53
Barcela Amon, 28
Bikini Bar, 55
Billy Boys, 58
blackjack in, 25, 26–27, 36, 40
Brennes' poker club in, 32
Camino Real, 22, 46–47
canasta in, 25, 39, 45, 52
casinos in, 24–25, 34–54
casinos *vs.* Vegas casinos, 24
clothing in, 21–22
Colonial Casino (*see* Colonial Casino)
Corobici Hotel (*See* Corobici Hotel)
Costa Rica Marriott, 53
craps in, 25, 26, 39
Cuban cigars in, 58
currency in, 21, 24–25
deep-sea fishing in, 58
Del Rey Hotel and Casino, 51–52
El Presidente Casino, 25
El Pueblo, 10, 22, 54–55
entertainment and nightlife in, 54–58
food and drink in, 24, 36, 39, 42–43, 46, 48, 49, 50, 51, 53, 55–58
games in, 25, 35, 39, 42, 44, 46, 48, 49, 50
Gran Hotel Costa Rica (*See* Gran Hotel Costa Rica)
Holiday Inn Aurola, 24, 26, 27, 41–43, 53
Irazú Hotel, 24, 32, 34, 48–49, 53
La Hacienda Steak House, 57
lodging in, 34–54
Lukas, 57
Marriott (Costa Rica), 54

money plays in, 24–25
Pai-Gow poker in, 25, 26, 35, 47
Palacio (*See* Palacio)
Papapez, 56–57
poker in, 32–34, 35
prostitution in, 22
raffle in, 42
rain forest in, 58
restaurants in, 56–58
Rias Bajas, 57
Rommy in, 25, 26–27, 34–35, 39, 40, 52
roulette in, 25, 45
Royal Dutch Casino, 25
shuffle tracking in, 27
slots in, 32, 39, 42
Soda Perla, 57
sports betting in, 25, 27–31, 35, 39
transportation in, 23–24
tute poker in, 25, 26, 39
volcano in, 58
San Juan, 79–97. *See also* Puerto Rico
baccarat in, 83
beaches in, 97
blackjack in, 83, 91, 92, 93
Caribbean stud in, 91, 93
casinos in, 82
Cerromar Casino, 95
cigars in, 87
Club Babylon in, 87, 96
cockfighting in, 83–84, 90
Condado Plaza Hotel and Casino, 81, 82, 89–90
craps in, 83
currency in, 80
Diamond Palace, 93
El Chico Lounge, 86–87
El Conquistador Hotel, 81, 96
El Pueblo Casino, 22
El San Juan, 9, 10, 82, 84–89, 96
Embassy Suites Hotel and Casino, 96
entertainment and nightlife in, 86–87, 96–97
food and drink in, 85–86, 89, 90, 91, 92, 94, 96–97
Gallistico Club, 83, 84

San Juan (*con't*)
  games in, 82, 85, 93, 94
  golf in, 97
  Hampton Inn, 90–91
  Hyatt Cerromar, 97
  Hyatt Dorado Hotel, 95, 97
  "James Bond Package" in, 88
  Lupis Restaurant, 90, 97
  Mandalay, 89
  Marriott (San Juan), 91–92
  Max's Deli, 89
  Metropol Restaurant, 90, 96
  money plays in, 82
  odds in, 83–84
  Philharmonic Pops, 87
  Players Lounge, 85
  Radisson Ambassador Plaza Hotel
    and Casino San Juan, 92
  restaurants in, 85–86, 89–91, 94,
    96–97
  Ritz Carlton Hotel and Casino,
    90, 93–94
  roulette in, 85, 92, 93
  Royal Suite in, 88
  safety in, 80
  shopping in, 97
  Stellaris Casino, 91
  Tapas bar and grill, 89
  Tequila Bar and Grill in, 85–86
  Tony Roma's Ribs, 89
  transportation in, 81
  Westin Rio Mar, 97
  Wine and Cheese Bar, 87
  Wyndham El San Juan Hotel and
    Casino (*See* El San Juan)
  Wyndham Old San Juan Hotel,
    82, 94–95
  Wyndham Palmas Del Mar, 97
San Marcos Hotel and Casino, 163
Sands Hotel and Casino (Atlantic
  City), 247
Sauerhof Grandhotel, 184, 186, 187
Scheherazade, 235, 238
Schwartz, Howard, 268
Service, good, 10, 272
Servicios Internacionales de
  Informacion, 28–29

Seven Eleven, European, 180
Seven-Stud Hi-Lo, 234
Shoe, defined, 14
Shooter, defined, 14
Shopping
  in Aruba, 135
  in Atlantic City, 255–56
  in Curaçao, 168
  in Las Vegas, 271, 289
  in Mar del Plata, 78
  in Moscow, 221
  in San Juan, 97
Showboat Casino, 242–43
Siegfried and Roy, 275
Silver Slipper, 284
Sinisalo, Jyrki, 197
Skiing, 186
Sklansky, David, 125
Slots
  in Aruba, 130
  in Atlantic City, 232, 242
  in Bonaire, 142
  in Costa Rica, 9, 32
  in Curaçao, 160, 163, 165
  defined, 14
  in Las Vegas, 267
  in Moscow, 213
  in Panama City, 104, 107, 113
  in San José, 32, 39, 42
Slovenia, 177
  Hit Casino, 178
  Nova Gorica, 199
Soda Perla, 57
Soft, defined, 14
Soft Seventeen, 14, 127
Sonesta (Aruba), 133–34
Sonesta (Curaçao), 147, 160–61
Spearmint Rhino, 288
Split a Pair, defined, 14
Sports betting
  in Aruba, 129
  in Las Vegas, 257, 267–68
  the lottery *vs.*, 30–31
  in Moscow, 216
  in San José, 25, 27–31, 35, 39
  in Vienna, 188
Stage Deli, 237, 238

Stand, defined, 14
Starbuck's coffeeshop, 237
Stardust, 272, 278–79, 284
Stellaris Casino (Aruba), 127–28
Stellaris Casino (San Juan), 91
Stewart, Payne, 135
Stibilj, Stasko, 199
Stripped Deck, defined, 14, 15
Stuck, defined, 14, 15
Stupak, Bob, 257
Super Bowl betting, 257, 280
Surrender, defined, 14, 16
Sushi Bar, 237

T
Tapas bar and grill, 89
Telephone wagering, 30
Tennis, 186
Tequilla Bar and Grill, 86
Texas Hold'em. *See* Hold'em
Ticos and gringos, 36–38, 46
Tipsy Seagull, 142
Toke, defined, 14, 15
Tony Roma's Ribs, 89
Tournaments. *See* Gambling
    tournaments
Treasure Island, 270, 272, 276, 289
Tropicana Hotel and Casino, 233,
    235, 244–46
Tropicana Poker Club, 233, 244
Trump, Donald, 229
Trump Marina, 229, 252
Trump Plaza, 229, 250–51
Trump Taj Mahal, 225, 229, 235–36
    best craps ambiance, 10
    poker tournament at, 226,
        233–34
Tute poker, 25, 26, 39, 52. *See also*
    Caribbean Stud poker

U
Ungar, Stu, 281
United States, 223–89. *See* Atlantic
    City; Las Vegas
United States Poker
    Championships, 237

Uston, Ken, 226
Utopia, 287, 288

V
Van der Valk, 141, 143
Venetian, 271, 272
Video keno, 107
Video poker, 107, 111, 160
Vienna, 178, 187–88
    Austrian Classics in, 188
    Concord Card Casino, 39, 178,
        187–88
    sports betting in, 188
    World Series of Poker Trial in,
        188
Vigorish (Vig), defined, 14, 15
Volstead Act, 30
Voodoo players, 7, 8

W
Waggoner, Marsha, 214, 215
Waterfront Hotel, 192
Westin Rio Mar, 97
Whale, 15, 29
White House Subs, 254
Wild Wild West Casino, 9, 229,
    243–44
Williams Hospitality Group, 82
Wine and Cheese Bar, 87
Wong, Stanford, 8, 27
World Series of Poker, 177, 188, 266,
    282
World's Fair Casino, 229, 250–51
Wyndham El San Juan Hotel and
    Casino, 9, 10, 82, 84–89, 96
Wyndham Hotel and Casino
    (Aruba), 125, 130–31
Wyndham Old San Juan Hotel,
    94–95
Wyndham Palmas Del Mar, 97
Wynn, Steve, 181, 229, 263, 275, 276,
    289

Y
Yamato, 86
Yo Tu El Pizzas, 77

ABOUT THE AUTHOR

JESSE MAY has written for *Poker Digest* and *High Stakes Magazine*, and is the author of the novel *Shut Up and Deal*. He is the voice and play-by-play commentator on the British television series "Late Night Poker." Originally from New Jersey, he now lives in Copenhagen, Denmark, but can usually be found wherever the best game is.